MADAME QUEEN

Also by Mary Kay McBrayer

America's First Female Serial Killer:
Jane Toppan and the Making of a Monster

MADAME QUEEN

THE LIFE AND CRIMES OF HARLEM'S UNDERGROUND RACKETEER, STEPHANIE ST. CLAIR

MARY KAY McBRAYER

PARK
ROW
BOOKS

PARK ™
ROW
BOOKS ™

Recycling programs
for this product may
not exist in your area

ISBN-13: 978-0-7783-1065-5

Madame Queen

This publication contains opinions and ideas of the author. It is intended for informational and educational purposes only. The reader should seek the services of a competent professional for expert assistance or professional advice. Reference to any organization, publication or website does not constitute or imply an endorsement by the author or the publisher. The author and the publisher specifically disclaim any and all liability arising directly or indirectly from the use or application of any information contained in this publication.

TM is a trademark of Harlequin Enterprises ULC.

Park Row Books
22 Adelaide St. West, 41st Floor
Toronto, Ontario M5H 4E3, Canada
ParkRowBooks.com

Printed in U.S.A.

For Madame Queen of Policy

MADAME QUEEN

CONTENTS

AUTHOR'S NOTE

I learned about Madame Stephanie St. Clair by a stroke of luck. During my first trip to New York City, I had to see about the Museum of the American Gangster. It's in a former speakeasy, so like the true rube that I was, I walked past it on St. Marks three times before I clocked it. Madame St. Clair's history was even more elusive.

Her photo hung inside the private museum alongside big-name gangsters from the '20s and '30s, like Al Capone, Lucky Luciano, and Dutch Schultz. Theirs were mug shots. Hers was the black-and-white equivalent of a thirst trap selfie: this stunner was on the edge of someone's writing desk in a sparkling dress, legs crossed at the knee, and gorgeous mule pumps slipped over her silk-stockinged feet. She looked away from the camera, midspeech, her left hand, mysteriously bandaged, about to gesture a directive to someone just out of frame. She was the only woman on that wall, and she was one of about three persons of color (Bumpy Johnson and Frank Lucas were pictured, although I later learned that those guys were her direct descendants, criminally speaking). When I tipped the docent after the tour, I asked her to tell me everything she knew about Stephanie St. Clair.

She took my money and smiled and said, "I just did."

If I'd gotten a fuller answer from her, this book might not exist. As a naturally defiant person, I took that docent's hard "no" as a "try harder." The first few internet searches yielded equally captivating images of St. Clair, posing hands on hips in a turban and a fur-collared wrap coat. I could never make out what animal her furs were from, but I always imagined them to be wolf.

A little deeper into my research, and I unearthed the reason why she'd taken those photos at all: in the early 1930s, after her numbers racket boomed and got the attention of both organized criminals and corrupt police officials alike, she took out ad space in the local Harlem paper, the *Amsterdam News.* That's where she wrote open letters to judges, mayors, and her neighbors, not only defending her honor, but citing specific advice, like what to do when the police tried to search your home without a warrant, or even how to report badge numbers from the cops who did that. She basically created her own PR campaign. After learning all this, I was deeply invested, and I tapped every research vein I could think of: I accessed archival articles through the university system library where I taught as a limited-term English professor; New York Public Library's Schomburg Center; and the special collections down the street from my house in Atlanta at Clark, Morehouse, and Spelman. I bought out-of-print books about Harlem in the 1920s and '30s from secondhand websites on the off chance she might be mentioned in a chapter or two. I scoured the (auto)biographies of her contemporaries, even fictional representations of the time and place, just hoping to catch a glimpse of her. But even with all that effort, information about her remains scant. She was absolutely glamorous. She was a philanthropist. She was a West Indian immigrant, a woman who bootstrapped herself into success in spite of the odds. A folk hero. A genius. All these things are true. And so are the facts that she was a businesswoman, and her business was illegal. Let me clarify: she was firstly a business woman, not a criminal, but because her business happened to be criminal, she had to engage with criminals. Like the adage goes, when you hang around shit, you get shit on you. The criminals she had to deal with were no small potatoes. They were those infamous villains whose names are still known, whose mug shots hung in the museum.

The more I learned about her, the more enthralled I became, the more I wondered, *Why had I never heard of this woman before?* I love gangster shit. Fictional and historical alike, I like to think I'm pretty well-versed in the lore. I may not know the details of every criminal's home life or the nuance of their relationship with their parents, but usually their names at least ring a bell. So, to my question above, *Why had I never heard of her?* I drew the obvious answers. Racism. And sexism.

For sure, those are huge impediments to getting credit where it's due, but Madame St. Clair was different from her contemporaries. The criminal nature of her gambling racket was incidental. That's not the case with other gangsters. Many of them were criminals by trade, too mean or too mouthy to work a regular job, and they almost always *wanted* you to know their name. They wanted that clout, and that's ultimately what brought them down—their own mouths. Or, on a long enough timeline, someone else would rat them out.

When I ran out of things Madame Queen said about herself, I had to go to what other people said about her. It was other people who started calling Stephanie St. Clair "Madame Queen" in the first place. Once in a while, she appears on a list of donors to a particular cause. She has a cameo in Dutch Schultz's story written by his lawyer Dixie Davis, which I include in these pages. Her "world" is represented in Shirley Stewart's book, *The World of Stephanie St. Clair:*

An Entrepreneur, Race Woman and Outlaw in Early Twentieth Century Harlem. She has a paragraph in Selwyn Raab's compendium *Five Families.* She's also a peripheral character in the Francis Ford Coppola movie *The Cotton Club* and *Hoodlum* starring Laurence Fishburne—but no one points the lens right at her, even though she was the only illegal business owner who didn't get burned by her own game. (She did get burned, but more on that later.)

This book is my attempt to fill the void of her presence. When I couldn't find credible references to tell the story, I took some intuitive leaps based on adjacent research. The narrative opens at her business's height, featuring one of the advertisements she placed in the *Amsterdam News.* I like to think of that article as her debut: when the police she'd been icing for years decided she was too successful, and they needed a bigger slice of her pie, she turned the tables by announcing she had paid them bribes. From there, we retrace her steps from the first evidence of her existence in Guadeloupe, when she immigrated to the States in steerage on a cargo ship, which is also her first PR spin. She was thirteen at the time, according to birth records, but the ship's muster records her age as twenty-three. Do I know for sure that she lied on purpose? No. But after learning all I could about her and her character, I can deduce that as the most accurate explanation for the discrepancy.

And that happens often in St. Clair's story, that ambiguity between intentional discrepancy and discretion.

Madame Queen was good at her job, and she was nothing if not discreet. To be good at a job like hers, you can't talk about it a lot. You have to be careful what you say, how you say it, and to whom you say it. Sometimes, no matter how much I leaned into a source, no matter how many adjacent narratives I could find, Stephanie was just *not there.* In those cases, I used the best information I could find to make the likeliest narrative. (I might not be able to prove that's wolf she's wearing, but right next to one of her letters is a printed advertisement for a wolf collar, so it was, at least, an option. And look at the striations in the photograph. Is it a printing error? Could be. But do you think it's likely that she would have identified more with a mink than a wolf?) I will always do my best to distinguish when I have the cold hard facts versus when I'm only pretty sure what happened. Any dialogue that is not verbatim from a source has been reconstructed as authentically as possible with an ear toward the era, region, and character of the speaker.

This book is a work of creative nonfiction. It's always my intention to tell the truest, fullest story that I can, to really resurrect Madame Queen, because while she might have wanted to fly under the radar during the interwar period, times are changing, and now we can celebrate her for the true boss she was—and I hope to learn more about her, for more of her to surface even if it's too late to put in this book, because she is so much more than a character on a page.

Mary Kay McBrayer
January 24, 2024

PROLOGUE:

AIN'T NOBODY'S BUSINESS IF I DO

If Madame Stephanie St. Clair greeted Sugar Hill every morning like she was its queen, it's because she was. November 24, 1928 was no different. She lifted her brightly wrapped head from her silk pillow, swung her bare legs over the side of her bed, and slid her feet into fuzzy bottle-green mules. She wrapped a gold robe round her shoulders on the way to draw open her lace curtains. From her window, she watched her people starting their day on Edgecombe Avenue, five stories below, already bundled in their wool and gloves with a copy of the *Amsterdam News* or the *New York Times* wedged underneath their arms. The newspaper boys accosted every pedestrian, swarming each car on the street that so much as tapped its brakes. The smallest child would flatten the newspaper to the windshield while the others barked its contents until the driver eventually cracked his window and slid out a nickel so he could get on his way. St. Clair studied the newsboys' hustle for a few minutes every morning, in case she should need new recruits. Even though she already knew the news before it was reported, Stephanie always bought a paper, too. She read them like any good citizen—even if she did it for different reasons, to learn which journalists were reliable, or simply to keep her story straight. She skimmed the headlines now while she brushed her teeth.

She swept over to her waterfall vanity and continued her routine, cinching her dressing gown tight at the waist before perching on the upholstered stool. Stephanie removed the cold cream and Vaseline from her face with the warm, damp rag her maid, Mildred, had left at the basin. She massaged her newest scent into her hands, face, and neck, thinking of how she would evaluate it to A'Lelia Walker, the cheerful heiress, next time they passed in the lobby. After a moment, she slid one darkly polished fingernail through the ring pull of the left-hand drawer and withdrew her Rider-Waite deck.

It was a typical morning for Stephanie until this point. Then it became newsworthy, as she later described it to the *Amsterdam News.* She didn't say exactly which cards she drew, only that they warned her of a betrayal. Because she had the eye for detail that only a seamstress turned criminal in a new, strange land could possess, I imagine it happening with the full drama detailed here. Even if she was the only one to witness her own performance, everything from the set to the costume to the flourish of her graceful fingers as she turned over each card would have been intentional and deliberate, because anything worth doing is worth overdoing.

Stephanie cut the deck once and then dealt herself three cards, face down. Their blue-and-white-checkered mandala seemed to pulse with impatience. Stephanie's gaze caught on the half-moons of her fingernails as she felt her eyes glaze over in anticipation. During the Depression, women painted around the half-moons to make their polish last longer, but she would have had her nails manicured this way because it was on trend, not for the sake of thrift. She made eye contact with herself in the mirror's round face to center herself before she turned over the first card.

Her throat constricted at the Ten of Swords. All ten rapiers stabbed parallel into the backside of a fallen corpse whose face turned away from her. She glanced over her shoulder, patterns in her wallpaper racing as she tried to discern what danger might lie in the rest of her apartment behind the closed bedroom door. All was quiet except for Mildred's soft step as she readied the morning's coffee and breakfast. Stephanie squeezed her eyes tight again and opened them onto the card. Her vision focused first on the yellow horizon running through its center: *a sunrise*, said the voice in her head. She let her focus shift from the background to the fore, where the swords stood in varying heights. *The shortest sword is not the shortest: it is the deepest driven.*

It looks worse than it is, she thought. *It is a mere anxiety.* She inhaled to settle her nerves before she overturned the second card.

The Chariot. *It is staying.* Drawn by its Black and white sphinxes, though it moves at the orders of its charioteer, it is here to stay. With the city behind it, an afterthought, with the sun having risen to expose its movement. *Someone*, she thought. *Someone I trust has acted against me. The treason is in motion already. It cannot be stopped. It is underway, in front of God and everyone.*

When she revealed the third card to be the High Priestess, Stephanie exhaled sharply and set her jaw as hard as the woman portrayed on the card. Stephanie saw the jewels above the High Priestess's head as a pomegranate half eaten. *I will descend*, she thought, *by trickery*.

———

She heard a light tap on her bedroom door and swept the cards back into their drawer as Amelia, her newest maid, opened the door barely an inch and said, "Good morning, Madame Stephanie—are you sleep?"

"Amelia," she said, and turned her face to greet her. "Bonjour, ma chérie." Amelia smiled broadly as she carried in the inlaid tray of coffee, cream, and sugar to set it on the right side of the vanity. These were her normal duties becoming her habit, and this day was unlike any other so far, so she would have completed them as she would have any other day.

She walked behind Stephanie and untied the scarf at the nape of Stephanie's neck. As Amelia unwound and folded it, she said, "Mildred says your breakfast will be up shortly. I put the hot comb on the stove, but I don't think we need it today. These pins laid the front down nice. I don't like to put on too much heat if you don't need it. Might burn your scalp. Especially since we just washed it day before last. No oil in it right now, really. What you think?"

Stephanie barely lifted her chin to signal that she agreed.

"That smells nice, what you got on. That what Miss Walker give you last week?"

"It is."

"I still go weak-kneed when I see her in the hall. Think, her mama was Madame CJ! That cream rinse holding up good, too. No rats in the kitchen, even with what all restlessness you been doing," she laughed, gesturing to the unmade bed behind them that looked as though Stephanie had slept in a thunderstorm. Amelia ran a silver comb through Stephanie's forelock and then brushed out the finger waves in the back, as was becoming the fashion.

"Amelia," Stephanie said.

She stopped moving and her black eyes flicked up into the mirror. "Yes, ma'am?"

This part we know for sure. She trusted Amelia, and she warned her of what she read in the cards.

"There is danger here. I do not know what it is." She stood. "I must dress quickly. Be mindful of whom you open the door for today. Remember: police cannot legally enter unless you give them permission. Do not give them permission."

"Yes, ma'am," said Amelia.

"Let me hear."

"Today I'll be real careful about who come in. No police. If they ask, I say no. No, sir, you can't come in."

"Bien. Merci. Help me dress. Quickly."

Stephanie pulled her gray drop-waist dress overhead, the one with the deep V that exposed her yellow slip beneath; and as she fastened her hose to their belt, she slipped her foot into the black T-strap shoe while Amelia buckled the tiny clasp at her ankle. She pinned a baby blue cloche to the part in her hair before whipping past Mildred out the front door and throwing the fox fur around her neck. I don't know all these wardrobe details for sure, but knowing her like I do, I feel good about them. They feel right. I'm leaving them in. In the floor's hallway, she eyeballed an old woman sitting by the stairs. She seemed as though she wanted to follow Stephanie onto the elevator, but when the operator, Jim, greeted her as Madame, the woman held her place, recognizing in his own mature face someone familiar with and intolerant of all types of bullshit.

"You looking lovely this morning," he said, and Stephanie pulled her kidskin gloves on with a small smirk. After he secured the doors, he asked, still facing forward, "Do you know the woman on the stairs, Madame St. Clair?"

"You mean the badly dressed woman who seemed to be following me?" Stephanie asked.

I don't know that Jim was his name, but I know that they had a good relationship, because anyone in Stephanie's line of work had to be on close terms with the building's security. And "James" was the third most popular baby boy's name in the 1880s. And doesn't that name just make you feel like you'd be safe around him?

Jim chuckled. "I'll have her removed soon as we get you in the car," he said.

"There is no one better at your job than you are," she replied. He levered open the elevator doors for her in the lobby, and her heels clicked on the penny tiles as she moved across the foyer—the foyer of 409 is still tiled this way—where the valet held the set of doors open for her to exit. Her limousine waited at the entrance to take her one mile down Lenox Avenue to her policy bank at the corner. She could have easily walked there. Most New Yorkers would have walked. She was not most New Yorkers.

———

Not half an hour later, three policemen commandeered the ladder from the bodega on the corner beside her apartment building. They tipped it up to the fire escape at the far side of 409 Edgecombe. They were discreet, but not discreet enough to evade the eyes of the children who peddled papers by morning and ran numbers by noon. It stands to reason that one wise and opportunistic boy slipped away from the pack as the six men scaled the five floors. The valet at 409's entrance hesitated to admit the boy until he said, "Got to get a message to Madame St. Clair, sir. I don't got to see her, just got to tell Jim." That would have opened the doors like abracadabra at the Cave of Wonders.

The child wiped his feet carefully on the mat before he jogged up to the front desk, where the man in the pillbox hat looked up. "What you know good?"

"Mr. Freeman—" again, I don't know that this was the desk worker's last name, but the odds are in favor of it since so many people who achieved freedom assumed that surname, "—there's three white men in uniforms climbing the fire escape round the side of the building. It didn't look right, and I just wanted to get the message to Jim so he could let Madame St. Clair know, in case she don't," and without confirmation, the boy slipped out the side exit and back into his fold, returning to anonymity just as three more policemen pushed into the building past the same valet.

Meanwhile the first three men arrived outside the bedroom window of Mrs. Mary Lightfoot in apartment 5-H. All this is on the record. Lieutenant Pfeifer stood back as Officers Tait and Baccaglini wedged their batons under the window where it was cracked and pried it open. Lieutenant Pfeifer squeezed through the window much more easily than his reporting officers, and Mrs. Lightfoot shrieked when she saw the three uniformed officers pour out of her bedroom, through the sitting room, and then out onto the back fire escape again. Her maid ran to her side from the kitchen, and even as the tea kettle screamed at being left unattended, Mrs. Lightfoot was already dialing Madame St. Clair. Mrs. Lightfoot's maid, Winifred, took the service hallway to St. Clair's apartment on the opposite side of the building. She arrived at the kitchen entrance just in time to hear glass shatter on the other side, and she pounded for Mildred to let her in.

On the opposite side of the building's fire escape, Officer Tait was the first through Stephanie's bedroom window— but it wasn't easy to lift. Pfeifer had them stand back while he smashed it with his baton, and then he directed Tait in before him. Tait grasped the broken pane at the sill, shards so sharp he didn't realize he was bleeding. At this point, with the whole beautifully curated house tossed by police illegally searching and seizing, it seems to me like Amelia would have changed her mind, since she was just looking for a quick break and didn't have this new level of loyalty to Madame Queen when she first tipped off the police. When Amelia heard the glass breaking, she flung open the door to Madame St. Clair's bedroom. "Get off that rug!" she shouted. "Y'all can't be in here tracking in all over the Oriental rug! And you—you stop that bleeding before you get it all over her nice things!"

Officer Tait looked right at Amelia as he grabbed Stephanie's dressing gown from its hook, wiped his bloody hands, and dropped the gown on the floor. He stood on it as he broke the lock off her dresser with his baton. Baccaglini and Tait rummaged through the drawers till they found the tin box. Tait opened it and pocketed the $400 inside.

"What are y'all doing!" Amelia shouted. Panic entered her voice at the destruction of her employer's apartment. "That ain't yours, and y'all ain't say nothing about stealing—you need a warrant to be in here!"

"Quiet that gal," said Pfeifer. Baccaglini and Tait seized Amelia and dragged her into the kitchen, blood smearing on her collar. Baccaglini cuffed Amelia's wrists behind her back while Tait patted her down. She continued to protest, "This wasn't what y'all said. This ain't what we talked about," as

Mildred whistled, washing dishes at the sink. I know that each of these people did each of these things because it's written in the local paper. I might not know exactly what each of them said while they did it, but a snitch like Mildred definitely would have whistled and thought all the while, like a cartoon character, that whistling makes you look unsuspicious.

With the hallway free, Pfeifer kicked in the door that led to the parlor, and he admitted three more officers waiting at the front door. Winifred and Jim arrived from their respective stations in the building and pounded fruitlessly at the service entrance. Just after the new officers paraded into St. Clair's apartment, the service workers watched helplessly and trailed behind, hesitating at the fringed floor runner in the parlor. Winifred ultimately followed the officers into the kitchen, where Amelia leaned, handcuffed, against the counter while she wept. Winifred watched as the officers briefly frisked Mildred, then opened the service entrance door to allow her exit. She clocked that Mildred did not look surprised at all.

Jim stayed in the hallway and watched Pfeifer unlock the hall closet with a key. Pfeifer broke the other locks, but he had a key for this one. Jim relayed this fact to Madame Stephanie later. On the floor of the hall closet, placed carefully atop a stack of hat boxes, was a burlap sack full of policy slips, original receipts with coded names, numbers, and amounts written in ink. Winifred and Jim exchanged an embittered glance before standing aside to allow the six officers to exit the main entrance. They knew someone had planted those slips. Madame Queen would never be so sloppy, and more objectively, she had no reason to bring the receipts *from* her bank *to* her home. On the way to the elevator, Lieutenant Pfeifer arrested the old stoolie woman on the stairs for no recognizable reason, and she meandered along behind them, Amelia also in tow. As soon as they left, Winifred rushed down the hall to Jim, stating, "We got to help Madame St. Clair clean up this mess."

"Freeman already called down to her at the bank. She said don't touch nothing, she's sending a photographer. She said for us to lock it all up till she can get the man over here. Then we clean it up for her. You go ahead on back to Mrs. Light-foot. Tell her I'm locking up, and I'll come by after this to see how she's doing. I'll let you all know when she gets back, or when I hear anything." When Winifred hesitated to leave, he said, "I'll be sure to let her know you witnessed. She'll call on you, too, I know it. She knows we're good people. She knows we appreciate her."

—————

Before the policemen and their charges arrived in the lobby, one of the gang of newspaper boys had already picked his way the mile down Lenox to warn Madame St. Clair, too. Rather than return home, she tipped the boy, lit a cigarillo, and called her lawyer. If the people of Sugar Hill didn't already know who their queen was, they would soon enough.

IT DON'T MEAN A THING

Stephanie St. Clair's father had been dead for two years in 1911 when her mother, Ancelin, booked her a single, one-way passage in steerage from Guadeloupe to America. Stephanie was thirteen years old. Ancelin was far from destitute. Even in steerage, with a work contract, any option to travel to America existed only for a select few. Besides, social convention still weighed heavy, and raising four children alone must have been overwhelming and expensive. What mischief were these boys getting into? And the girls were too pretty, growing into women too fast to be left alone. Ancelin may have been trying to remarry herself, and rather than marry off Stephanie, she shipped her away. More likely, though, Ancelin saw the passage as an opportunity for a shrewd girl like her middle daughter to spin straw into gold.

The facts about St. Clair's immigration are sparse, but all of them imply a strong-willed woman. Leaving everything and everyone you've ever known is not for the irresolute, and a change like this one was impossible without detailed forethought, especially in the case of young women traveling from the Caribbean to North America. Stephanie's voyage had many stops, first in the Caribbean itself, to collect other passengers. Then, she spent days at sea until the ship docked at Ellis Island. The contract her mother had secured provided her a place to stay with other Black women arriving to New York City, a few weeks of training in domestic skills, and a sponsor to escort her through the confusing transportation system. After that, because her first language was French, Stephanie took a final train passage to Montreal where she would work a contract as a housemaid with the Du Boises for a few years, and then she made her way back down to Harlem. That's all we know for sure about her particular passage, but the route was so particular in the way that it doubled back, I can determine a few specifics with some confidence.

Stephanie would have packed sensibly with her mother's help. Neither of them cried. Neither of them said much of anything. Smaller rolls of neat dresses, stockings, underwear, and enough soap to last till she got where she was going stuffed her bedroll. Sewn into the bottom of her right shoe were a few bills to use only in case of emergency. She carried a coat of her father's, turned twice and tailored down to fit her shoulders. It still smelled like his pipe and rum. Because she left on a Sunday, July 23, 1911, Stephanie likely said goodbye to her brothers and sister before they left for Mass. Only her mother went to see her off. They wore their neatest, cleanest dresses on the trip to the port, even though that short trip alone soiled them.

When you were small, a palm reader confused you for my third son, Ancelin said as they walked down the pier. *Before I could correct her, she said, No. A girl. A strong, very strong girl. You could have been a very successful man, my dear. As it is, you will have to use the disadvantage of being a woman to your advantage. Do not forget that you are a lady. Even when you climb the back fence, even when you are tired and dirty and you feel too young or*

small to matter, never forget that you are a lady. And put on your
cleanest dress when you reach the port in New York.

=====

The SS *Guiana* wasn't the largest boat docked, but it still
loomed black and white above everyone on foot, as Stephanie climbed the stairs alone, the stack and the beams coming
into view as she rose. A man in a double-breasted coat with
shiny brass buttons looked at her ticket and directed her to
the lower deck. Families who embarked with tickets in steerage on the *Guiana's* earlier stops like Trinidad and Jamaica had
already made camp with a shade propped overhead or a little
pile of blankets.

The Quebec Steamship Company advertised to the New
York upper-class that the *Guiana* was a luxury cruise liner,
and it was, for them. The ship had electricity and double
berth rooms with space to walk between the beds, for passengers who paid for those luxuries. Those were the white
people who gathered on the top deck, gloved hands clutching
at the railing as the ship disembarked smoothly into the sea.

Stephanie must have realized almost immediately that the
ship did not make its profits on those first-class passengers, nor
even those who rode in steerage. Once boarded, she peered
over the ship's stern to see a wide ramp where men sweated
as they packed huge wooden crates into the hold. The SS
Guiana might be a luxury liner on top, but a look around
back quickly revealed its cargo ship foundation. Stephanie
held her bedroll primly in front of her and waited in the line
that snaked between exhaust pipes and ropes for her turn to
speak to the ledger man.

In the ship manifest, he took down her age incorrectly.
That's a fact. How it happened I had to infer. Could it have

been sloppiness on his part? A tired man performing a tired job? Maybe.

Or, at his podium, he asked her name in English. She did not speak English yet, but she deduced his question from the response of the young woman in front of her. "Stephanie St. Clair," she said, slowly enough that his pen could keep up. "Age?" he asked without looking up. She said, "Twenty-three." He said, "Next?"

Stephanie stepped aside and smirked a little when her little lie landed. Her mother's lesson was confirmed: she would decide what people thought of her. A step further, she could be whomever she chose.

━━━━

Official records state that the SS *Guiana* stopped five times total in the Caribbean before it continued up the east coast of America. The sea spray speckled the steerage passengers, and the salty air dampened them again between gusts off the waves. The brine collected and dried into a crust on Stephanie's skin, and her hair at the temples and nape of her neck curled and peeked from beneath her wrap. She could only imagine how ashen the salt made her skin look, and she fretted over it not from vanity but presentation. How could anyone believe she was a lady if not even her personal hygiene reflected that status? She found a bit of oil or grease from her tray at the end of a meal and massaged it into her knuckles and lips, smoothed back her hair, never mind if the oil went rancid before the chance to truly bathe. Everyone smelled the same, or at least, one in a crowd did not stand apart. Stephanie was cordial to the other girls who bedded down on the deck, but she kept her distance, even as they waited in line at mealtimes. Instead, she lingered nearer to the English-speaking people who boarded in St. Lucia and Barbados so she could glean everything possible before they docked at Ellis Island, where all the Caribbean immigrants like herself were deposited before the luxury liner continued up the Hudson River to Pier 47 in the West Village. When she disembarked, she and her fellow passengers filed into queue behind the immigrants just off another ship. She paid the closest attention to the children because they spoke the slowest and with the least inhibition. Any language in the world was represented in that line, from Arabic to Finnish to Swahili—and they were all spoken loudly, everyone panicked to be understood. New immigrants stood in line for hours, waiting like cattle in their chutes. Some may have tried to discern from where their neighbors might have arrived, why they smelled so distinctly of a particular spice they couldn't place, why their clothes were too dark, too bright, or too many, but most of them were probably concerned with themselves, their families, whether they'd come all this way for a new chance at life or if they'd be turned away at the threshold.

The gauntlet of tests everyone faced upon arrival at Ellis Island has been documented at length by many of the thousands of immigrants who were processed at this station. Tension was high for everyone, and the epithet Island of Tears preceded the institution. So did the six-second physical on which everything depended. Immigrants were often deported for reasons they couldn't help, like mental health, old age, and handicaps. Illnesses like tuberculosis, favus, and trachoma earned others weeks or months of quarantine on Swinburne Island south of Staten Island. If they didn't succumb to the illness—which they often didn't even know they had—then they waited, children and adults, sequestered, alone, indefinitely.

Much of this fate was determined in that initial physical examination. These six seconds were among the most important in Stephanie's life. When it was finally her turn, Stephanie climbed the large, wide entry stairs with her possessions while the doctors leaned over the railing to watch her from above. She never wrote or spoke about this period of her life. Later, she told most people she was French, from Marseilles, because what business was it of theirs where she was from? Because she was a slippery sort, and she later made her living off being a slippery sort, here's my best approximation of how her entry to New York might have happened. One doctor marked the shirt of a woman ahead of her with a piece of chalk. She was weeping openly, and the mark made her cry harder as she was sorted off the line for further medical examination. Stephanie then stood in front of the doctor with her chin tipped up, and she looked the white man in the face while his eyes passed over her, lingering first at her scalp, and then at her belly. "Bien, merci," he said after just a few seconds, and she stood there, surprised at the brevity.

"Viens par ici." A man in black gestured around the corner, where she found herself face-to-face with another white man who used a buttonhook to turn each immigrant's eyelid inside out. The physicians lingered the longest on her eyes, asking questions in a French accented so weirdly that she paused before answering. *If you are checking for contagious disease, why are you using the same rod on everyone?* she wondered, but knew better than to say aloud. At the time, trachoma was one of the most serious diseases they screened for, as it had no cure, was very contagious, and could cause irreversible blindness. Soon after, conjunctivitis, or "pink eye" like this would be treated with a simple dose of antibiotics, but now, it could mean the end of her journey if she were infected.

After a quick look, the doctor nodded at her, and she

moved past him into another queue where hundreds of immigrants waited their turn. She had completed the twenty-
nine–question survey on the ship. She was careful in her
answers, and she made sure her writing reflected both her education and her gentility. Stephanie clutched the form now
in her hands while she waited. Another hour passed before
she crossed to face the man in the tall chair behind the desk.
She had memorized the full form and her answers before she
finally passed it to the first medical examiner.

Her pauses after the questions alarmed the translator. "Bon-
soir, comment t'appelles-tu?" he asked.

She paused. He was speaking French, but she was bewildered at the strange accent again. It was not an English nor
American accent, which she expected. "Stephanie St. Clair,"
she answered, slow and clear.

The man scanned the ship manifest until he found her
name, and he asked, "Quel âge avez-vous?" This was the answer that made her most nervous—she didn't know yet that
white people could not see age on dark skin.

"Vingt trois ans."

"Quelle religion?" he continued.

"Catholique."

"Ancienne résidence?"

"Pointe à Pitre."

"Pointe à Pitre . . . ?"

"Oui, Pointe à Pitre."

"Où se trouve Pointe à Pitre?" the man asked, confused.
"Pouvez-vous m'entendre?"

Stephanie started to panic. "Oui, oui, Je t'entends, monsieur."

"Pourquoi ne réponds-tu pas, alors?"

The man next to him, who spoke in a more familiar accent,
overheard the conversation and said, "Pointe à Pitre . . . en

Guadeloupe, oui? She doesn't understand your crazy accent, man. He's from New Brunswick," the attendant said, as if that should explain it to her. "Il vient de la Nouvelle-Écosse. Qui vous rencontrera ici, mademoiselle?"

She breathed with relief that the officials had sorted out their miscommunication. Stephanie understood that she needed to identify a sponsor in New York City, and while no existing records indicate whom she had listed, it was likely that she arranged to stay at the White Rose Home, or another such home that specialized in acclimating girls to America, New York City, housekeeping skills, and the kinds of domestic jobs they'd work. She struggled around the odd, English words, "Ze Welcome Stronjerr Cloob take me to White Rose Home," and then for clarity she said it again in French, "Le club L'étranger Bienvenu m'accompagnera jusqu'à la Maison de la Rose Blanche."

"Ah, bienvenue en America, Mademoiselle St. Clair," the first man said, and gave over her landing card, her golden ticket, the permit to enter New York City. The whole interrogation lasted less than two minutes.

———

While she waited, Stephanie scrutinized what she could see of New York City. It was dirty and gray. Unlike the July she had left in Guadeloupe, here, the heavy clouds held in the moisture, trapping it to her body so that her sweat never cooled her off and never quite dried. When the mandatory sponsor that her mother arranged arrived, he escorted her to the White Rose Home for Colored Working Girls on East 86th Street. She wobbled as her sea legs adjusted to the pavement, and although she normally could keep her face placid at any stimulus, her eyes widened with marvel when they boarded the subway, and when the screeching behemoth started to move, she nearly panicked. A short walk from the stop, they arrived at the home.

The White Rose Home had fourteen beds for residents, and Stephanie's was probably a small, wrought iron–framed mattress, maybe in the corner of the dormitory. It housed women with many different stories. Black women and girls from all over landed in the White Rose Home in New York. One, an old woman up from the South. At least, Stephanie would have thought she was old. In reality, the woman had been born into slavery, emancipated as a child, and then sharecropped for years to earn passage north. She was only in her forties. Even she was not sure of her own exact age. This story is true. I have no way of knowing who Stephanie's roommate was—or if the White Rose was the home where she acclimated—but because of the diverse backgrounds of their residents, it's not unlikely, and if it happened, it would have played out this way. That woman followed Stephanie into the room, and rather than introducing herself, she fussed at Stephanie in an accented English that Stephanie couldn't understand. When the woman exclaimed, thinking Stephanie would set her bedroll on the clean spread, Stephanie met her with a steely side-eye, which changed her anxious rattling into a singsongy ramble. Even though her travel had taken less than a week, Stephanie wanted to wash her laundry clean first of all. She communicated through snatched phrases and gestures that she'd like laundry to be the first among the home's classes that she attended.

Each resident only stayed at the home for a few weeks, so after just a few days of extended bedtime prayers and snoring so loud Stephanie thought she was suffocating, that woman probably moved out and a second neighbor moved in. This is another true story, though I can't be sure it overlapped with Stephanie's stay. This new girl had walked to New York City

from Philadelphia. She was just a little younger than Stephanie's actual age of thirteen, but unlike Stephanie, she acted her
age. Her mind wandered during the cooking class that the
White Rose Home provided. The girl scalded the lard in
the pan and let the biscuits burn on the bottom. Stephanie
never understood unfocused minds like that, especially not
after watching the girl run over her finger with a sewing machine needle. Stephanie did fine with cooking, but she was
excellent at sewing. She mastered the machine and its main-
tenance after the first lesson, her hand stitches were tiny and
precise, and she had a knack for putting patterns together that
matched the skills of accomplished dressmakers. Though she
excelled there, she stunned everyone at the Penny Provident
Fund during that first lesson. I'm backwalking here: Stephanie was an expert seamstress and mathematician. That kind
of prodigy doesn't occur suddenly. Her talents would have
been present much earlier, and to develop the way they did,
someone had to realize it and help her hone those talents
into skills. It tracks that Stephanie's home would have offered a class like this one, even if it was not this one. The
class was her first introduction to the way money worked.
Although English came to her slowly, she understood numbers immediately. The formula kept her mind moving while
her roommate wept at her throbbing hand. Stephanie faced
the opposite wall, sweating, and in the light of the streetlamp
shining through the single-paneled curtains, she traced the
mauve floral wallpaper with her eyes, which in its reproduc-
tion of nature somehow made the city seem even more urban, while she multiplied in her mind the domestic problems
her classes presented her . . . how many eggs to feed breakfast
to a family of four? What if the eldest son came home from
boarding school without notice? How to squeeze in enough
for the servants to eat just as well but not raise the tab? How

could she schedule the milk and eggs to arrive at the same time and avoid paying for an extra delivery? How long could the milk keep between purchases in the summer? In the winter? New York City was hot, but when she made it to her final destination in Montreal, would it be hot, too? Did they have cellars to keep provisions cool? Those variable equations drowned out the bunkroom noise and put her to sleep.

In the daytime, while she learned important but boring tasks like how to darn a hole in a sock or how to get blood out of silk, her mind tumbled topics she learned about in the classes taught by the Penny Provident Fund. The class had many volunteer teachers who, once they had a little success of their own, wanted to pay it forward to the upcoming generations. Her specific teacher is not listed. One teacher in the program was Mr. Stephen Bowman, who was young and eager to help working-class people learn how to manage money, save, and eventually retire, and I can see him regarding Stephanie as an ideal pupil for those objectives. The concept felt so exotic to so many students he often had to explain it several times before his pupils fully grasped it. Every class, he showed up fresh in a suit and introduced new topics. Stephanie's favorite thing she'd learned so far was compound interest. She enjoyed percentages and probabilities as well, but the concept of earning money by doing nothing except being wise was particularly attractive. At the start of each class, she slipped out of the line filing in, hovered by his desk at the front of the room, and asked him hard questions in simple, limited English until the matron scolded her and she scurried back to her seat. Eighteen years before Black Tuesday, Stephanie wondered about bank runs and federal insurance, though she didn't have the terms for them. She asked things that blue bloods never questioned, or never wanted questioned: Why do people want to buy shares of a company when they are valued at their highest? Do people take advantage of and prey on that ignorance and hope? Statistically, it doesn't make sense for one person to win at every investment. Surely those who always win are cheating? How are they cheating? With information, or just stealing? Why don't they get caught? What happens if everyone withdraws their money from the bank at the same time? Won't the banks run out of money, if they're investing it, too? What happens when the bank runs out of money? Does anyone have insurance?

Mr. Bowman would have been fascinated with her mind, and he likely couldn't always answer her questions. In fact, she made him resent the rest of the students a little, when he had to explain and re-explain the simplest concepts of check-book balancing while Stephanie almost vibrated with energy, the problems on the blackboard long completed and resting neatly on the slate in front of her. The teacher spent the time between their classes working up harder problems, more practical applications, larger scopes of the financial world for her to try. Sometime during her adolescence, Stephanie picked up the skill of probabilities in the most practical way a child might have applied those principles. I think it would have happened like this:

Once when she took out the trash after supper, she saw a group of five or so men huddled behind the dumpster in the alleyway next to the home. Mr. Bowman was one of them. She was surprised and delighted to see someone she knew outside the context of the White Rose Home. Stephanie trotted down the stairs to the other side of the dumpster and watched for a moment before she held up a palm in greeting and quietly called, "Meesterh Bowmaan."

The young man was grinning at the game the men circled around and he when he glanced up, he had to do a double take to be sure it was her. "Just a minute, friend," he said. He called all of his students "friend." And he threw something on the ground that bounced against the wall of the brownstone. The other men shouted and he raked a stake of coins toward himself. "Don't touch anything, y'all hear? I'll be right back."

"We can't just be waiting on your ass," one of the men hollered at him.

"How about if I just take my pot and go home then?"

"Nah, we can wait a second, now," another man said loudly, "we got to at least have a chance to win it back."

Mr. Bowman held out his hand to shake Stephanie's.

"What is this?" Stephanie asked about the circle.

"We're shooting dice," he said. "Come on over, I'll teach you how to play."

"She got to ante up, too. Ain't no free looks," said the first man.

"Calm down, Junior," Mr. Bowman said and shoved two pennies from his growing stack to the center of the circle. "Look here," he said to Stephanie. "The goal is to win the pot by guessing the probability outcome of what number the shooter will roll. The pot keeps growing through the game, so the longer the game goes . . ."

"The more money," Stephanie said.

"Exactly. So what we do next is, everybody rolls both dice to see who the shooter is. The shooter is the one who will roll the dice for the game. For this group, it's whoever rolls the highest number. See there, Junior, he rolled a four, so we can be pretty sure he won't be the shooter."

Stephanie stood, absorbing every word, as the men each rolled their turn.

When the dice made its way to her, Mr. Bowman said, "Now when you throw it, make the threes into a V shape, like this, and then throw them side arm—they both have to hit the wall. There you go! Eight, not bad."

When the next player rolled a ten and became the shooter, Stephanie looked at Mr. Bowman.

"Now, Joe will put up whatever amount of money he wants to bet on himself. What we're betting on is one of two things that might happen on the first roll. The first roll is called the 'come out.' So we're betting on one of two things: Joe will either pass (that means roll a seven or an eleven), or he'll crap (that means roll a two, three, or twelve)."

Stephanie looked at him and said, "A twenty-one percent probability to . . . sixteen, no, seventeen, sixteen and a half percent?"

The circle around them stopped talking and looked up at her.

Mr. Bowman grinned and shook her shoulder a little, saying, "That's my girl, doing probability outcomes in her head! So what do you think Joe will bet on?"

"Joe should bet to pass."

Joe blinked suspiciously and said, "That's what I was gone do anyway, all right."

"See, Joe put up twenty cents. So it's up to the rest of us to match his twenty cents. We call that 'ante up.' See, they all put in a nickel, so if I want to bet some more, then I'll have to do a side bet. But let's just sit this one out and see what happens."

Joe shot his dice again against the wall, and he passed with a seven.

"That's the game. Joe wins," Mr. Bowman announced.

Stephanie frowned. "So short."

"Sometimes."

"What if he shot a four, five, six, eight, nine, or ten?"

The men were surprised that she could keep all the figures straight in her head and murmured to each other.

"Oh, that's when it gets real interesting, Stephanie. That's called the point."

They anted up and waited two more games, another pass and one crap, before the shooter—Joe again—rolled an eight.

Stephanie looked up at Mr. Bowman, though they were both crouching now.

"Okay, now, the number eight is the point. The only two things that matter now are the number eight and the number seven. So, if someone bet that he'd pass before—"

"Joe," Stephanie said.

"Right. So, Joe bet to pass before. Everybody else bet that he'd crap. So now, Joe's betting on seven, and everyone else is betting on eight."

"Those odds are very close," Stephanie said.

"Yes, they are."

"And what if he doesn't roll a seven or an eight?"

"Every time he rolls, we get to bet more money."

"And the probabilities change."

"Exactly."

"Because the probability of *not* rolling a seven or eight decreases, depending on how many shots or what the other shots are."

"Exactly."

By this point, the men in the circle all bore expressions of struggled comprehension. They were following conceptually, but not practically. They knew the idea of what she was saying, but the tables and charts weren't unspooling in their heads the way they did in the eye of Stephanie's mind.

"But we aren't betting," Stephanie said.

"Naw, uh-uh, y'all can't bet together," Junior said. "You got to play your own hand."

"Yes, sir," Stephanie said, and got very quiet.

Joe said to Mr. Bowman, "You know, Stephen, all this time I just thought you was a lucky son of a gun. But now I see, you just doing math."

Joe rolled an eight, and while they were divvying up the pot, Mr. Bowman said, "Do you want to play, Stephanie?"

"No, sir, thank you."

"You can play, if you want to."

"No, sir."

"I'll stake you."

She looked at him, confused.

"I'll give you a quarter to play with."

"No, sir, I couldn't take your money."

"When you win, you just pay me back."

Stephanie thought about this before she said, "With five percent interest."

"Four percent," Bowman countered.

"For neat math." She smiled.

"One more thing, though." At this his face looked serious. "You got to spend what you win on something important. Not just candy and ribbons."

Stephanie said plainly, "I thought I would put it in the stamp bank, like you taught us, sir."

He held out his hand to shake.

To say that Stephanie was a natural would be an understatement. The truer statement was that she understood the rules so well that she knew how to skate up to the very edge of them. She didn't bet big until she got comfortable, but by the second time she was the shooter, she put in all of her money but two cents.

As soon as her winnings mounted to fifty-one cents, she turned to Mr. Bowman and placed twenty-six cents in his hand. "Thank you," she said.

"You cashing out?" said Junior, a little too relieved.

"Let her play!" Joe protested.

"You can keep on," Mr. Bowman said. "Go ahead."

Inside of an hour she'd tripled her money. She lost track

of time until Mr. Bowman saw his watch and swore. Stephanie looked over from her growing stack of coins. "I better see you back to the home," he said. When she stood up, her knees cracked as blood rushed back into her feet. She picked up the handfuls of coins and dropped them into her pockets. They were so heavy that her dress looked like it might slide off both shoulders. Each of the men in the circle shook her hand as she left, and Mr. Bowman walked her around to the front of the building. "Just follow my lead, all right? The matron might not like it that you were playing dice, so—"

"*Dice?*" the matron gasped from the front stoop. "We have been worried sick about you, Miss St. Clair. You didn't sign out in the book or let anyone know where you were going. Anything could have happened!"

"I'm sorry," Stephanie said, too happy to show any contrition.

"And now you've been out *gambling*. Lord forgive you."

At this new word, Stephanie looked perplexed. "Gambling?"

"Relying on luck to earn your money is a sin."

"Oh! No, it's not luck," Stephanie said, smiling now that she understood. "It's probability. It's mathematics. Not luck."

Mr. Bowman bit his lip to keep from laughing when the matron glared at him. He gave a small shrug before he admitted, "She's right. And madame, if I might say so again, Stephanie is *very* gifted with figures." Before she could butt in with a punishment, he added, "She's been learning a lot in the Penny Provident classes. Stephanie said she wants to buy stamps from the bank with her winnings. I mean, earnings."

This seemed to shut the matron up, or at least set her back. "Still, you left the house without signing out—"

"No, madame. I took out the trash. I was behind the house all along."

"And now, this impertinence. Straight to bed with you. You'll be scrubbing baseboards tomorrow."

Stephanie grinned big as if to say, *Worth it*, and made to dash away before she remembered herself, turned around, and shook hands with Mr. Bowman again. "Thank you for teaching me," she said, and darted up the steps, coins jangling against each other all the way. Stephen Bowman couldn't help but be happy with himself, even though it seemed like the matron might bore holes into him with her glare alone.

———

Bowman was nearly driven to tears when his star pupil had to leave a few days later. He sent with her several books on probability and statistics, all that he could get on short notice. She wouldn't take them with chalk on her hands—Stephanie was adamant about not wiping dirt into her skirts—and he waited while she withdrew a handkerchief from her sleeve and wrapped it around them chanting *merci* over and over.

Since her arrival stateside, Stephanie had spent nearly all her time at the White Rose Home—especially after her punishment for gambling—so when it was time to leave for Montreal just a month later, she saw the city with virgin eyes. When she made her way to Grand Central Station, she caught snatches of every language, strange clothing. Greasy hands. Smells of garbage and coffee and new spices from the street vendors. She boarded the express train to Montreal with specific instructions on where to transfer, where to sit on the train, and whom to find when she arrived. While she rode on the hours-long trip, she scoured the immigration contract her mother had signed, which had been released to her possession only on this leg of the voyage.

Stephanie arrived in Quebec less than a month before the Cabinet of Canada passed Order-in-Council P.C. 1324, which declared that "the landing in Canada shall be and the same is prohibited of any immigrants belonging to the Negro race, which race is deemed unsuitable to the climate and requirements of Canada." Even after the order, other women like Stephanie continued to arrive via the Caribbean Domestic Scheme—and while the documentation of Stephanie's indenture has been lost to antiquity, many women in her circumstances, working-class women of color from the Caribbean, immigrated through this program. Although the government tried to keep them out, women from Guadeloupe continued to arrive, much to the relief of the Canadians who relied on servants. White girls either would not do service work at all, or they asked for a fair wage, which was far too much for the upper middle class to sustain, so the Canadian government made exceptions to their own rules when immigration involved importing a new servant class. The Caribbean Domestic Scheme was the most likely reason why Stephanie stopped through New York City only to continue on to Canada, when, for many immigrants, New York was their final stop. This scheme recruited young women from Guadeloupe. Canadian employers paid their $80 passage to Canada, and in exchange, the women worked for one or two years for $5 per month. The scouts for the scheme had likely duped Ancelin into believing that jobs in North America were scarce for domestics, that no one in New York could speak French, and that the wage they proposed was firm and high, even with cost of living adjustments. Ancelin had contracted Stephanie to work in Canada as a domestic servant for two years in exchange for the passage and room and board on the SS *Guiana*. Domestic servants lived with the white family, which meant long hours and no community interaction. Stephanie also learned that under this contract she would never be eligible for Canadian citizenship. With the best of intentions, Ancelin sent her daughter to a holding cell, from which, if she ever escaped, she could be immediately deported. Stephanie only learned the details of the contract while she was en route, and she naturally started to plan. And she started to count. Her documentation stated that she arrived to the home of her Canadian employer, the Du Bois family, after just four weeks in New York. She arrived knowing exactly what she was capable of, and exactly how much of that capacity to reveal to the ones driving her.

Stephanie learned English well, though she never lost her accent completely, since even those from whom she learned spoke French as their first language, too. She soon grew accustomed to the weird French-Canadian accent she'd first heard at Ellis Island. While she was at the Du Bois home, she cultivated the skills she learned at the White Rose Home, skills that were always in demand. She was especially eager to dress the woman of the house, and her clothes fit—and displayed—the mistress so well that she was the envy of all her friends. Madame du Bois would have probably felt generous when she let Stephanie use the remainders of the fabrics for her own dresses (as long as they didn't match her gowns too clearly), and because Stephanie excelled at mathematics, she could almost always squeeze another, less extravagant frock from the remnants, or at least a set of practical undergarments. She let out her own dresses with gussets and other tricks as she grew; she studied the books Mr. Bowman at the Penny Provident Fund had given her; and she kept count of the days.

Because she held her cards so close to the vest, it stunned the Du Boises when she announced one evening after the table was cleared that her contract term had ended, and she would be leaving their employ. Despite Monsieur du Bois's predictable stuttering rage, she continued evenly that she wanted to try her hand at dressmaking. She felt that she had a real talent for it, and she told them she planned to serve a two-week courtesy notice to ease the transition.

Monsieur du Bois did not notice his wife's small smile when he stood so fast that he nearly overturned his chair. He said that Stephanie should be gone by morning, and he wouldn't provide a reference. Because she had intuited that he would react this way, Stephanie had already packed her bag in her apartment upstairs. She withdrew politely and bathed in preparation for her return journey to New York. When she rose before dawn, Madame du Bois waited at the foot of the back stairs, where she hand delivered a letter of reference detailing the exquisite creations Stephanie had styled for her, sketches of Stephanie's that she used to illustrate some of the especially complex gowns, and a small sum of money. Stephanie made the walk to the station and used the parting gift to buy passage on the Adirondack Express. Best to get out of Canada on her own terms before Monsieur du Bois thought to deport her to the Caribbean. She arrived back in Manhattan alongside a host of other immigrants and refugees in the Great Migration.

———

Many Italians fled Fascism and Mussolini for America, New York in particular. Even more people left Sicily when they could, and although Sicily was already officially a part of Italy, its culture was far different from that of the mainland. Sicilian was a pidgin language, of Italian and Arabic. Sicilians looked different. Their customs were different, and their government was doubly oppressive: even though they were under legal governance by Mussolini—who went from prime minister to the Fascist Il Duce in 1925—they were also subject to the vendettas of the long-standing unofficial local government

known as Cosa Nostra. Silly as it might sound to call the government "our little thing," the Cosa Nostra, or mafia, was no
joke. If Italians fled the dictatorship of Mussolini whenever
possible, Sicilians fled both Fascism and the mafia.

Other nations on the Continent saw exodus, too. Through-
out the 1920s, German policy officially encouraged Jewish
emigration. Germans left their homelands for America where
whole neighborhoods devoted themselves to immigrant populations of Italians and Jewish people.

Before all this, though, there was the push for outlawing
alcohol. The Women's Christian Temperance Union of the
1910s had linked unemployment to alcohol consumption, and
with alcohol consumption, homemakers saw domestic abuse.
They lobbied for Prohibition with several religious groups,
factory owners who sought to increase worker efficiency and
prevent workplace accidents, and reformers who sought to
increase government involvement in daily life. The promise
of Prohibition paradoxically led to increased immigration, especially among bootleggers. When the 18th Amendment was
ratified in 1921, it opened up a whole new field for people
who were criminals anyway.

Career criminals bootlegged alcohol into the city from
Canada. A lot of recent immigrants still had business connections on the Continent, so they orchestrated the big-picture
smuggling. When business of all kinds boomed in the 1920s,
everything was great. The big guys hired unemployed refugees
to do the hard part, like driving a truck full of contraband
over the frozen Great Lakes, or paying off border police.

=====

While other immigrants found their place in the city, Stephanie St. Clair retraced her steps to New York City. Records
don't specify where she went exactly, but it makes the most

sense that she revisited the White Rose Home first, and she likely arrived unannounced. I imagine the matron of the home viewed the decision as rash and unthoughtful, but Stephanie would have planned this return from the moment she left for Montreal. The matron would have remembered Stephanie, and she would have been surprised to hear Stephanie speak easily to her in English. Her appearance had morphed into a poised young woman, and although wrinkled from travel, she was especially well-dressed. Perhaps the most surprising element, though, was simply that Stephanie had come back at all. Almost no one returned. Before the matron could think to ask about a disgrace or ingratitude, Stephanie explained her plan. She offered to rent a room at the home until she could find employment at a dress factory and rent her own place. At the mention of her living alone, the matron would have stopped her cold. They had no empty beds at the moment, but they could fix up a cot. Stephanie rose. "I will make the bed. I remember where things are," she said, and put the one dollar and twenty-five cents into the matron's hand.

———

Stephanie secured a position at a dress factory in the garment district within days, but the matron at the White Rose Home still insisted Stephanie live with them. To live alone as a woman was to be a woman of ill repute, she said, or a widow who would soon become a woman of ill repute. She would have no protection, no people, no support, and the matron wouldn't allow it.

Other expectations came with permanent residence, though. Stephanie taught a few classes on sewing and math until she lost her patience, and then the matron made her attend the child-rearing courses. The cooing nonsense, scraping

excrement out of cloth diapers before boiling them on the
same stove they used to make dinner, and bouncing someone
else's infant who screamed directly into her ear till her back
ached drove her to distraction. "Please," she asked the matron.
"I can't spend my time doing this."

The matron lived by the ideal that idle hands are the devil's
playthings, and Stephanie was no one to stay idle besides,
so this is one way that Stephanie might have surfaced at the
Roman Catholic Church. The matron sent her to serve at
the kitchen they hosted. Stephanie attended Mass regularly
all her life, first in Guadeloupe, then in Montreal, and now
she went with the rest of the residents at the White Rose
Home since she started working there. She genuflected before entering the pew, and she paid rapt attention through the
homily, kneeling prayers, and hymns, though she sometimes
abstained from taking the sacrament because she seldom arrived in time to confess beforehand, and with folded arms
took the blessing instead. It's likely that this Roman Catholic
Church is where she met George Gachette. On Ash Wednesday while she waited to confess, a tall young man with bright
eyes asked her name. "Where are you from?" he asked.

"Marseilles," she answered, and looked away before she
could see him frown.

"Your name is Marseilles?"

"I'm from Marseilles."

"The Tiger from Marseilles." He waited.

"My name is Stephanie."

"I'm George Gachette. I come to this church with my
mother, but I live in San Juan Hill."

She said nothing.

"I see you when I visit. I'd like to come call on you."

He waited again.

"My mother said you stay at the White Rose Home. She

said the teachers she knows there know you. Can I come talk to you sometime? I like smart women, and they say that you're smart."

"I'm a lady," she corrected him.

"That's what I meant—smart ladies," he blurted, eager now that he'd gotten a response. "Can I come call on you?"

"It's my turn," Stephanie said, and turned away.

I don't know that this is the exact dialogue that happened between them. No one knows exact dialogue this many years later, even if they were the ones who had the conversation, and even if Stephanie told me directly, based on what you already know of her character, what are the chances she wouldn't edit the interaction to tell the story she wanted to tell?

Same with George. Young dating-age men always come across more gallant in their retellings than they are in fact. Later, George would have told his mother he was going to call on Stephanie at the White Rose Home. His mother had seen their conversation, and she was skeptical. "She didn't say no," George told her. "She's a lady. She couldn't say yes, but she didn't say no."

———

Stephanie made no mention of George Gachette in her later life. The only way we know he came into her orbit is from legal records. A marriage certificate. Immigration data. His later death certificate. For that reason, I feel like I should remind you that I've recreated all interactions with George. Documents state that all these interactions happened, but there is no personal record . . . unless Stephanie detailed them in a letter or interview. Like I said before, I'm working backward, knowing the person she developed into without knowing for certain *how* she did it—we know the end point and the start point without the journey between. Based on the stories she told, I can intuit the indomitable persona she wanted to display for the world, a façade that she could stand behind while she took care of her own business in private. With that in mind, I ask you to trust me that Stephanie did not like that George came to court her where she lived, even if the other girls peeked out at him from behind the sitting room screen to admire his pretty, wavy hair while he signed the guest book. She was not moved by his charm the way the others were, but she still walked with him through the park when he came to call. She was a lady, and she did not want to embarrass him by turning him away, not in front of other people. George seemed like a nice man. Official records show that he was an immigrant from Dominica, and he had gone the opposite route from Stephanie. He and his family landed first in Canada and then made their way down to New York, where they heard of a neighborhood called Harlem. He rented a room there, by himself, and he supported himself by working as an engineer. He would have told her all this as though reading his résumé to her aloud, proud, but trying to get her attention with something, anything. "I take jobs in Manhattan, Hell's Kitchen, Flatiron, Financial District—"

She glanced over, as if realizing for the first time that he was there.

"It's just as easy to get downtown as it is across Harlem," he explained.

"Why?"

"Why? Subway only goes north to south. I guess they figured we'd only want to get in and out of Harlem, not from one place to another inside it."

"There is no bus?"

"Oh, sure, there are buses . . ."

"Damn the buses."

He looked at her again as they walked, and he almost laughed. "Damn the buses," he agreed. "They are never on time."

"They're filthy."

"Somebody always eating egg salad or cutting their toenails."

They said in unison, "I could walk there faster."

They paused as George trotted down a few steps ahead to offer Stephanie his arm down the stairs. She took it, even though she didn't need it.

"What interests you, mademoiselle?"

"What?"

"I keep talking, but I can't figure you out. It's starting to make me feel vain, all this talking about myself."

"The future, I think. I think the most about the future."

"What does your future look like?"

Stephanie smiled.

"That's the first time I've seen you smile."

"You like my gold tooth."

"Sure."

"It's expensive."

"It's gold."

"No, my future is expensive."

George laughed.

She shrugged. "You asked."

"So, you like money?"

"Money is interesting. But I only like money because money gives you options."

"You mean it gives you stability?"

"Yes, but it lets you choose what kind of stability you want."

"You know, some people would say marriage does that."

"Those people choose that kind of stability."

"You won't choose that kind?"

Stephanie shrugged. "I don't see how it is better than any other kind. It might be worse. It's very permanent."

"If you marry me, you won't pay for nothing. And if you don't fall in love with me by the time you've saved up your right amount, you can leave whenever you want."

Stephanie stopped walking and looked at him incredulously. "Your marriage proposal sounds like a business proposal."

"That's your language."

"It's no risk for me. You have all the risk. No reward. It's a bad deal for you. Why would you do this?"

"Because even if you don't love me right now—"

"If? I never talked to you before Sunday. If."

He pursed his lips. "Even though you don't love me right now. I know you will."

"How do you know this? You don't know me."

"Everyone falls in love with me," he said simply.

"I don't do that," she said.

He continued on, "And I know myself. I will love you as long as you let me."

For most women, that would be more than they ever thought to ask for. For Stephanie, it was not enough. She negotiated: "I will not be your housewife. I will not ever be a housewife, and I do not want to be a mother."

"You'll change your mind."

Stephanie turned on her heel and walked away.

"Wait—"

She said over her shoulder, "I will not change my mind. I know my own mind."

"Maybe not about being a housewife, but women always fall in love with their babies."

"I don't do that."

"Do what?"

"Love. I don't do that. It makes no sense."

"Just because you haven't done it yet doesn't mean you 'don't.' *That* doesn't make sense."

"Be reasonable," she said.

"It is reason. But it's still wrong. You can be logical all day long and still be wrong."

"George," she said, with the French accent, the way the name was originally pronounced. He grinned when she said it, a mouth full of perfect white teeth. "George," she repeated. "I'm not going to change my mind, either. But if your mind is still decided at Christmas . . ." She tsked. "We will see at Christmas."

George didn't change his mind. I invented the conversation above, but they did marry in the Roman Catholic Church on Epiphany, January 6, 1915, thirteen days after she turned eighteen.

━━

Few people in Harlem know about this part of her past, or really any part of her past. It was easy to obscure in favor of more relevant information. In Stephanie's mind, her history was full of stuff that had already happened. Stephanie's eyes were on the horizon, and she didn't have the patience to acknowledge, let alone answer, inane questions about the details of her success. "Where'd you grow up?" her hairdresser might ask in the kitchen while the lye warmed on Stephanie's scalp.

"Don't come at me sideways, my dear. You want to know where did my money come from, yes?"

The woman would laugh as if embarrassed at the confrontation.

Stephanie probably responded in the cryptic ways that seemed so rational to her, "The answer is always the same: work and smarts. Where do you get your money? Work and smarts. And it helps to be lucky. How do you lose the weight?

Diet and exercise. But it helps to be thin already." Though her answer stayed rote, the rumors of her wealth swung wide, a pendulum moving between the privilege of inherited wealth ("I heard her family had they own sugarcane plantation in the islands, one a them slave rebellion colonies, and then she came up here for to just see what all we about") to infant sacrifice and zombie priesthood ("How else she got secret big money like that? Ain't like she invented what all Madam Walker did. And what a good-lookin' woman like that doing without no husband or family?"). In reality the truth was somewhere between those two extremes, and she was being truthful: it was equal parts work and smarts, but it helped to have a little luck. Stephanie St. Clair knew, of course, that the luck was the most important element. Not only was she so intuitive and sensitive to energies that many revered her instinct as witchcraft ("Don't you know that woman's touched? Stay out from round her or she'll put your future on you."), but her mind extended in the patterns of mathematics, too. When she couldn't sleep at night, she counted by prime numbers—arithmetic branched in every direction at once, the way a drop of blood spreads on a white linen, sure of itself and indelible. The luck was possessing these two talents, but the smarts was incorporating them.

Stephanie could have only been in Sugar Hill with George for so long before she learned of the ubiquitous numbers racket. 1915 might have been right in the middle of the Progressive Era, but tenement living was the norm, and we can assume that a frugal man like George would have had an apartment on the top floor of a walk-up, and a domestic worker like Stephanie would have hated the stairwell—not because of its height, but because of its stench. Fine for the too-many smells of stove pots to seep into the hallway, but this one smelled like someone urinated on the fifth floor and it spilled the whole way down, and the corner of every stair was piled with cat hair. She moved through the transitory space as fast as possible, and by the time she reached either the top or bottom, she was always breathless. While she didn't mind doing her share of the housework (exactly half, no more and no less), she would not approach the dumbwaiter for the trash. It was a concentrated amalgam of the hallway, and she would only describe its smell to George as "pure evil," and the many-kneed roaches that scurried out of the dumbwaiter made her cringe to her very core. To her, that kind of filth should only be handled by a man who put himself in its proximity. George didn't mind. He was doing it all himself before she moved in, and he liked the way those bugs revealed her softness. He seldom saw it elsewhere.

She saw the policy racket firsthand and dismissed it as total chance. That, she thought, was what the White Rose Home matron meant by "gambling." But based on other memoirs of the time, the room they rented would have been so hot by late spring, even with the window open, that the whole street was up on the roof, just trying to catch a breeze while the sun set. Those same memoirs say the numbers runners hopped roof to roof taking penny bets, so she might have watched the gangly man lope from group to group, eventually coming to where she and George were stretched long. "Can I put something down for ya, George?"

"Sure," he said. "What'd you dream about last night, honey?"

"I dreamed I was a queen bee mad that you were talking about my honey."

George looked back to the runner. "What's that, insects or royalty?"

He shrugged. "Could put a nickel on both."

"A penny is all. We'll go with royalty," George said. "What's that in the dream book? One fifty?"

"I got you," he said, jotting something on a long strip of paper and pocketing George's coin.

"What's this?" Stephanie asked him. "What's this game?"

"You must be new to town. You ain't played the numbers? Well, here's how it goes: every number is three digits. Always three. . . ."

After a drawn-out explanation, Stephanie deduced that the first winning digit came from taking the last digit of the sum of the payoff total for the first three horse races that day, the second digit came from adding up the payoff total for the first five races, and the third digit came from adding up the payoff for the first seven.

"So, for example," he said, jotting down the numbers as he explained, "if the payoffs on the winning horses in the first three races added up to $315.60, the first five was $731.20, and the first seven was $913.40, then the number that hit that day would be 513. Of course, if you can spare more, then you bet more. Lots of people combinate, too, to get more chances at a win. So, for example, if their lucky numbers were 3, 7, and 9, they'd play 379, 793, 937, and so on, a penny or a nickel or whatever they could afford on each number. The more you stand to bet, the more you stand to win. You follow me?"

Stephanie understood, and she understood just as well that if most people "combinated," then most people were not using probability outcomes to place their bets. The same as with the dice game, they thought it was all luck. She thanked the runner for his explanation, and when he asked if she'd like to put something down, she looked at George as if asking permission before she said, "Let me think about it."

The runner bandied to a couple more groups before he jumped over the alley onto the neighboring roof rather than walk all the way down to the street level, over one address, and then all the way back up the stairs. After that, she saw those men everywhere she went. There were several runners for every numbers bank, and banks shared territory. Different banks held people's preferences the way some people preferred Lucky Strikes over Camels. It wasn't better or worse, just a matter of taste. Even if she hadn't met her first numbers runner in this way, she was absolutely introduced to the game somehow.

Stephanie probably watched George play without any strategy for weeks, studying the outcomes like a cautious person would, before she went down to the butcher shop to place her bet with the runner who propped himself outside. She went in and ordered her soup bone and ground beef from the Jewish owner right afterward, as if nothing had happened, but she felt a rush of promise, and at the counter I think she might have splurged as if celebrating, and she changed her order to sirloin.

At some point, a quick trace of probabilities told Stephanie that even if she did win, the bank wouldn't be able to pay out. Her own building's tenants likely hit several times, big, all in one week, and that led to folks playing nickels instead of pennies, and then dimes instead of nickels, doubling down on their ordinary combinations, She placed her bet in secret, only because she couldn't have sweet George tracking her money with every win: you never can tell when men will start to feel entitled.

She hit big several times in a row because she knew how to play the odds—like when she learned the rules of dice, it came naturally to her. She could read the pattern of which numbers in sequence had already hit. Though the probability outcomes were so much more complex for the numbers game that she couldn't keep them all straight in her head, she could still read the potentials.

Although records aren't clear on whether the George Gachette born in Harlem in the summer of 1915 was George
and Stephanie's child, if he was, then George Sr. would have
often found Stephanie scribbling at his tiny breakfast table by
the window, hunched over her newly pregnant belly in the
glow from the streetlight. When he looked over her shoulder,
he couldn't decipher a single figure. Not the numbers whose
odds she calculated, and not the names of the employees for
each bank. He'd just smile, hug her, kiss the top of her head
and ask her to come to bed, which she wouldn't.

At first, she spread her bets across the neighborhood, and
then she got strategic. Stephanie placed bets with everyone who came to see her on her childbirth bed. Because
the women she knew were from church and from the White
Rose Home, they all lived in separate apartment buildings
now, and the buildings sat in the territories of different banks.
Over the next few weeks, her number hit several more times.

Her triumph in accumulating capital didn't happen overnight.
She lost sometimes, as everyone does, but soon enough, her
winnings piled high enough to play her own hand. In a very
predictable scene the following summer, Stephanie might
have held her cardboard suitcase while George held their
son, demanding to know why, and how could she. Stephanie
pursed her lips and said matter-of-factly in a way that anyone but her would perceive as cold, "George, we both kept
our agreement," and left them forever. If George Jr. was their
child, she probably sent money to them both, especially once
she got really wealthy, because that's who she was. That's if
the boy survived to adulthood, and some documents say he
didn't. She wouldn't have left George Sr. for any reason other
than business because she was honorable and honest, and

business was always her first priority. In fact, they never did divorce on paper. She was a generous person, and she realized that without generosity, with the whole community competing against one another, no one could succeed. Still, no one knew about this part of her life. No one knows still. It looks as if that chapter had been struck from the manuscript. It was just part of the journey, compulsory only in its assistance toward the destination. Some people claim it never happened at all, that a lady like Madame Stephanie St. Clair might have left an old husband, but she would never abandon her child, and maybe they're right.

———

Regardless, at last, Stephanie rented her own room in Harlem, closer to the main line that took her down to the dress factory where she worked, and with a hallway kept immaculate by the super. She didn't have a doorman yet, but she had sense enough to rent on the far side of the building, an apartment with its own fire escape so she could have two routes of egress, just in case. She sat out on that platform often, and although to anyone watching it may have seemed like she was daydreaming, her mind was scheming, manifesting, plotting her next move to rise into the position she wanted. Stephanie spent her days at the dress factory, but that job alone wasn't enough to live on and save up. It makes the most sense that she kept playing the numbers, and she kept winning. We know that she hit it big several more times. She won enough times to draw attention from the bankers whose doors she temporarily shuttered. And we know that at some point, she cut her teeth working as a clerk for someone's bank. Which one she worked for isn't written down, but it's pretty obvious.

How she got recruited isn't clear, but I think one way is the most probable. Stephanie made her living off probabilities, so I feel comfortable taking this gamble. Plus, this way is the most fun one, and she was at ease in changing her own narrative. One day when she came home from work, it wasn't the runner sitting on the stairs grinning with her payout, but the banker himself. She'd never seen him before, but she knew it was him from the too-much grease in his hair, how clean the middle part, the rings on every finger but the married one. And she had seen his face in the papers. A great philanthropist, they said, and between the lines, a gangster. She drew her heels together and held her purse in both hands. The door was right behind her. She could make a getaway if she needed to—she'd have no trouble outpacing this man in his uncreased suede shoes, she was sure, and she could always give some kid from her new building a quarter to come gather her important things. She thought of all this, scouting potential defensive weapons in the loose staircase spindle or even the fountain pen in her purse. With a plan in place in a matter of seconds, Stephane raised her eyebrows once under her hat's wide brim and said, "Good evening, Mr. Holstein."

He didn't stand, and her prey-like mentality vanished. Now she just thought he was trash.

Casper Holstein didn't say anything, not for a long time, but she waited him out, elbows pinched to her sides.

"How'ah you doing this?" he asked.

"Excuse me?"

"How is this, that this same woman keeps winning?"

"I don't know what you are asking me."

"Who do you have on the inside at the horse track?"

Stephanie laughed so wide it was like her jaw unhinged in one, shocked guffaw.

The boss shifted his weight.

"You flatter me," she said, covering her mouth with one

hand. "You think I'm cheating. I do not do that. I do not cheat. I am a lady, monsieur."

"I can see that. How you doing it then?" He leaned forward, still feet above her on the staircase.

"It is only mathematics, sir." She murmured something in French, thought for a moment, and said, "It's what you call . . . 'the law of large numbers'?"

Holstein offered her a job on the spot.

Stephanie had conditions before she accepted. Two among them: she could keep her job at the factory and work second shift for him, and she could leave with one day's notice. He agreed, and when the awkward silence extended long enough to make clear that she would not be inviting him up for dinner, he left. Stephanie was so excited that she couldn't sleep. The hunger she had felt when leaving the factory had vanished, but hearing her stomach, she chewed on a roll from the day before while she thought of what she might wear on Monday when she started work as clerk for Casper Holstein.

She was a quick study. She absorbed all the information she could from her new boss, including his own history. He wasn't as close-lipped as she was. Casper Holstein had been in New York since he was in elementary school, when his family emigrated from the British West Indies, so he knew its ins and outs better than she. He got his first significant job as a bellboy at a Manhattan hotel, and while that position had pulled back the curtain to the elites, his real break came when his mother sent him to deliver a message to a servant at the Chrystie house—that's Mr. John A. Chrystie, of the Chrystie and Janney firm, one of the wealthy Wall Street tycoon families of New York. While Casper waited in the kitchen for a reply, Mrs. Chrystie asked him to deliver a package to 124 Putnam Street. When he arrived at the address, Casper realized it was the wrong one. Rather than turn back, Casper knocked on every door with a four in its address till he found the right place. By the time he reported back, saying that the package was delivered, Mrs. Chrystie also realized she'd given the wrong address. "Wonderful! How did you manage it?" He explained what he'd done, and she was so impressed by his tenacity that she persuaded her husband to hire him in their house. Because Mrs. Chrystie's mother was blind, they ultimately hired Casper to read to her every afternoon. That little job got Casper in the Chrystie family's good graces, so much so that they hired Casper as Chrystie's valet. He worked in that role until he joined in the Great War and served in the navy for four years. Then, he came back to the bellman's job, where he learned so much about the stock market and horse racing as a fly on the wall that people say he's the one responsible for creating the numbers game as they knew it.

From this story, Stephanie learned that her break could come from anywhere. Anything could be an opportunity if she looked at it with one eye half-closed.

===

Still, if and when Stephanie went to work for Holstein's bank, she took the second shift, adding an income stream rather than taking on more risk. She expected to learn the trade of the numbers business, and she did. She uncovered how its machinery worked, where the gears ran smooth as well as where they ground with inefficiency. Bankers could evade taxes by banking offshore, and this worked especially well for Holstein because he was a Virgin Islands native. To Stephanie, though, that offshore banking meant that when a bettor hit big money, or more than one bettor hit at the same time, and the bank paid out, the banker had to make a run down to the Caribbean to wire funds back, in person, before they could get back up and running. That travel took days if not weeks, so the bank stayed down until the money arrived. And when the money hit the account, it took a little while longer for word of mouth to reach all the employees. Time was money, and the bank lost customers to attrition every time they went under. They lost employees as well because everyone had mouths to feed and bills to pay, and very few of them had the education Stephanie had gotten from the Penny Provident Fund when she was young about how to save, budget, and invest. Stephanie was always glad she'd kept her first-shift job at the factory for this very reason: she didn't need the Holstein job, so when it dried up, she would still be all right, even if she was living month to month, which she wasn't. Banking did pay better, but only when it was paying. She didn't like the inconsistency. No one liked it. She had identified a major employee retention problem in the business practice.

Not to mention that while banking offshore was mostly legal for Holstein, at some point, the government always comes sniffing around for more money. Even if it was completely legal to bank how he was banking, which was most likely not the case, when the taxman inevitably audited him, the bank got a whole lot more attention. She didn't want that attention. No illegal business would be comfortable with that. Stephanie didn't know for sure, but when that audit rolled around, she figured Holstein would have to grease more palms to back them off, and would that balance out financially with not paying taxes? She doubted it, even if most West Indian–run numbers banks followed the same practice. Bribes were a high-ticket item, but they were necessary when you had to appease the corrupt Tammany Hall officials. The Democratic organization had started off in the early 1800s on the grounds of representing white working-class men otherwise

overlooked politically, and in the 1850s they became a pow-
erhouse of Irish politics who helped poor families with coal
or food. Tammany exploited the support by stuffing ballot
boxes and exercising power anywhere it saw an opportunity,
and its political machine continued to flourish through the
1920s and '30s. Maybe not everyone knew their taxes were
funding huge salaries of officials that enabled—or were part
of—the mafia, but most people knew. Most businesses had to
pay for protection to mafia dons, as well, which was in fact
protection from the mafia itself and simple extortion. Costs of
doing business were high all around, but she couldn't justify
not doing her moral civic duty. At the very least, on a practical level the costs of doing business were harder to account
for, and Stephanie didn't care for sloppy figures.

She also learned that the old adage "There is no honor
among thieves" was only somewhat true. Stephanie stood out
among Holstein's employees as the only woman. Not the only
woman clerk; she was the only woman. Not even the sec-
retaries were women. For that reason, I deduced that there
would have been some tension at her presence, and I think it
may have played out in a scene like this one:

"Who's this broad?" one of the runners asked the comptroller right in front of her desk, as if she wasn't there.

Stephanie stood up and said, "I'm Madame Stephanie
St. Clair. I'm the new clerk. You can call me Madame St. Clair.
And, you can give that package of bills to me to count, Mr.
Jackson."

"That ain't how it works around here," Jackson said. "The
runner gives the money to the comptroller. Then the comptroller gives it to the clerk." He handed the package to the
comptroller.

She held out her hand, and the comptroller gave it to her.
Stephanie found the day's calculations of winning payouts

and sat down to count Jackson's submission against the figure while Jackson and the comptroller chatted about her right in front of her. "She got a mouth on her, but she cute, though. I like how she holds that pencil."

Stephanie compared the two sums and then looked up again from the tidy short stack of bills and coins, and the policy slips. She said that he was thirty-four cents short. "Also, I am a lady, and I'll thank you to keep your comments about my person to yourself, Mr. Jackson."

"That ain't short. Count it again."

"You're thirty-four cents short," she repeated.

"Count it again."

Stephanie kept eye contact with him while she picked up the stacks of coins with one hand and set them back down. "You're thirty-four cents short."

He stared at her.

She stared back.

"I'll count it my damn self," he said.

"Both hands above my desk, please."

He swore the whole time, counted the stacks, and came up with the same figure, much slower than she did.

"What did you count?" she asked.

He stared at her with a clenched jaw, not admitting that she was right.

She said nothing.

He dug both hands into his pockets, where he found a few pennies. He checked his breast pocket, and the pockets of his coat, but he was still short.

"What's that come to?" he asked.

"Twelve cents short," she replied.

The comptroller looked on.

"Well, I don't have no more change just hanging out on me," he said, exasperated now.

Stephanie just looked at him.

He scoffed. "What you want me to do, here?"

"I can't accept this drop without the full amount, Mr. Jackson."

"Aw, girl, it's just a few cents."

"Madame St. Clair," she corrected. "I cannot turn in an incomplete drop."

"What I'm supposed to do, girl?"

"There are two options. The first one is that you pay the full amount that your records stated you collected here to me now—or to your comptroller here, and he can hand it to me, if you would prefer to follow exact protocol. The second option, you can refund each of your customers according to your records." She gestured at the log of policy slips next to the pile of coins.

By this time, the whole bank had quieted down to hear the confrontation between the new clerk and the longtime runner.

Jackson said nothing.

"You may take your time with your answer," Stephanie said politely, "but my job requires that I log a full report of every transaction. In case that information helps you decide."

She quickly copied over his bets while he hemmed and hawed, shifting from one foot to the other until finally he withdrew his own billfold from an obscure pocket within his winter clothes and produced the remaining change.

"Here is your receipt," Stephanie said immediately after, and tore out the perforated carbon copy.

"Thank you, Madame St. Clair," he murmured before he scuffed out the back way.

She knew everyone was watching. They'd been staring at her from the periphery since she hung up her coat that afternoon. What she didn't know was that Jackson had been skimming his take for weeks, and because everyone else was friendly with him, they'd been letting him slide. Stephanie knew better than to become actual friends with any of her colleagues—that was how people got dragged down, mixing business with personal, punching each other's time cards till they got lazy about it out of habit, and they got caught.

Stephanie quickly established how she was to be treated, cordially and with respect, though her coworkers tried her a few more times first. She held fast that there would be no gossiping with her. No shooting the shit about Mechanics' Night at the Cotton Club. She was strictly business. Still, a few of the comptrollers invited her out for drinks after work as a gesture, but she politely declined. She did have an early morning, after all, with her second job. They all assumed she was working a nine-to-five and a six-to-ten to make ends meet, like everyone did. Most people made only enough to survive, or at least they thought so, having no information otherwise, and what little was left over went toward trying to win more at the numbers racket itself. Stephanie was as frugal as anyone else, but she knew how to save, and she always thought ahead. They could not fathom how big her plans truly were. Stephanie had no intention of becoming one of the boys. She was not interested in joining the boys' club . . . though she did learn that boys loved to be a part of a club. The more exclusive, the better, but any club would do, as long as it was men only.

Casper knew that, too. He was a bootstrapper, and he was a West Indian immigrant, which set him apart from the Colored families who had been established in the East Coast for generations. When he saw the opportunity to help fund Harlem's Imperial Lodge of Elks—which women and non-members called simply the Elks' Lodge—Casper knew it was a foot in the door. This sort of bought belongingness might be the most important thing Stephanie learned from working for Casper Holstein because she did not anticipate its necessity. The cold fact was that he ran an illegal business in two countries, so it was important that he was also a huge philanthropist, and that everyone knew it. Holstein sponsored the building of dormitories for colleges in the Islands even though he hadn't lived on St. Croix since he was a child—actually, he hadn't lived there since the island was a part of the Dutch West Indies rather than the renamed US Virgin Islands—he developed that community, as well. He invested in everything from the national band to hurricane relief funds. That kind of generosity inspired reciprocity. Madame St. Clair took note.

Holstein did as much in New York, too. He was the biggest patron of the Harlem Renaissance, funding literary prizes that ultimately went to the likes of Countee Cullen and Claude McKay. Casper Holstein did an amazing thing . . . he was accepted on both sides of every line in the sand: he was American and West Indian. He was a worker and a patron. He was a criminal, and he was an angel. He had a loyal following, so much so that even when people lived in the territories of other bankers, they'd go out of their way to come find his runners for their bets. More importantly, if anything went wrong for him—if he got tied up by the cops or his bank closed up after a big win, people rallied behind him. He was essentially buying their loyalty, but he never said so. It was like the white gangsters said it would be when they extorted protection, except that he actually did support the community. He's where Stephanie learned the power of vigilante justice, and much more.

Though she didn't have the kind of capital to invest in her community yet, Stephanie championed several causes while she worked for Holstein, starting with rent control in 1919. When slumlords tried to price out their current tenants after

the Great War, she organized protests and petitions on behalf of the cause. During 1922–23, she protested landlords
illegally dispossessing people from their tenements and apartments for the sake of driving up costs of living for their own
profit. It was a disgusting business tactic that she was glad to
fight against.

Casper Holstein had the gentlemanly equivalent of St. Clair's
gentility, having served four years in the navy. He didn't cheat,
he didn't smoke, and he didn't drink. That didn't mean he
wasn't at the party, though. He knew how important clubs
were when it came to fitting in, and he owned several speakeasies that boomed as soon as Prohibition was enacted. When
the government outlawed liquor in 1920, it was easier than
ever to get people to part with their money for the numbers.
People were drunker and more depressed, and playing the
numbers gave them hope.

Stephanie worked for him for three years, and she was one
of his best employees. She admired him and respected him,
especially how, after getting his first big break as a numbers
king, he diversified into other ventures and made them just
as profitable. In 1923, he opened the Turf Club at 111 West
136th Street, and it was a stunner. Five stories of a brownstone outfitted in everything related to horse racing from
prints of the jockeys to polished brass bits. Those spring balls
and Christmas parties were talked about for seasons, because
entertainment was a form of supporting the community,
too. If other verticals were stable, then there was never a full
dependence on just the oscillating numbers racket. Casper
could have done that, stabilize the numbers with his other
ventures . . . but why hadn't he? Was it possible that he just
hadn't thought of it? She may not have cared for clubs, and

certainly not boys' clubs, but Stephanie was inspired by the idea of running several businesses at once. When she thought through this new business model, she realized she had out-grown Holstein's operation. She had passed him. That meant it was time to go into business for herself. She kept no records of this, though, because even receipts could be incriminating.

Timing was everything. And surprise was almost as impor-tant. So when St. Clair started her own bank in 1923, I doubt that she gave Holstein a courtesy notice, but she didn't break him like she broke the other banks in her path. His bank was so established that she might not have been able to break him even had she tried. The small banks all had to go under at once. Not forever, just a brief shutter all at the same time. The numbers racket, Stephanie had taught herself, was only lucra-tive if there were enough people playing. She had to hit big, and she had to hit hard, and she had to hit them all. It was a big buy-in for her, but she didn't look at it like gambling. It was no more gambling than the dice game. She was investing in her future, and she trusted her own intelligence to play the odds.

The banks couldn't pay out all her winnings, not right away, and when they closed temporarily according to her plan, to get their feet up under them, to flit off to the Carib-bean and wire some cash back onshore, Stephanie moved in on their territory. She snaked their runners and their comp-trollers, too. The workers still had the same expenses, so she gave them a job. When the bosses came back, bewildered that their business had disappeared in a matter of a few days, Stephanie offered them jobs working for her. Most often, they were too proud to accept, and they moved into other illegal lines of work. In 1923, there were plenty of those occupa-tions to choose from. Unlike Stephanie, most of them were career criminals. They specialized in crime, not mathematics.

She didn't do that to Casper Holstein, though, and he

didn't exactly fit the description of the other bosses because of his philanthropies. Holstein contained multitudes, and people wouldn't switch over to her if she hurt him like that. Everyone fell at the same time. Except Holstein and St. Clair. They were the big two left standing.

The small size of the banks was also, however, the way that they circumnavigated the law. If they were quiet enough, they could buy off the local police without the issue of legality escalating any higher. There had to be a big quantity of small amounts for the brass to turn a blind eye. Timing and surprise were the most important elements for success, but discretion was right behind.

She used $10,000 as startup money. Its origins are not completely clear, but because she would not have wanted to be beholden to any investors should she acquire any, the capital likely came from her winnings at the numbers. That cash was gone almost as quick as it'd come. First stop was icing the police. She wouldn't seek them out, but they'd find her, sure enough. She made sure to set aside what she estimated Casper had been paying, for when that time came. Dealing with the authorities was inconvenient, but necessary, even with the bootlegging and rum-running to distract them. On a long enough timeline, everyone would serve some time, but these payoffs delayed the inevitable.

The thing that took her the longest to sort out when she set up her own bank was figuring out how she could avoid getting done to her what she had done to everyone else. She had to defend against some other savvy opportunist sweeping in, taking her business, and running it without her. She had to make her employees assurances that there was more to working for her than just having a job. She developed a plan that paid the runners a percentage of their bettors' winnings, too. This measure incentivized the runners to find more bettors because the more bets they took, the bigger chance that someone whose number they ran would win, and then they'd win, too.

To fund those down periods, it seems like Stephanie had to invest in a straight business, as well. It wasn't exactly laundering, but it wasn't *not* laundering, either. Because of her caution and savvy, I think the most likely purchase would have been the dress factory where she had worked. Ten thousand dollars was already a lot back then, but where she got the money for this second venture, no one knows. Best guess, a bank loan from a clerk who knew her, Casper, or at least his business. She likely opened a dress store front at the location of her bank, too, to keep up appearances.

The next, most important issue, was how to keep everyone honest. There was no regulation. No legal system to keep the owners like her honest, much less her employees, even though she paid them well and offered more job security than any other bank—more secure than most straight lines of work, too. It was still a criminal enterprise, which meant it was rough, and I think it would have required a bit of muscle to keep her workers in line. Something like this, if not this exactly:

She overheard her comptrollers discussing the latest headline of such dishonesty when she arrived in the bank one morning. They both hushed when she walked into the bank through the back of the dress store. "Good morning," she greeted them before hanging her hat and coat and walking over. She hopped onto the desk between them and lit a cigarette before she asked, "You're discussing Mr. Caldwell's murder?"

They fell quiet, unsure of how to answer. "I saw it in the paper, that he hit on two dollars. He stood for a big payday. And then the banker changed the last digit of the winning number." She paused. And then gestured for them to pick up the story.

"He was mad as a hornet and went to cussing the banker. He caught two bullets for his trouble and died in Harlem Hospital last night."

"It's a shame," Stephanie said. "Did you know him?"

They both shook their heads. "Knew him, but didn't know him like that."

She dragged her cigarette and exhaled through her nose. "He did nothing wrong."

This surprised the comptrollers a little, her siding with the bettor.

"He only wanted what he won. That's fair enough. Who can say he is wrong for demanding the winnings that would have changed his life?"

"How long you think till something like this happens to our outfit?"

Her eyes darted to him. "It ought never happen. If you hear any of this, you tell me. Day or night, well or sick. Find me and tell me, and I will handle it."

―――

While Stephanie's bank picked up new bettors, she set about ensuring that when the time came, she could serve a sentence without her absence affecting the business—after all, if your business can't run without you, then you don't really have a business. You just have a lifestyle.

She knew every employee on a first-name basis, knew their spouses and children and which in-laws were staying with them, whose sister did laundry for which rich white lady downtown, and whose brother was a pimp on 118th Street. She remembered birthdays and gave bonuses on holidays. Still, with her company expanding, she continued to hire, and it was probable that one of these new hires who thought her rules were more so suggestions first had the nerve to test her.

Let's call him Alfred. Imagine Alfred decided not to pay out to a winning bettor.

It was midmorning when the comptroller heard about the fight from the clerk, who overheard the runner bragging about not paying out when he turned in the day's slips. Stephanie stopped figuring and locked eyes with her comptroller during the story. "Alfred got into it with Mr. Baldwin. Mr. Baldwin, he said he bet on the hit, 424. Alfred said he didn't, said he bet 429. He wouldn't pay because on the slip it said 429—least that's what he says. Looks like it could go either way, to me. But they got into it, fighting in the street and Mr. Baldwin, he got his eye blacked before he backed down the street cussing the bank." All while he caught her up, Stephanie didn't stop moving. She slid her chair from under the desk, pushed it back in behind her, walked to the coat rack with her pocket book and put on her hat and wrap. She greeted the ladies in the dress shop when they passed, and she said, "I assume Alfred is outside the barbershop? Walk with me."

She carried on at a clip down Edgecombe and turned on 137th till she spied Alfred leaning against the stoop and carrying on with some younger boys. He pretended not to notice her approaching, not until she walked right through their game of dice and he heard her pull back the hammer of the revolver in her purse. Then he backpedaled so fast it looked like he was falling downhill, and she kept up with him until he had wedged himself against the wrought iron fence and she had the barrel pressed into his groin. "Miss St. Clair, I don't know what you heard—"

"You know exactly what the fuck I heard. Unless you want this to be the last thing you ever hear, you better listen to me."

Everyone on the street fell silent, and she never raised her voice.

"Madame St. Clair's bank *always* pays its winners. Our bettors are more important than anything else in this world. Mr. Baldwin's winnings will be taken out of your final commissions, and you will repay any remainder to me in cash before the sun comes up on Friday. Tell me you hear me."

"I hear you."

"You hear me what?"

"I hear you, ma'am."

Stephanie released the hammer of her pistol and stepped aside, facing the street, which did not pretend it hadn't heard everything she said. "I won't condescend to any of you. I know you heard every word, too, and I know you saw what happened between Alfred and Mr. Baldwin, which I only just learned. Mr. Baldwin will receive his full winnings and more for his trouble. Please, tell everyone you know that Madame St. Clair's word is true. And I apologize for interrupting your afternoon." Stephanie walked around the dice game and motioned for her comptroller to match stride with her.

"Damn," he said. "I never knew you had a gun." No one knew.

"You never needed to know," she said calmly. "Now, Mr. Baldwin. He lives on Eighth Avenue? Do you know where?"

"No ma'am, not exactly."

"No matter." She walked into the butcher shop on the corner. "Buongiorno," she greeted the butcher, and when he asked how she was, she said, "It has been a hard day. I need to make good with Mr. Baldwin."

"Mr. Baldwin," he said. "A good customer."

"Will you wrap up two of his favorite cuts, please?"

"Sì. You know he has a-three children?"

"How old?"

"Ehh . . . twelve? Fifteen?"

She smiled, smelling the upsell. "Their favorites, as well."

"We going to Mr. Baldwin's house right now?" her comptroller asked.

"Oui, of course. Now."

The butcher wrapped her cuts and thanked her for her
business. "Grazie," she said. "Grazie mille, signor."

"You just know all the languages, huh?"

"No," she said, reading the address on the package and
turning left out of the shop, "Only a few words of Italian. But
people like it when you show effort for them. It makes them
feel important. More important than they are. And you never
know when you might need a friend." It helped, too, especially dealing with the white folks, to remember what her
mother told her: she was a lady. As she foresaw, word of how
she reconciled the disagreement spread fast. The number of
people betting with her spiked, and when she made good on
her word—and continued to make good, week after week,
month after month, the amount of money they wagered increased just as steadily.

———

1926 saw the roar the decade became so famous for. Henry
Ford championed the five-day work week for his employees.
He hypothesized that by paying his workers well and giving
them Saturday off, they would have more time to rest, which
would lead to greater productivity during working hours.
With their extra time off, now known as the "weekend,"
he hoped that they would become heavier consumers, and
while they spent time with their families, they might stimu-
late the economy as well as spend some of their money on his
vehicles. His hypothesis quickly became theory. St. Clair was
probably happy to adopt Ford's model when the idea proved
effective, though she would have had to give some employees
Monday off instead of Saturday to stagger the force, due to

the nature of her business. If they worked six days, she'd pay them more, plus their bonus or incentive percentage.

Stephanie also returned to the fight against unfair rent inflation. Since the Great War, New York City had been protesting housing conditions. During the war itself, construction halted, even as the city continued to grow, which led to the housing shortage. Tenement owners often had only oral contracts with their tenants, which allowed them to hike the rent whenever it suited them, which was often, with the high demand. They themselves never even had to break the news to their renters, but made the building manager, who often lived in the building himself, conduct the collections or evictions. Rent strikers made gradual progress over the next few years, pushing for reforms like the April Laws which allowed tenants to prove their rent should not be increased by more than twenty-five percent, and then, the shift of that burden of proof onto the landlords. Those laws had since been renewed twice, but now the tenant associations were losing strength in their numbers. The current law said that rooms renting at more than $20 a month were exempt from rent control. St. Clair worked to prevent lowering that ceiling. She even wrote to Mayor John Francis Hylan and the "happy warrior" Governor Alfred E. Smith, complaining about the slumlords who reigned over Harlem from the Upper East Side. After she pushed for the subsequent investigations, lawmakers compromised: the laws were extended, but they did lower the limit to apartments costing less than $15 per month. These small victories were still worth fighting for, since they affected so many of her bettors if not Madame St. Clair directly.

———

She saw the situation firsthand because of the tea pads. St. Clair didn't frequent the raucous speakeasies or the clubs that entertained white guests with Black stereotypes. Sure, she may have dropped in once a month or so, but it would never be her scene. She was there to show face, and showing face meant being watched. Being watched meant she couldn't relax. But a tea pad was a different ordeal. A tea pad was basically a rent party, a party hosted out of necessity, to raise enough money to pay the host's rent. They were the opposite of flash. The lights were turned down so low you couldn't make out a face if you wanted to, most times. That's if the lights were on at all. Most times, unless it was really cold, the electric company had already cut off the power, so candles flamed on every surface, stuck out of Coke bottles. Incense smoked through the apartments. Usually, a women sat behind a deck of cards that explained your life to you in a way you couldn't understand till they said it. I think it's more likely than not that Stephanie would have chosen tea pads over a dance club, if only for the sake of practicality. She'd have been swarmed immediately at a club—it would have been like a celebrity showing up—but tea pads had more discreet and intimate guest lists. She remembered the other seamstresses talking about tarot cards on occasion, but she didn't see it for herself until the tea pads. She watched from afar as people sat down across from Madame Zora. Stephanie only ever confirmed the outcome of the following vignette as fact, so I recreated its occurrence in a way that I think is in keeping with her character.

Stephanie would have picked up tarot reading the first time she saw it, so the next time the fortune-telling woman saw Stephanie, she pulled a deck from her handbag and gave it to Stephanie. Stephanie protested. Nothing came for free, and she could buy the cards herself. Madame Zora then informed her that one's first deck had to be received as a gift. "Don't forget to smudge them between your readings . . . otherwise the energies will get confused, and that's when they get dangerous."

"Smudge?"

Zora withdrew a seashell and a dried bundle of sage from the same bag. It smelled like the incense, but cleaner, somehow. Through this brief mentorship, Stephanie learned how to channel her intuition through reading the cards. Unlike Madame Zora, she wouldn't read cards for others, only for herself, and only as a means of processing her inherent clairvoyance. This is a fact. After a little while, Stephanie barely needed the cards to access her clairvoyance. She might not have learned this craft at a tea pad, and maybe not from Madame Zora either, but she learned it somehow, and this is one way she might have happened upon the profession.

=====

Tea pads were also the places where Harlem's entertainers tried out new material, before they took it to the clubs. Bands crammed into the corner of a New York City apartment until the neighbors who weren't at the party because they were too old or too young banged on the ceiling with a broom. Or a new record spun on a gramophone—if the place still had power. Sometimes a comedian held court. If she went at all, Stephanie St. Clair only went to a few, select tea pads, and only after her comptrollers vetted them and made sure the only marijuana supplied was from Mezz, the white "Mayor." Of all the substances available, reefer would have calmed her anxiety without dulling her senses, if she timed it well and paid attention. But of course, this pastime was another illegal one, and therefore unregulated inoculation, so there was always the chance she'd get too tight.

That's what may have happened this night. Kind of like we know Stephanie learned to read cards, but not where she learned, we also know that she started icing the police due to Mustache Jones, but we don't know *how* he got her. From what I know of her, I think the tea pad provides the setting for both of these events. While she reclined on a chaise longue to the crackling, canned keys and banter of Fats Waller on a low-key night, grass-stenched smoke unfurled from her fingertips, and the man folded on the floor at her feet inched his hand over her ankle. He fondled the tiny buckles over her arch. She kicked him away before curling her feet under her, and then his face was too close to hers. She felt his breath on her face just before he kissed her, first on one cheek and then the other before brushing over her lips. Her eyes opened to suspicious slits. He looked familiar, kneeling in front of her, his shirt unbuttoned to the breastbone. She frowned and sat up, brushing him aside. "You know who I am?" he said, too slow. She squinted at him. "I could arrest you right now," he said.

She scoffed. "You have no charges."

"You high, Madame St. Clair."

She laughed again and looked around the room. "Compared to what?"

"Why don't we just mosey down to the station on 123rd and talk to my lieutenant."

Stephanie leaned in until her nose nearly touched his and said with her eyes half-closed, "Yeah, why don't we do that. Why don't we talk to your lieutenant."

Half of her assumed he would take her to his apartment as a detour, that "his lieutenant" was a euphemism. She could shake him there if that was the case, but the other part of her knew they would actually go to the station. His actual lieutenant, a little Sicilian man, extorted her for $300 protection a month, to be delivered to him through a courier named Mustache Jones, the same plainclothes officer from the tea pad who opened the station door for her as she left, and muttered, "What, you think we was going back to mine?"

She walked up to him again, too close, smirking when she chided, "Mustache, all whores should get paid," and stalked out, alone, into the night. That's how Madame Queen got roped into icing the cops like any common gangster. That Mustache Jones was the one who snitched her out to them is the only confirmed fact, but doesn't the rest seem just as real?

Anytime she was extorted by a purely criminal enterprise, she knew not to trust them. They said your fee was for protection, for assurance that they themselves wouldn't attack—even, sometimes, to keep the law off you for you. In the event that you saw an opening, you could always risk squealing to the police. But when the law extorted her themselves? They could do whatever they put their mind to with no regard to recourse. Because what were you going to do about it? Blow the whistle on them . . . to them?

Make no mistake, Stephanie always knew not to trust the law. Men in groups could not be trusted, as a rule. The more exclusive the club was, the less trustworthy. There was no one to keep them in check, so they fed into their own bullshit until they were so caught up in it, they couldn't tell which way was up. There were still tactics to bring these clubs to heel, though. For one, the inexplicable loyalty among the groups could be called on as a whole if you hit the right note. Or, if you managed to tweeze them apart, pick off a weak link, or foment some kind of mistrust among them, you might be able to rally them to your aid. As a last resort, you could misdirect everyone. Never give the full, whole truth, and never by itself. The truth always needed a side dish of dazzle, just to confuse it.

Stephanie watched Casper Holstein deploy all of these tactics the autumn he got kidnapped. He was such a quick hand that the whole thing gave off a kaleidoscopic effect. No one ever realized the full truth of the conspiracy, and they still haven't, not to this very day.

By September of 1928, Stephanie hadn't worked for Holstein in five years. When she left his bank in 1923, he was already big in the Elks' Club, racing and sporting circles, especially boxing, and he'd started the Turf Club. Since then, he'd remained the Turf Club's president, developed real estate to a huge profit, and separated from his wife—whom Stephanie never really knew anyway, which was itself pretty telling. In short, Casper Holstein was a forty-five-year-old childless bachelor with a lot of disposable income.

Thursday, September 20, 1928 was a night like any other. After an evening at his Turf Club, he called up his lady friend, Mrs. Gomez Whitfield—who was also estranged from her spouse. He said he'd be there in twenty minutes. Keep it warm. He left the brownstone, got in his Lincoln sedan, and had his chauffeur drive him to her place, 225 West 140th Street. Mrs. Whitfield said she never saw him that night.

So far, all accounts of the events were consistent, but this is where they diverged. One account said Mrs. Whitfield wasn't home. One account said Holstein didn't make it to her door, but he was seized in the hallway. His official statement said he left her apartment on foot around 1:00, in the early morning of Friday, September 21, but didn't say why. He was almost home when five white men and two white women drove up and forced him into their car at gunpoint. They pretended to be policemen, saying he was wanted at headquarters.

But if that was true, what of Holstein's chauffeur's statement that he chased the offending vehicle until he lost sight of them? Holstein said on the record that his own driver was nowhere nearby. Because the records conflict, and for that reason, all the quotations used in this episode's retelling are verbatim from source material, even when they directly contradict each other. Even when they seem too good to have been actual quotes.

Holstein also said that he cooperated as the kidnappers "hustled him into the machine," though he didn't get a good look at what kind of car they had. It must have been roomy if there were five men and two women in there. Or was it six men and one woman? Regardless, all of them were white.

By Holstein's account, even though he cooperated, one of the men pistol-whipped him, and the others beat him too before gagging and blindfolding him. Or was it that they put fogged glasses on him? Glasses sound more chic. By his second interview, he stuck with the glasses.

Holstein said he lost consciousness and then regained it before the car pulled up at a house. The kidnappers took him inside and put him in a bedroom, and then they took the bandage (or later, glasses) off his eyes. They took his money— either $2,000 or $3,000, or $72, depending on when you read which papers during this five-day debacle—and his diamond ring (worth $2,000). They bound his hands and feet with wire and cloth. They laid him on the floor, and two captors stood guard over him.

A few hours later, he was moved to another, nearby house. One source said this was when the kidnappers called Charles King, the Turf Club's secretary, and they put Holstein on the phone. He heard Casper's voice shaking when he said, "For God's sake, give these men $70,000 or they'll kill me." But can you really trust the *New York Age*? When the *Times* made no mention of a phone call and listed the ransom as

$50,000? A quick calculation makes it sound like the *Age* is embellishing by forty percent. An even quicker intuition says someone's trying to buy time, but whether it was Holstein or the kidnapers, it's hard to say.

Holstein was held at that house all day Saturday, and then they took him back to the first house that night. His captors offered him food several times, but he could not eat.

This much was definitely true: his friends were panicked. He was the president of one elite club, and he'd helped found another. Both groups rallied to his aid without being asked. Holstein had also helped so many people with money or clothing over time that several hundred volunteers searched for him through New York for a full day before alerting law enforcement. They correctly assumed that because of Holstein's businesses, police intervention might bring about punishment or death to Holstein. They gave themselves about twelve hours before electing Mrs. Edna Davis to finally call in the kidnapping Friday evening.

Police at first treated the case as a missing person, but after an anonymous "tip," they soon changed tactics to investigate it as a kidnapping.

A different story says that Saturday morning—twenty-four hours later—was when one of the male kidnappers telephoned Charles King, the secretary of the Turf Club. The caller told him to go to an office in a store at 1251 Washington Avenue, in the Bronx (later identified as the office of Michael Bernstein, thirty-two years old), and he demanded "$17,000 ransom." Well, that's a big difference. If the papers can't keep that big of a dollar figure straight, what else are they missing?

Detectives later learned that before the kidnapping, Bernstein had gone to the branch of the American Exchange–Irving Trust Company at Southern Boulevard and 167th Street in the Bronx to ask if a check drawn by Holstein on a branch of the Chelsea Exchange Bank (for $3,200) would be honored. The tellers said they would not cash the check. So, rather than fraud, it appeared like Bernstein would orchestrate a kidnapping instead. Or, it would be made to appear that he had orchestrated a kidnapping.

When King went to the office, presumably to pay the ransom, Bernstein proved that he had custody of Holstein by showing him some telegrams Holstein had on his person, sent Thursday afternoon. Afterward, he increased the ransom demand, raising the price to $50,000.

Late Sunday night, they returned Holstein's ring. They kept his cash. The captor said he'd be returned home without being harmed.

"You got a raw deal," the kidnapper told him.

Holstein said he didn't call anyone, and to his knowledge, no demand was made for money. That made no sense to anyone—what was the point of a kidnapping if not to extort a ransom?

The *Age* reported that Secretary Charles King said detectives trailed him to the rendezvous where he was to pay the ransom, and the kidnappers did not appear to claim their money. But who can be sure if King really said that?

The newspaper then reported that he was a well-known philanthropist, and just before his kidnaping he "sent a large consignment of lumber to negro storm victims" in the Virgin Islands. He also tried to raise funds for similar relief which should have happened on the day the newspaper reported. Just in case any readers were doubting the altruism of this criminal.

This is when Stephanie got invested in the story. Of course, she didn't want anything to happen to her former supervisor and now colleague. But this spin was incredible. No one knew who to believe. She was sure it was because of a clever

circumvention on the part of Holstein himself, because even
if journalists were friendly, they knew that throwing mud
could result in them being backlisted, especially when such
powerful people were involved. The question for Stephanie
became not "What happened?" but "How did he do that?"
And perhaps more importantly, why was he obscuring the
identity of the people who had kidnapped him? Why did
they deserve his protection? Was it a favor to someone powerful? Did he undergo this hostage situation and come out
with the proverbial one in the bank?

====

Five white male suspects were arrested the night of Saturday,
September 22, in front of the Commonwealth Sporting Club
on 125th Street and Madison Avenue when police identified
the car used by the kidnappers. But how? How did they identify it with no eyewitnesses?

The suspects were grilled in the West 135th Street station,
and while that was happening, one of the kidnappers called
Holstein's friend, Dennis Armstead, of the Monarch Lodge
45 with the Negro Elks. He put Holstein on the line, and
Holstein told Armstead, "The police should get out because
if they continue all you will get will be my dead body."

The suspects were held in the Manhattan municipal jail
known as "the Tombs."

Sunday night, his captors blindfolded and gagged him and
drove him "a long way."

At 2:00 a.m. on Monday, September 24, Casper Holstein
was "freed" at 140th Street and Amsterdam Avenue. His captors gave him three one-dollar bills for cab fare to his home
on 144th Street and sped away so that he couldn't get the tag
number of the car. He didn't go home, though. Instead, he

went to his Turf Club. Clubmates and friends "greeted him enthusiastically" after fearing he would be killed.

Then, Holstein went to the West 135th Street police station to give his statement, which lasted more than an hour. Tuesday morning, he could not identify any of the five men in a lineup who were held as suspects in his kidnapping.

=====

By Tuesday night, September 25, Casper Holstein was back in the sporting circles. "Tailored to the last crease," reporters said, and as suave as ever. A pile of telegrams congratulated him on his return, and men clustered around him to shake his hand. At the Turf Club, one reporter asked him, "Didn't you recognize any of your captors?"

Holstein smiled and said to the reporter who immortalized it on the record, "Well you know how it is. I could—" he winked "—but I can't."

It was genius. No one knew what to do with it. Everyone directly involved felt like they were in the right, and they'd done their part to uphold justice. Everyone on the outside was so frustrated and confused that they just rubbed their eyes at the newspaper column and moved on to the next thing, be it an advertisement for a fur-collared winter coat or more news about some corrupt judges.

Stephanie was in a unique, adjacent category, close enough to see how Holstein had deployed the smoke and mirrors, but far enough away that she did not know what was behind them—it was safer not to know, and she didn't mean to find out. She had problems of her own, now, and she wanted to address them in the skillful, practical way that Holstein had done.

November 24, 1928, about two months after Holstein's

kidnapping, was when Madame St. Claire's house was raided.
She waited almost a full year to tell her side of the story to
her people, but it went like this, naming names and badge
numbers:[1]

> The raid of Nov. 24, 1928, was caused by information from
> the stool pigeons, whose names were Mustache Jones, Mil-
> dred Brown and Ethel Small. Mildred Brown had been
> working for me as a general worker since March, 1928. She
> duplicated my keys and gave one to Lt. Pfeifer, one to Mus-
> tache Jones and one to Lucille Carter.
>
> On the morning of the raid, Mildred came to work as
> usual. I, Mme. St. Clair, told her that I believed she was
> working with the outside enemies to frame me. She replied:
> "No Madame." I then returned to my bedroom, took up my
> deck of thirty-two cards and shuffled them, and laid them
> out carefully on the bed. The cards directed me to make a
> short journey immediately as the enemy was near, so near,
> that I looked around to see if they had surrounded me.
>
> A few minutes later Amelia, also known as Sarah Scott,
> who worked for me as a maid, arrived. I quickly dressed and
> told her that there was danger, but I did not know what it
> was. That she should be careful and not open the door for
> anyone. I did not know that Mildred Brown was the Judas
> and that she had been offered $500 by Mustache Jones to
> place a bag of policy slips in my closet on the morning of
> the raid; the same offer was made to Lucille Carter, but she
> refused.
>
> I left the house at 10:15, and as I came out of the door,
> I saw a badly dressed dark-skinned woman sitting on the
> stairs. As I walked to the elevator, she followed me but
> did not take the elevator down. I afterwards recognized
> this same woman in the 32d Precinct and knew that she
> was Lt. Pfeifer's stool pigeon. From witnesses' testimony,
> they were in the apartment between 11 and 11:30, gaining
> admission by going through Mrs. Mary Lightfoot's apart-

---

1   I have reproduced the content of contemporary newspapers in this book.
     That content often has unconventional or variant spellings. I have edited for
     clarity, but only where necessary.

ment, 5-H, raising her bedroom window and climbing the fire escape. They smashed the window to my bedroom and entered the bedroom. They broke the chiffonier lock and stole $400 out of the tin box which was in the chiffonier. They then opened the door leading from the bedroom to the sitting room, which was locked with a Yale lock and went to the front door, opened it and admitted three more officers. Witnesses testified that they walked to the kitchen and pretended to search Mildred Brown, then let her go out of the apartment.

They then placed Sarah Scott and an old lady of 65 years under arrest. The officer who smashed the window cut his finger, spreading the blood on the bedroom rug. There was also blood on the tin box that contained the $400 and some change. This officer's name was Sidney D. Tait, Shield No. 11,968. Other officers' names were Patrolmen Hunter and Baccaglini, and Lt. Pfeifer. They did not give the names of two other officers that were with them.

═══

"The hell was she doing with bettin' slips at the house?" one of the paper sellers on Edgewood may have wondered as he flipped through the *Amsterdam News* and leaned on a stoop that wasn't his.

Another boy, Red, for his hair, cuffed him on the back of the head before he answered, "You know she ain't have 'em in the house."

A third boy, Elijah, snatched the paper out of his hand. "He got the newspaper right in front of him and can't see the truth. You out of your rabbit-ass mind if you think Madame Queen dumb. They planted that shit on her."

The first boy sucked his teeth and said, "Well why's she goin' a jail then?"

"Chill, chill, he's just up from Michigan, Lige. He don't know what it's like yet."

But it was a rare occasion that any of this had to be explained to a Harlemite. However new they were to town, few could afford to be so green as to believe Stephanie St. Clair had not been framed. After all, why *would* a banker have numbers in her own home? And she was walking home, *away* from the bank. She hadn't even been at the bank, according to this. She was visiting with a friend talking about a charity. The boy straightened the newspaper in front of him and said, "Man, damn. They just looking to catch her on something."

"Yeah," said Red. "She bad, though. You can't break Madame Queen."

MY HI-DE-HO MAN

On another man, folks might have named this kind of meanness Little Man Syndrome, or a Napoleon complex, saying the reason why a short man was aggressive was because he felt inadequate, like he needed to compensate for his unintimidating frame, or more. Nobody even so much as whispered that behind Ellsworth Raymond Johnson's back. He wasn't paying on some kind of deficit the way people might assume. Truth told, he wasn't aggressive, and he wasn't small. He might have been only 5'8', but he was built like a stack of bricks with eyeballs, and he looked like he wished you would run slap into him. A lot of Harlem thought him short-fused, but he didn't have a temper. He wasn't even mean. He was just bad. And he was good at it.

They called him Bumpy from the time he was a kid, and that rolled off his back, too. The name stuck to him, all the way up from Charleston, South Carolina, and through a few wage-earning jobs that he got bored of quick. That's the thing with boys like that, when they got all the smarts and no feelings, they get dangerous.

He was fifteen and a half years old in 1924 at his first arrest, just after Madame St. Clair opened her own bank. They booked him as eighteen. Even that young, this wasn't his first time playing bodyguard to the Numbers Kings. On the night of his first arrest, he and one other bodyguard were escorting the Cuban banker Alex Pompez back to his limousine after a night out in Spanish Harlem. Bumpy and his second stood on either side of Pompez. They didn't loop arms with him, but Pompez pinballed between the two, staggering in his drunkenness. Out from an alley stepped a man with a gun. "Hand over that wallet, fancy man."

Bumpy didn't wait for the demand to register with Pompez. He just pulled his switchblade and slashed the mugger across the face. The robber screamed and dropped his gun while Bumpy opened the back door to the town car and shoved Pompez inside. The car idled and waited for the bodyguards to do their job. When Bumpy turned back to the mugger, he was now unarmed and screaming in fear of losing sight in his left eye. He whimpered, blue-black blood thick and hot between the fingers of his left hand. The second bodyguard looked on. It seemed to him that the job was done. This guy wasn't going anywhere. He wasn't saying anything about anybody but himself. But that's not how Bumpy ran his ship. He dragged the switchblade across the robber's Adam's apple before stabbing it to the hilt in his gut twice. A policeman nearby heard the screams and came running, so Bumpy dropped his blade, and his second kicked it into the sewer.

"What's going on here?" shouted the policeman.

Bumpy said in his slow Carolina accent, with his hands tight around the robber's neck, "I come up with my friend, and I just see this man on the sidewalk tryin' a shove his guts back in his belly. I'on know who did all that to him . . . I know he's scared to lose that eye, and I'm over here trying to hold the fella's throat shut with my bare hands. No telling what kind of germs. . . ."

The policeman looked baffled and went over to the car to try to question Pompez. Bumpy stepped between them, up to his elbows in blood. He said, slow and heavy, "He don't speak English, sir." He said to the other bodyguard, "*Sal*," and the second jumped into the passenger seat as the driver screeched off.

It dawned on the copper that Bumpy had tricked him, even as the man on the sidewalk wailed like his guts were spilling out, which they were. The policeman said, "Out of the way—" and before he could push past, Bumpy had jabbed him right on the button. They brawled in the street, Bumpy and the policeman next to that bleeding mugger until more police heard the racket and broke up the fight.

The neighborhood maintains Bumpy didn't know who was who when it went down, but it was the thing that put him on the map as the best heavy in the racket . . . and anyone with good sense and a good sense of who Bumpy was would know better than to believe that. It didn't surprise anyone that he was convicted of disorderly conduct. The cop who booked him put eighteen on Bumpy's rap sheet to try him as an adult, but the truth won out, and because he was so young, he got just a year of detention.

Bumpy fell on this grenade so Pompez could get out from under the police. It was the job of a bodyguard, to throw their own body in the way of danger for the one they protected. Bumpy picked the fight with that policeman as a way of keeping the police off Pompez himself, who was a very wanted man. Madame St. Clair read the papers every day, but she knew about this incident long before it made print, and she made a note to keep an eye on Bumpy Johnson. Someday, he might be a useful ally.

═════

Of course, it didn't matter whether Pompez was a wanted man. Plainclothes police made a habit of stopping, searching, and seizing anything off anyone, all they had to have done was be Black and nearby. To the best of Harlem's knowledge—most of Harlem—that was a totally legal practice. Stephanie St. Clair felt like that should not stand, not in a country that prided itself on freedom, like the United States of America, so she wrote out the situation in a letter. One of the many Negro authors in her building edited the first draft. Her secretary reviewed the second and retyped it on carbon paper.

Madame St. Clair then took a crisp sheet of stationery from her secretary desk, a green border all the way around and her monogram printed in a serif font centered at the header, with her full name and address below. In racing green ink, she handwrote the letter again, folded it into the matching envelope, and mailed it to Mayor Jimmy Walker. She did not know Walker personally, but she knew he was a Tammany Hall official, which did not bode well for her cause. It was an open secret that everyone in Tammany Hall was corrupt, if not directly on the take from the Italian mobs. Still, government officials had so little to do with Harlem, an important part of their constituency if only in number alone, that she thought she might appeal on behalf of his voters.

She waited a week for his response. When she did not receive one, she sent a carbon copy to the more neutral police commissioner Grover Whalen, who was notorious for enforcing Prohibition laws. He did not respond, either.

Stephanie St. Clair may not have had quite the philanthropic clout of the model Holstein yet. She did make regular donations to humanitarian organizations, but she was less vocal about her monetary contributions. She thought that on a practical level arming people with knowledge would prove at least as helpful as throwing money at them. When Mr. Bowman had taught her to play dice, it served her much better than if he had handed over twenty-five cents and left her to her own devices. "Give a man a fish," and all that.

Stephanie St. Clair was unlike most people in a whole host of ways, but the most relevant one here was her proximity to legal experts, both the corrupt and straight ones. So, when her white lawyer, Frank Stanton, showed up to her office right on schedule in mid-August, unbuttoned his sports coat, and sat down across the mahogany partners' desk to discuss the regular bonding fees for when her runners got arrested, something happened to put him on her shit list. Based on the letters she wrote afterward, I think it went down like this:

She first leaned back against the green tufted seat and then slammed her palms down on it in a rage. "I am so sick of this shit. Frank, I wrote to the mayor and the police commissioner, and they won't respond. Police just lie! They say they're the gas man or the electric man and barge into people's apartments. They flip the place and take whatever they want, or frisk them on the street whether they're breaking the law or not! It ought to be illegal!"

Frank looked confused. The corners of his thin mouth turned down. "Madame St. Clair . . ." he started, with his posh Manhattan accent that sounded patronizing even when—like now—he didn't intend it to, "that is illegal. It's illegal search and seizure. Even a detective needs a warrant for that. Beat cops can't do a search without probable cause, and plainclothes police can't do it at all." He paused for a moment while he unpacked his briefcase. "Well, by law they can't do it. But like you said, they still do. And don't get me started on the bail bondsmen that are on the mob's payroll. I don't know how anyone could untangle this level of legal perversion."

St. Clair pressed a button on the brass torpedo statue at the corner of her desk, and it dispensed a cigarette. Frank scrambled to light it for her, and she stared at him while she drew on it. She said, levelly, "If justice be by the law, then Christ died for nothing."

Stephanie always came across as mysterious, but this was the first time Frank could remember her drawing a curtain between the two of them, and his pulse thudded in his fingertips still on the wheel of his lighter. He knew better than to ask what she meant, whether she had identified him as one of the crooks making her world more dangerous, or if she was resigning herself to corruption of law enforcement. Frank said only, "Galatians?"

Stephanie said nothing. She left her lawyer sitting at her desk and told her secretary to get the *Amsterdam News* on the phone and find out what it cost to run an advertisement. On September 4, two full weeks after she sent the letter to Mayor Walker, she took control of the situation where her legal support had failed her, and she had the letter published as an ad in the newspaper, just below a half portrait of herself. In the photograph, she wore a stylish turban, a pearl necklace, a wolf-collared coat with gauntlet cuffs, a jeweled ring, and a frown.

AMSTERDAM NEWS
WEDNESDAY, SEPTEMBER 4, 1929
Advertisement Advertisement
Mme. Stephanie St. Clair

MME. STEPHANIE ST. CLAIR
409 Edgecombe Avenue
New York City

August 21, 1929
Hon. James J. Walker,
Mayor of New York City,
City Hall,
New York City,

Dear Sir,

I am writing this letter to let you know about the terrible conditions of my race in Harlem and what they are going through with the City Detectives.

The colored people are crushed, robbed, and jailed by those detectives. Your door bell will ring, when you got to the door and ask: "Who is it?" The answer will be, "the gas man," "the electric man," or "the insurance man." When you open your door, four, five, or six detectives will rush in your house, brutally force you to sit down, then take full possession. They search from one end to the other. Sometimes, if the door is not opened for them, they will climb up the fire escape and break into a window. Also, they will stop men and women on the street, whom they suspect have policy slips, take them to some nearby hallway and search all through their clothing, inside and out, even taking off their shoes. After a thorough search, if they do not find anything and feel like taking you down, they do it. When they reach the 12th District or the 5th District Magistrates' Court with you, you will be surprised to know that they produce an envelope with a paper with three figures, called policy slips. The Judge will say $1,000 bail for Special Sessions, and you have no choice in the matter, no change to prove that you have been framed by the detectives.

Sometimes the detectives find these policy slips in their search, but if you pay them from $500 to $2,000, you are sure to come back home. If you pay them nothing, you are sure to get a sentence of 60 to 90 days in the workhouse.

If they raid a place known as the bank, or where the work is done and find adding machines and hundreds of the so-called policy slips, they then call themselves doing big business. They will take from $1,500 up and walk away and say nothing, or make no arrest. Many times they protect these bankers and are sometimes on the weekly pay rolls of these bankers. A recent case of their frame-up happened at 180 St. Nicholas Ave. A crippled colored man, who was wounded in the World's War, was a collector. They knew it and protected him. Many of the officers played with him every day. When the combination of 211 came out recently, one of the officers had a 10c hit. The boy's banker was a Jewish man and ran away and did not pay his collector. The officer did not get his money and a lot of excitement was made over the hit and the amount of money due the officer. He threatened the boy's life, saying; if he did not get his money he was going to get drunk and come back and shoot the boy. He later did nothing when he found out truthfully that the banker had run away.

Another recent case happened at 239 W. 141st St., two uniformed policemen, disguised themselves as detectives and rang the woman's door bell. Upon being admitted, they asked for the policy slips or a big sum of money. The woman called to someone and when they came, rang the doorbell, the officers hearing the belly became frightened and jumped through the window, down the fire escape to the yard and ran away. These two officers have been doing this for years. They co-operate with some person who tips them off where to go. About two weeks later, the doorbell of this same woman at 239 W. 141st St. rang again. She asked, "Who is it?" Her answer was a terrible banging on the door. Becoming frightened, because of her previous experience only two weeks before, she went to the telephone and called Police Headquarters and asked them to send her protection as she feared there were burglars at her door. In about 10 minutes, officers from the 16th Precinct came, rang the bell and to her question as to "Who is it?" said: Officers from headquarters. When she opened the door, two white officers and two colored officers entered her apartment. One of the colored officers said: "I hate you West Indians anyhow, give me those policy slips." The husband was getting ready to go to work. They searched the whole place and found nothing. Going down the hall to the room of a lodger, they searched the lodger's room. In a few minutes they called the husband and when he came to them, they placed him under arrest with a piece of paper with three figures. The husband is now under a $1,500 bail.

Now Your Honor, I beg you with tears in my eyes and a broken heart full of sorrow, to please do something for these conditions which my people are going through in Harlem. If you will investigate, you will find these and many more like cases going on. I am writing to you, because I believe you do not know of these brutal mistreatments, for if you did, they would have already been stopped. My people cry: "Oh, we can do nothing for there is no law, no mercy, no justice for us." I tell them, yes, there is a law and mercy and justice, and plenty of it in New York City, but you have to look to the right persons for it.

Your Honor, you do not know how thankful we are to you for the great work you have done for us in keeping down the subway fare. Sometimes we can hardly make the 5 cents for the fare to our work, so where will we get the 7-cent fare? Also, we are thankful to you for what you have done to stop the raising of rents in Harlem. The moment you took the matter in your hands, it was stopped right away.

You Honor, I am going to organize my people in Harlem to work and support you in the coming election. We want and need you to be re-elected Mayor of New York City, and I am going to do all I can to help you.

I close my letter with tears in my eyes, and, again, I beg of you to please do something to remedy these terrible conditions of mistreatment to the members of my race.

Yours very truly,

(Signed) MADAME STEPHANIE ST. CLAIR.

She didn't need Walker to win the election. He lay snug in bed with the corrupt Tammany Hall officials, and they kept her business competitors, the mafia, in their breast pocket. If he got re-elected, though, she did want Walker in her corner. Men like him, self-interested and connected, were a dime a dozen. He was simply the one in charge, and as such, she had to get his attention. And everyone knows the best way to rally a man's loyalty: appeal to his ego. So, when the whole neighborhood agreed with her, and they started sending him letters that echoed the message of her own, she realized that her success and wealth had put her on the level with the men who elected Walker to protect them. The local cops whom she could once pay for protection no longer allied with her because the guys running businesses on her level wanted her out of the game. They couldn't handle her as competition. Madame St. Clair might not have the law on her side, not yet, but she did have influence.

The same day she talked to the *Amsterdam News* about the advertisement, she went to the New York Public Library on 135th Street and looked up "illegal search and seizure." She had to inform herself because after that publication, Harlem didn't just write to Mayor Walker. They wrote to her, too. Airmail envelopes from Strivers' Row, cards from operators and handymen and maids working in her building, child-like handwriting on ruled paper torn out of spiral-bound books with sketches of her in the margins, even other mono-grammed stationery from neighbors in her own building. Everyone asked her about it. Most specifically, they wanted to know: How can you tell a police officer no?

The second most popular question was whether she heard back from the mayor or police commissioner. When the officials did respond, which was in a matter of days after the article ran, their letters didn't contain anything worth mentioning. Just empty promises that they would look into it, how they took her concerns seriously, yadda yadda, without any practical plan to change anything at all. So, she wrote another letter. These were again edited by friends who spoke English as their first language, writers who could help straighten out her syntax and adapt the rhetoric. This time, she'd complicate matters for them. See how these officials liked it when civilians not only knew but exercised their rights. Two Wednesdays passed before the paper had space among their advertisements, enough time for her to get a new photo taken. She called one of the young men who wrote to her about the newspaper. His letterhead had been stamped beautifully—but still stamped—and she saw an opportunity to invest in her community by hiring him. This time she wore a different turban, a light-colored dress, and bejeweled earrings because he said they caught the light from the window. The young photographer had made up her face so that it looked garish in person, but he insisted that on film, and reproduced in the newspaper, this kind of stage makeup would make a big difference. He was right. The photo was much clearer when the *Amsterdam News* ran her next letter as an advertisement on page six, right next to an ad for Dr. Frank Palmer's Skin Whitening Preparations:

NEW YORK AMSTERDAM NEWS
WEDNESDAY, SEPTEMBER 18, 1929
Advertisement Advertisement
Mme. Stephanie St. Clair

TO THE MEMBERS OF MY RACE:

I have been asked by many persons if the Mayor and the Commissioner of Police have replied to my letter to the Mayor about police brutality. These men have too much respect for the members of the race not to reply. Both the Mayor and the Police Commissioner have replied and the matter is being carefully considered.

Now my friends, I have made a careful search of the law to find out if it is legal for the police to treat you as they have been doing. The Civil Rights Law, Bill of Rights, is as follows:
Sec. 8. Right of Search and Seizure.
The right of the people to be secure in their persons, houses, papers, and effects, against unreasonable searches and seizures, shall not be violated; and no warrants can issue but upon probable cause supported by oath or affirmation, and particularly describing the place to be searched, and the persons or things to be seized.

So if officers meet you on the street and suspect you of anything, do not let them search you on the street, or do not let them take you to any hallway to be searched. Do not resist arrest, but let them carry you to the Police Station, where they have a legal right to search you.

Also the police have no right to come to your house without a search warrant, beat you, and sometimes kill. If they

meet you on the street and say that they suspect something
is going wrong at your house, if you say, come and see, if they
find anything wrong at your house and should arrest you,
without a search warrant, you have nothing to say, because
you invited them to your home.

If the police should ring your door bell and you open your
door, refuse to let them search your home unless they show
you a search warrant.

In conclusion I will say: I am going to continue fighting
until the members of my race are freed from these mistreatments.

From:
MME. STEPHANIE ST. CLAIR,
409 Edgecombe Avenue,
New York City.

In the time before Stephanie St. Clair had boarded the
SS *Guiana* and charged into her adulthood, she had to have
learned some kind of cruel, formative lessons that built her
into the woman she later became. She would have been one
of the many children around the fire in Guadeloupe, picking vivaneau meat from rib bones, crunching on the fried
fish fins that potato chips would later recall to her. Not long
after eating, the children might have danced and watched the
hands of their elders on goatskin drumheads. They might
have had stories and songs on Sunday nights, and on one
night, at this kind of dusk, she might have listened to an old
former bondswoman who had lived on the Nile before she
was sold. Maybe not. Maybe this didn't happen, but the timeline adds up, as does the geography, and who better to teach a
lesson of survival than a woman who clearly remembered her
emancipation? The most ancient people of the motherland,
she might have told the children, worshipped the crocodiles.
It is like the kayman, she said in French, *but it is bigger, and it is*

meaner. They worship the crocodile because they fear it. When the floods come in the ancient days, the waters are full of crocodile, and the waters bring them into the towns. When the waters withdraw, no, the crocodile, they stay. They eat the weak. They eat the slow. They eat the small. When the men try to hunt or kill the crocodile, they eat the men. That is how big the crocodile. So, the men, they build temples and carve spells to protect themselves. They move their world to fit the crocodile. But still, the monsters eat the people. Do you know why? Her honey eyes blazed into Stephanie's at this moment. Of all the children, she settled on Stephanie.

Stephanie said, *Because they are monsters.*

The woman's kohl-rimmed eyes crinkled at their edges. *And what can one expect from monsters?*

Monsters are monsters.

The crocodile, she said, *they tunnel underground, waiting. It flood underground first, habibti, and the crocodile feel it first because that is where they live. So, they crawl, the crocodile, elbow out, before the floods return. And the people. The people, they said, the crocodile are prophets. The crocodile are prophets come to tell us when the floods come.* At this she paused unblinking and stared across oceans and decades and asked, *But, what?*

But they were just monsters.

Yes.

The drums beat in the past until Stephanie found her words again. *Should we strive to be man? Or crocodile?*

No, the woman snapped her fingers, and then wagged one between them. *No, my dear. Be the flood. Inevitable and necessary. Everything relies on the flood.*

Stephanie couldn't stop now. She had to raise the water level if anything was going to happen, so in the same method as before, she wrote a letter to the governor of New York, Franklin D. Roosevelt.

NEW YORK AMSTERDAM NEWS
WEDNESDAY, SEPTEMBER 25, 1929
Advertisement Advertisement
Mme. Stephanie St. Clair

(Copy)

Hon. Franklin D. Roosevelt,
Governor of New York,
State Capital,
Albany, New York.

Your Honor:

I am enclosing a newspaper clipping of a reprint of my letter to Mayor Walker of New York City, because I believe you do not know of the big graft which this involves.

Uniformed policemen, seeing the plain clothes men making so much money through graft, become jealous and when off duty disguise themselves as detectives and for information given them by persons known as "stool-pigeons" scare the people into giving them from five hundred to two thousand dollars bribery for fear of arrest.

Through these cases of graft and bribery detectives, colored and white, in Harlem are getting rich. The lawyers and bondsmen are making plenty of money. The city is the biggest loser and the poor colored people are sufferers.

After the arrest, when you call to employ a lawyer he will say: "I will fix the case for from five hundred dollars up." Many cases are known to cost one thousand dollars because some detective will not take money direct from the defendant, but take it from the attorney, which makes the fee very high. When these poor people are taken to jail they are taken care of by the city, thus adding a great unnecessary expense to the city.

Your Honor, I close my letter believing that you will do all in your power to see that these terrible mistreatments are stopped.

Yours very truly,

MME. ST. CLAIR

TO THE MEMBERS OF MY RACE:

Last week in my letter to the public I quoted a section of the law (Sec. 8: RIGHT OF SEARCH AND SEIZURE) and asked that you not allow the police to search you on the street or carry you to a hallway to be searched. I understand they are still searching colored people on the streets. Again I ask you to refuse to let them search you on the streets or carry you to any hallway. If for any reason you are suspected insist that they carry you to the station house and search you there. If they do not find anything on you, there is a law for that.

If these searches on the street are not stopped in my letter next week I will publish the officer's name and badge number, also the name of the "stool pigeon" who has been giving this officer the information.

Yours for justice,

MME. STEPHANIE ST. CLAIR

Dear Mr. Lee:

Your letter to the Editor of the Amsterdam News was very carefully—

Here, the text block was interrupted by advertisement headline, "Noted Indian Doctor Discovers Preparation that Grows Hair Two Inches Longer in Two Months," as if to either remind readers that these open letters were paid for by their author, or to block the coming tide against the paper's readership.

—read to Mme. St. Clair, who directs me to answer your letter and say that you are still asleep. Please wake up, for this is the 20th century.

Mme. St. Clair says the members of her race are brutally mistreated by the police and that these mistreatments should be stopped. The police of Harlem do not know their place. They do not know that they should have the same amount of

respect for a civilian as a civilian would have for them. They
are forgetful of the fact that they are the hired servants of the
public. The police should do just what the law orders them to
do, and no more.

Secretary to Mme. St. Clair

If anybody thought Madame St. Clair would back down
from a fight because a "Mr. Lee" wrote to the editor to
complain about her writing, they thought wrong. Stephanie treated these weekly advertisements almost like a regular
newspaper column, and they seemed to affect her business
positively. Harlem appreciated the education she provided to
them, and they appreciated someone like her—a fellow citizen, but well informed in such matters—taking the time to
inform them. Not even people who were elected and paid
to inform them did so with any reliability. Out of respect, or
maybe from a sense of reciprocity, people of Harlem sent her
more letters. Letters of thanks, letters professing their love,
letters asking about her beauty regimen or diet, and letters of
warning. Harlemites weren't informed on the law, but they
knew the street-level happenings. They knew enough to know
that Stephanie was sticking her neck out for them, and while
they appreciated the risk, they wanted to make sure she knew
how big that risk was.

Her enemies got in touch as frequently as her supporters.
They knew they were at risk of exposure for extortion, assault, battery, as well as gambling and alcohol consumption,
depending on who they were. They rang her up at home or
sent anonymous notes by courier that threatened to expose
her criminal ventures.

Stephanie knew she was a criminal. Everyone knew she
was a criminal. She never carried on about it at length,
though, to look the part of a badass the way the gangsters

did at the speakeasies. Never anything so blatant. Her business was more of an open secret. She didn't talk about it out in the open (It didn't make sense: *If you run a business that is illegal, maybe don't tell everyone about it?*), but people knew, and because she invested so much of her profits back in her community and genuinely cared about her neighbors and their well-being, the illegality of her business didn't dissuade anyone's loyalty. Because she operated outside the law, no one enforced ethics on her, but she was ethical regardless, because that was the right way to be. People with legal businesses often treated them worse, just because they could. Even the police remembered who wrote their checks, so to speak, and they had more important crime to attend to than the little numbers racket that wasn't hurting anybody, and the letters were transparent. Stephanie herself could never take anyone seriously who didn't sign their own name to something, so she held herself to that same standard. She signed everything.

NEW YORK AMSTERDAM NEWS
WEDNESDAY, OCTOBER 2, 1929
Advertisement Advertisement
Mme. Stephanie St. Clair

TO THE MEMBERS OF MY RACE:

Many persons have said they are afraid for me and that I should be careful. I am not going to be any more careful than I have been. Please have no fear for me. I only ask that you listen to my advice and to do what I have told you. I have no fear of anybody. I respect everybody and shall expect respect from them.

Enemies have telephoned almost every night and said they are going to give me a ride and bump me off. When they say such things over my private wire I just laugh at them, because such things sound silly and simple to me. My enemies are now planning to frame me by saying that I carry a gun on my possession. These, and many more things, they are planning to do, but they will have a hard job to be successful. Because from three to seven days before anything happens, I have a warning of it.

In conclusion, I will say that I am going to continue to fight until the members of the race get their just and legal rights.

MME. STEPHANIE ST. CLAIR

Stephanie didn't let off the gas. She kept her advertisement column going, since people seemed to enjoy it so much, and her business kept growing. People came to her looking for jobs in everything from domestic work to dressmaking to bookkeeping. Sometimes people from other walks of life came to her—not because they thought she needed a porter or a tutor or a seamstress on the staff necessarily, but because she might know somebody who did. She nearly always knew somebody to match, employer or employee, and if not, she probably knew someone who knew someone. Understand, Stephanie didn't provide references for just anyone, but she had no problem pointing members of her community in the right direction. A job was anyone's to lose.

People in her building came to her for a different reason: could she see how the super was letting everything slip? She could indeed. And yes, she would be happy to help lead the committee charging the owners with delinquency and demand resolutions for the fourteen problems they stated. She would be honored to serve such a role at a building so prestigious as 409.

She also learned that two corrupt police officers had been arrested for abusing their authority, and she relished telling the people about their cumulative victory. True, they hadn't been convicted, but this was a big step, one that deserved to be celebrated.

NEW YORK AMSTERDAM NEWS
WEDNESDAY, OCTOBER 16, 1929
Advertisement Advertisement
Mme. Stephanie St. Clair

TO THE MEMBERS OF MY RACE:

I have the satisfaction of knowing that two of the officers who have been framing many members of the race have been arrested and are now under $2,000 bail each, the hearing will take place in Magistrate's Court, 12th District, on October 18th. Many more of these officers will be in the same predicament, if they do not stop framing colored people.

Again, I ask the members of my race not to allow officers to search their homes without a search warrant. These searches are not done by detectives, but are done by police officers in civilian clothes. Detectives are not allowed to bother with these so-called policy slips.

MME. STEPHANIE ST. CLAIR

Two days after her advertisement ran, she appeared in court to look those defending officers in the face. Right afterward, she wrote about it for the *Amsterdam News* again, as if she was a journalist viewing it from the press section, but also a celebrity among the numbers bankers who did not have her courage. She called them to action in print, this time with a different photo, facing the camera square with a cloche hat, a beautiful round ruby broach, and a new, dark coat.

NEW YORK AMSTERDAM NEWS
WEDNESDAY, OCTOBER 23, 1929
Advertisement Advertisement
Mme. Stephanie St. Clair

TO THE MEMBERS OF MY RACE:

I am asking you again to co-operate with me in order to get justice for all. Some of the so-called policy bankers say they are afraid. If that is so, then why aren't they afraid to do business? Heretofore, many of them had been shook-down by the officers each week and were obliged to pay out large sums of money. This has now been stopped. Before they were making more than a dozen arrests each day, but now many days pass without a single arrest for the so-called policy slips.

On October 18th, while in the 12th District Magistrates' Court, at the trial of the two officers about whom I made mention in last week's paper, a shabbily dressed man by the name of Mr. Ellenvoke, who I afterwards found out was one of the defendant's attorneys, approached me and said: "Are you Madame St. Clair?" I asked him, "Who are you?" He replied, in a very sarcastic tone: "That's all, that's all." During the trial this same attorney did not know enough to ask for a motion for dismissal. I am not pleased to have strangers approach me and try to make me identify myself to them.

I am making this fight without prejudice. If the colored officials were doing what some of the white officers have been doing, I would report them also. The colored officers are too well known in Harlem to disguise themselves as plain clothes officers.

MME. ST. CLAIR

The following week saw the biggest news break since the end of the Great War. Up to this moment of the roaring twenties, the US stock market expanded wildly, due to speculation—meaning people bought a lot of stock in assets with a high likelihood of loss on the slim possibility of a big reward. When the reality dawned, that production and employment were both in steep decline, the stocks lost their excess value, and the market went into decline, too. Friday, October 18, 1929, marked the biggest drop ever.

By Thursday, October 24, stockholders, brokers, and companies were all in a panic. Over twelve million shares were traded on that single day. Investors and bankers attempted to stabilize the market by buying up huge blocks of stock, so the following day, Friday, looked optimistic, but only for a moment.

On Monday, October 28, the market went into free fall.

The next day was October 29, better known as Black Tuesday, the day the stock market crashed. That market free fall was just one of the accelerants to the Great Depression of the 1930s. It was really as much a symptom as it was the cause.

Still, blue blood families bottomed out. The Chrysties, who had given Casper Holstein his leg up out of service work, fell on hard times long before the crash, but Black Tuesday launched them into direr straits. The ever-grateful and philanthropic Holstein kept them up for twelve years, paying for their apartment on West 93rd Street, the maid to serve it, and all their other expenses.

Nowadays, we know that a stock market recession only directly affects you if you own stocks. Maybe that's why Madame St. Clair made no mention of it in her published writing. She was not writing to Old Money, but exactly the opposite, the strivers.

In the 1920s and '30s, only the wealthiest of people owned stock. One would think that a crash would only affect the uber-rich, but because those people were the ones who owned companies and employed the working class at a time when the American middle class was much smaller, this crash affected everyone.

To public knowledge Madame St. Clair had not invested in the stock market so the crash had not directly affected her, and she seemed to prefer focusing on the matter at hand. Mayor Walker was corrupt, taking bribes and paying off police to look the other way while he worked with gangsters, but he was now helping Harlem with their problems, too. Walker likely was directly affected by the crash, and there is a chance his potential losses helped him focus on protecting his voter base in Harlem. It was rare for any official to prioritize the safety of Colored citizens, so St. Clair rallied in his favor. She did so in a fascinating way: she encouraged immigrants who had begun the legalization process to finish becoming American citizens, and then vote for Mayor Jimmy Walker. It didn't matter to St. Clair that she herself was not a US citizen. Hypocritical though it might seem, she might be doing more for the cause this way. It took a long time to complete the process start to finish . . . and she had not even begun. Regardless of her own shortcomings, Walker had shown and proved, and that was more than anyone that high up had done in a while.

NEW YORK AMSTERDAM NEWS
WEDNESDAY, OCTOBER 30, 1929
Advertisement Advertisement
Mme. Stephanie St. Clair

TO THE MEMBERS OF MY RACE:

It was a big surprise to learn that the colored population of New York City is approximately 400,000 and only one out of every ten are voters. Many of the foreigners, known as British subjects, come to the United States, take out their first papers and are afraid to take out their second papers. I have questioned many of them as to the reason why they do not want to become full citizens of the United States. They have replied that they know their English Consul will protect them in case they have any trouble. Dear friends, you should not feel that way. I want you all to become full citizens of this country. Please do not think about discrimination. It will be for the best, if we all become full citizens of the United States.

Dear friends, you will recall my first article in The Amsterdam News was a reprint of my letter to Mayor Walker. Mayor Walker is working very hard to better the conditions in Harlem. You can now see a big change. In order to continue this good work, Mayor Walker must be re-elected next Tuesday. In the same manner that I begged him to help my race, which he is now doing, I now beg you all to vote for Mayor Walker, regardless of any promises the other candidates may make to you. Mayor Walker has proved to be our friend in every way and we owe him our full support.

MME. ST. CLAIR

Walker did win the reelection against his challenger, Fiorello La Guardia. Like so many campaign promises, his commitment to helping prevent police brutality and abuse of power in Harlem evaporated from his mind, or at least from his list of priorities, once his next term began. Stephanie St. Clair was resolved to hold him accountable, though, and she said so in her advertisement directly following the election.

NEW YORK AMSTERDAM NEWS
WEDNESDAY, NOVEMBER 23, 1929
Advertisement Advertisement
Mme. Stephanie St. Clair

TO THE MEMBERS OF MY RACE:

On October 28th I received a letter from Mrs. Davis, of 438 West 163rd Street, in which she said she had been beaten up by the police and asked me to call to see her.

I went and found her walking lame, her face was badly bruised, her eyes were black and bloody and her hand was bandaged. In all of my experiences, I have never heard of a more brutal mistreatment of a woman. Mrs. Davis' statement to me is as follows:

"I had visitors at my apartment on the morning of the raid, and as I went to the door to see one of them out, five white men walked in. Without saying a word or showing a badge or any papers of any kind, one of the men began to search through my dresser in the bedroom. Taking up my pocketbook, he opened it and began to search through it. I rushed up to him, snatched the pocketbook out of his hand and asked him what right he had to come into my house and begin searching my things without showing a badge or a search warrant? My first impression of the men was that they were burglars. Smelling liquor, I said, you are drunk. One of them replied, yes, crazy drunk. I then insisted that they show me a search warrant or some means of identification. One of the men handed me a piece of paper. As I took it and walked across the room to a better light to read it, the man yelled to the others to not allow me to read it and to take it away from me. Two of them grabbed me, one of them bent my fingers back until I released the paper, nearly breaking my thumb.

"After they had taken the paper away from me, one of the men, whom I afterwards learned was Officer O'Neil, began to beat me and to call me vile names. He hit me on the head and in the face, choked me and kicked me on the leg, injuring me so badly that I am now under the care of a physician."

Mrs. Davis was placed under arrest by Officer O'Neil charged with violation of Section 974 of the Penal Law. The case was dismissed in Magistrate Court on November 5th.

Dear friends, I do not know how you feel about this case, but for my part, I am not going to let this officer get away with it and mistreat a woman as he has done. If colored people would stick together, these bad mistreatments would never happen. But our people are too selfish. WE are too much against one another. But I am determined to fight until these mistreatments to the members of the race are stopped.

November 11, 1929.

MME. ST. CLAIR

She had attempted to resolve the raid in court, if only to say she had tried. Now she was relying on her way. That's when she published the full story. What really got everyone's attention—civilians and police officials alike—was that she named the officers, gave their badge numbers, and accused them of perjury, all at once.

One year and three days after the frame-up, Madame Queen finally got the last word. The boys on Edgecombe yelled not the headline of the *New York Times*, but the details of another "advertisement" placed by Madame St. Clair on page 4 of the *Amsterdam News*. Under the heading "City News Briefs," wedged between ads for $65 fur coats, repaired dentures, and Dr. Palmer's Skin Whitener, was a small black-and-white photo of Stephanie St. Clair's smashed window, taken by the photographer that she had earlier taken an interest in. She had brought the same photos to court, but they weren't really considered. The only type of justice anyone like her could rely on was the vigilante kind, so St. Clair wrote the facts down for the public herself, naming names and badge numbers of all the policemen involved as she related the facts of the whole story as it had actually happened. She was so adamant that the truth came to light that she paid for its publication herself. The newspaper editors were only too happy to oblige.

Then, she repeated what the culprits told in court, perjuring themselves in addition to their numerous other crimes:

At the trial, Officer Tait told the court he cut his finger on the door of his automobile and that it was bleeding when he entered the apartment and that they did not smash the window. I have never heard such notorious liars, and to me they are a set of burglars, and a disgrace to the Police Department.

In Magistrate Court, Sarah Scott told the court she did not see a bag of slips and that she was the owner of the apartment. In the Special Sessions Court, she changed her testimony and said, yes, she saw Mildred give the officer a key and that he opened the closet door and took out a bag of slips. Later, I learned that Sarah Scott and Mustache Jones were sweethearts, and that the other women often visited at 570 Lenox avenue, where Mustache Jones was a lodger. The whole frame-up was planned by Mustache Jones and carried out with the aid of the officers and those women. The officers were accompanied by Ethel Small, for whom only a month previous I had carried her sick father to the Roosevelt Hospital in a private ambulance at my own expense.

So instead of getting me, they arrested one of their own. This case is still before the Police Commissioner, on the grounds of unlawful entry and burglary. I am going to continue this fight until I get justice and my money back.

MME. ST. CLAIR

After Harlem heard the full story, calls of support rang whenever Madame. St. Clair was out. She was always wrapped in silks and furs, behind shaded glasses or beneath the dipped brims of hats. It seemed to the outside world that she traveled incognito in a cloud of mystery to and from her places of business, but she knew that this demureness truly made her stand out more from her neighbors. "Fuck that Mustache!" she heard yelled from one side of the street to the other. More often still, she heard, "We hear you, Queenie!"

Letters poured into her mailbox again. Mr. Freeman, the doorman, had taken to delivering the parcels to her door rather than holding them for her in the lobby as he once had. He always joked with her, "Today's mail was smelling like cologne, Madame St. Clair."

As she waited for the elevator, she would smirk and ask, "Did it smell expensive?"

He invariably said, "No ma'am," and chuckled.

Not all of them were love letters. Some were letters of support, merely claiming that they would continue placing bets with her as long as she had her bank. Some sent foil-wrapped home-cooked dinners, the same as they would do for any member of their community; some sent home remedies for anxiety; some begged her to invest in their businesses; some asked outright for help. She did everything she could, for everyone.

In December of 1929, a year after the raid at her apartment and a month after she wrote about it, Stephanie St. Clair rode the bus home after meeting with her friend Mrs. Elam Berry about a potential charity venture. En route to her home, she said she had a vision. I think she recalled a fable like that of the crocodiles, from her childhood, something at least that warned her of a trap closing in around her. The plainclothes Colored officers Moore and Hunter followed her. They boarded the bus ahead of her, and they took the last two available seats. She knew what would happen before it happened: no man in their neighborhood would ever leave Madame Queen standing while they sat. It was like watching a wave crest high above her, a crash so inevitable that all there was to do was hope her preparations would serve . . . and that she could hold her breath till she surfaced again.

Her premonitions were more often of the future, a feeling enshrouding her rather than a scene transporting her spirit through time. Stephanie's rare reverie was so powerful and clear that it was more like a trance. The past only overcame her occasionally, when she needed to remember it. When it needed her full attention. It blocked out everything she could observe in the present, and to those in the present with her body, she was terrifying, like a standing corpse, swaying on a stinking brass pole in the middle of a city bus. She was suspended between the two spaces, as if she had one foot on a boat leaving a dock, but had to retrieve something vital before she disembarked completely. Her eyes locked with the old woman's embedded in her memory, stretching—when Stephanie finally blinked, she took a moment to get her bearings, and she realized that she had missed her stop. From the corner of her eye, she could see both officers staring her down over the tops of the *Amsterdam News*, the same paper which just the day before had printed her article condemning the officers for beating her neighbor, calling for justice. They did not realize the irony, and they did not seem like the types to read the papers, especially the local ones. She settled herself with a few breaths, and she turned toward the bus exit at its rear. The crowd parted to let her out, while the two officers nearly trampled everyone in the aisle as they rose from their seats to tail her.

Stephanie had only missed her stop by one, so she walked back up the street to 141st Street, to 7th Avenue, and into the hall of the apartment building before they rushed her. Dizzy Roberts and Officer Hunter came from nowhere and St. Clair let out the calmest, longest, loudest scream a pair of human lungs can muster as Roberts tried to open her clutch and shove in a bundle of papers. When they would not fit, and her scream did not subside, he pushed the bundle under her arm, instead. He took a step back, and when Officer Moore arrived from his hiding place to arrest her, he could factually say she was holding the evidence at his first sight.

NEW YORK AMSTERDAM NEWS
WEDNESDAY, JANUARY 1, 1930
Advertisement Advertisement
Mme. Stephanie St. Clair

TO THE MEMBERS OF MY RACE:

Well, folks, I have been arrested. Yes, arrested and framed by three of the bravest and noblest cowards who wear civilian clothes [. . .]. Suppose I was banking, I would never be foolish enough to have on me at any time anything that would incriminate me.

Suppose I was banking, what would I be doing on the street with a bundle of slips in my hand or possession?

MME. ST. CLAIR

The newspaper boys on Edgecombe read her letters, same as anyone, and they got eyes on them before the rest of Harlem. One doubtful boy new to town might have only caught a few scraps of the words before his eyes settled on the photograph next to the article, which took as much space as the article itself. No verbatim accounts of Harlem's reaction to her exposé survive, but the sentiments have been recorded. Based on those intimations, the following scene is how I imagine the neighborhood's reaction. "Wayminute," he said, holding his hand to his head and spiraling the curls there around his fingers. "Wayminute, man, I know this woman. This lady . . . she been in the papers a whole bunch." His city friends would have stared on as the connections dawned. "She the one . . . she the one that's saying to vote?"

The boys watched in silence.

"Ain't she the one saying if they won't hire Colored folks to don't buy nothing in they stores?"

They stared on as the meaning dawned.

"Ain't she the one telling people how the police can't just bust in on you with no reason? She the one said she paid the cops not to bust her and she got busted anyway! What's she doing taking slips *from* work *to* home? Talkin' 'bout now she's through for good. Man, please."

Red cracked a smile and looked Elijah. "I told you he'd get with it before long."

"What's gone happen to her, though? They sending her to jail?"

Elijah said, "Yeah, probably."

"Don't study all that," Red said. "Madame Queenie might go to jail, but she can jail, and when she get out? Everybody in trouble. Come on, man, let's go conk that head."

Thomas looked up from the paper, hand still at his scalp. "What you mean?"

"Can't be looking all wild like that now you in the City. Time to take that paper-slinging dough and get you some lye."

"What about Madame Queen?"

"What you gone do about her? She won't say nothing new in here till next week."

"Don't she got a trial coming up? Can we go?"

"We might can. If there's space."

Magistrate Samuel J. Silverman, the judge on St. Clair's case, was born in Odessa, Russia (now Ukraine), in 1908. He and his family immigrated to the US in 1913, just two years after Stephanie arrived, but likely for very different reasons. Though there isn't explicit documentation of the Silverman family's reasoning for immigrating to the United States, theirs occurred amid the many pogroms in Eastern Europe and Russia that were exiling Jewish people like them. And while we don't know for sure that the Silvermans were among them, tens of thousands of Jewish immigrants settled at least at first in the tenements on the Lower East Side. If Samuel J. Silverman had been living in the tenements in 1918, he would have seen how tight living quarters were, how hygienic standards fell in the cold of a January like the one of 1930, and how quickly a disease can spread. The influenza pandemic of 1918 killed thirty thousand people in the city of New York alone, not to mention how many people were ill for weeks or months as a result of its contagiousness. If he'd been in the tenements—or even if he hadn't—Silverman would have witnessed firsthand what kind of devastation influenza could wreak at its height and how fast it could take down even the healthiest people.

So when, on Madame St. Clair's court date of Monday, January 6, 1930, her lawyer, Frank, showed up to court with a doctor's note explaining that Madame St. Clair had come down with influenza, the judge granted a postponement. At the very least, he would have been aware of the newest influenza pandemic, and while the death toll of the current 1929 flu was not as high as others had been, two days seemed hardly a price to pay for the health of so many people who had showed up to witness her trial.

It didn't go over well with the crowd—"You don't have to go to work when you're sick? Your kids get to stay home when they have the sniffles?"—but they were glad to see Madame St. Clair much recovered two days later. Although she did seem weak in court, and her nurse sat right beside her in case of emergency, or maybe just to authenticate her story, her spirit was obvious and strong in the letter she had published just after the original trial date.

The next Wednesday, St. Clair made the front page for firing her lawyer—Harlem speculated as to why she did that, and the best they could surmise was that Frank hadn't kept her out of trouble in the first place. His intel about the illegal search and seizures surely hadn't helped her. What good was knowing the law if no one abided it? She hired Philip Levey of 521 5th Avenue, white, and Jewish at least in name, in Frank's place. They couldn't read the politics of his identity clearly. Was she pioneering against the growing interwar anti-Semitism? Was it a weird subversion of power, to show that she could employ him? Or was he simply the best in the game? Immaterial of the reason, Philip Levey, Esq. was the one who submitted St. Clair's plea of not guilty. Justices Voorhees, Nolan, and Salomon received the plea and continued bail to the date of the trial, February 21.

The real news lay in the last line: the *Amsterdam News* said, "She lays her arrest to her protests to Mayor Walker and Grover Whalen, police commissioner."

Deeper into the paper, on page four, was where they buried the real lede. Madame St. Clair's letter this time detailed the intrigue of the state inspector's investigation to find her and his questionable methods, which she portrayed as if they bordered on stalking.

NEW YORK AMSTERDAM NEWS
WEDNESDAY, FEBRUARY 5, 1930
Advertisement Advertisement
Mme. Stephanie St. Clair

February 3, 1930.
TO THE PUBLIC:

[. . .] He then said, "Now Madame, I guarantee you this, that the police will never bring any players to me, if any of them do so I shall transfer them to another precinct." [. . .] At this point Inspector Leonard asked me if I knew a man by the name of Henry Alexander [and said he wanted] a television telephone to see what was going on in my bedroom [. . .]. I looked at his hypocritical face, and I mumbled to myself, "God give me courage." If Chief Deputy Inspector can act that way, what can you expect of any of the police that are under his supervision?

MADAME STEPHANIE ST. CLAIR

Harlem was familiar with this type of hypocrisy, inconsistency, and ineptitude from law enforcement and politicians. None of the letter's contents surprised them. That the inspector couldn't keep his facts straight, didn't know his informants' names, tried to dismiss her evidence (and thereby her whole complaint) on conjecture that Stephanie disproved on the spot . . . none of that was out of the ordinary. But it was vindicating to hear that it happened to powerful people, too, because powerful people like Madame Queen might actually do something to rectify the problems.

Intentional or not, the pass that the inspector made at St.

Clair would have rallied young women and housewives to her cause on that principle alone. Men might have dismissed it then as they might now with an offhanded, "She just showed up at his office smelling all good like they do, what was he supposed to think?" "Dressing like that, what was he supposed to say? Nothing?" or "I don't know any men who don't talk like that." But not women. They knew Madame Queen, or they at least knew of her. Even if they weren't the progressive types, the types who would think that no matter what she was wearing or how she behaved she didn't deserve to be spoken to like that by a member of the police staff. Even if they didn't have that mentality—and a lot of them probably didn't, not yet—they couldn't possibly think someone with manners like hers, who dressed just so, whose romantic reputation was cleaner than anyone's, whose priority was to make sure everyone knew she was a lady, could have ever been asking for it.

So when a husband defended the inspector and said, "I don't know any men who don't talk like that," a wife would have shot back with a glare over whatever chore she was doing, "I better know at least one."

Madame Queen wouldn't let any support go to waste, and she wouldn't use it for anything unimportant. Her next letter specified just what someone like them should do if they wanted things to improve.

========

When Stephanie St. Clair showed up to her day in court on Friday, March 14, she wore a baby blue cloche cap, perfect kohl liner around her eyes, a full-length fur, and kidskin gloves. She was fully composed in front of the bar when courtroom photographer Edward Lewis snapped her candid photo.

NEW YORK AMSTERDAM NEWS
WEDNESDAY, MARCH 19, 1930
Page One
MME. ST. CLAIR CONVICTED
CONFESSED "BANKER" OF "NUMBERS" GIVEN
SENTENCE TO ISLAND
General Sessions Judge Refuses Jury Trial to
Harlem Woman Who Proved Thorn in Side of
Bluecoats for Year

The conviction of Mme. St. Clair [. . .] ended a battle of more than a year, during which time she fought the police of Harlem on the grounds [. . .] of improper conduct, unlawful entry and downright attempts to "frame" their victims. She contended to the last that she was a "marked woman" and had predicted months in advance that [a] plainclothes officer of the Sixth division, would "frame" her.

———

While Madame Queen served her six months' time in the penitentiary, it was like she went underground. We don't have much information about this period, which makes sense. Incarcerated criminals are sensible to lie low. But if a rapper can cut a record from behind bars, Madame Queen was certainly not out of the game. Her business seems to have run on autopilot, since it was waiting for her to get back behind the gears when she was discharged. She probably used this time for scheming, rerunning the stories she remembered from all the newspapers she had read over the years. When their hands are busy, creative, strategizing minds entertain themselves with stories they already know, rolling them over for new insights, new opportunities. The story about Bumpy Johnson defending Alex Pompez and assaulting policemen might have stuck in her mind's eye. All day while she fed fabric through a machine, she thought about this kid, Bumpy. She stretched her neck in the workhouse chapel's front pew, the sun al-

ready descending over the East River full of bodies dumped
by men far worse than she. Her head had been bowed over a
Singer sewing machine eight hours that day, and for the past
six months. She recited the Lord's Prayer as sincerely as her
fellow petty criminals, and she also prayed for special signs
through her cards, which had long ago been smuggled back
to her. She prayed for her champion to speak to her once
more, for strength, for patience. Amen. I imagine that even
with her head down, she was a fearsome fellow prisoner, to
be mostly avoided, and I think the other prisoners would
have found evidence to support their fear of her. She wrote
later of another vision she interpreted, and this is how I imagine the scene to have happened:

The women all struggled up from kneeling, unskilled
inmates having served the workday at much rougher tasks.
Knee joints cracked as the women trudged to the courtyard,
and then clambered in slow circles like misused ponies at a
rich child's birthday party. Welfare Island, St. Clair thought
as she rolled her neck, her fingers pressed back at the palms
under either ear, her elbows wide. Welfare Island, as if no
one knew its other names: Blackwell's Island, Damnation
Island—

Stephanie opened her eyes to see the island's lighthouse,
its beach barely visible over the cell blocks. The Tower, she
thought, and cried out, "We God!" She stared up at the light
flashing in the fading sun. The Tower. A change—a disrup-
tion coming. Barely visible now, but coming. She chanted
aloud unconsciously in her Creole as a woman in front of
her collapsed in the dirt. Everyone looking on swore she cast
a spell, but no one dared point the finger for fear of her
witchcraft. They would recuse themselves by agreeing with
a scientific diagnosis that the woman simply died of exhaus-
tion. St. Clair did not touch her. No, her hands were behind

her head, cuffed the whole time, as she stared up at the sky. There she saw Death, the second card of change. She would have been certain, in seeing that card, that the change would be big, sweeping, however far off.

———

Most criminals don't look at prison as safe, but most imprisoned criminals then were men. The women in prison then were seldom the violent kind, and they were even less often mercenaries whose violence against another woman could be bought. Generally speaking, when men have a conflict, they fight. They punch and kick and bite each other and wear themselves out, and then the conflict is over. That's not how it goes with women. Whether it's because people think that it's all right for men to fight, that they have to fight or they're sissies, or whether they naturally have that toxic violence in them, whatever the reason, men's main emotion is rage. They explode in a tantrum, and then they feel better. Rage looks like strength, so that one is all right for men. Women don't get that luxury. No one says it's all right for women to fight. And they don't get to show any emotion either—at least men get to have rage. Women, though. They're so adept at tamping their feelings that an adversary may not even know they're upset. They see farther ahead than men because they have to: men get to have strength, women get to have smarts, and that's why they have to play the long game. Women don't get to show it when they're wronged. What they get instead of emotions is memory. Women have long memories. It might seem like they have forgiven you, and maybe they have, but they never forget. When Stephanie St. Clair realized she was going down, she dragged down as many Tammany Hall corrupt officials as she could.

She knew all this about men, and she also knew how short their memory was. If her bank went under for even a weekend, all her runners would have new employment by Tuesday morning, so she made sure that everyone knew the standard before she surrendered at the prison: even in her absence, business was business as usual. They still did their jobs, and they still got paid for doing them. If they were skeptical, no one showed it. Her open letter in the *Amsterdam News* naming names and badge numbers was her last swing before she surrendered, and everyone working for her liked that tenacity. It renewed their confidence. She didn't serve a long sentence, and six months of labor wasn't even close to long enough for her to forget that the police she'd been paying for "protection" turned on her.

The newspapers celebrated her release on December 3, 1930, by sharing that she shook up the whole court within a few days. She said under oath that she'd been icing the cops, $6,000 to a lieutenant and plainclothes officers. Her employees welcomed her with big smiles, and bouquets of cut flowers waited on her desk when she came to work the first morning she was free. In her absence, the business had flourished. After all, the best thing a manager can do is hire talented people and let them work.

Other Harlemites chuckled at the bombshell and tipped their hats to her when the saw her, same as before, but this time with a twinkling eye at her vindictiveness. This is when she met Bumpy Johnson, and it happened so quickly after her release that I have to assume that Stephanie orchestrated it. Though his wife, Mayme, wrote a little of the interaction, the majority of the scene below is my best approximation Mid-December of 1930, Madame Stephanie St. Clair walked in a slight pump and a velvet-lined wool coat buttoned to its fox-fur collar through Colonial Park until she reached one of the near-frozen iron park benches. The young man seated there was reading what his wife identified as his favorite book, *The Black Phalanx*, and he rose when he saw her approach.

"Sit, please," she said, and they both did, gazing over the green foliage turning brown in the cold. "How do you like the book?" she asked the stranger.

"It's a favorite." He passed the book to her. "I've read it prob'ly ten times since element'ry school." She took the book in her indigo kid gloves from his wide-knuckled, bare hand. "It's about the Colored soldiers in our country."

She smirked slightly. "I know," she said, and opened to see the name Ellsworth written on the title page in childlike handwriting. "Are you a soldier?" she peered sideways at him from under her stylish turban.

"Yes, ma'am," he said.

"Ma'am," she nodded.

"My mama and sister would whoop me if I lost my manners towards a lady." The man had his big hands shoved in the pockets of his brown jacket.

"A soldier now. You no longer want to be a lawyer?"

His nostrils flared a little before he shrugged a little. "We ran out of money after my first year of college. Got to live." He glanced over. "Ain't you cold?"

She nodded. "But there is something about the wind now . . . I can't be away from it."

He nodded. "Cold's diff'rent on the outside."

They sat a moment, cold air blowing directly into their eyes, and neither face flinched. "You know me, then?"

"Yes ma'am." Her silence urged him to follow with, "They moved you from the workhouse to the state pen in April last year, and since you been out, you already shook up the police, telling the judge how you been icing those beat cops. First day free, already shakin' 'em up."

She lifted a palm and tipped her head. "Why waste time."

The young man grinned, wider than she expected. "You know me?"

St. Clair tipped up her chin. "You protect the businesses in Sugar Hill against the Italians and Jews. Your Alex Pompez, his lawyers persuaded your sentence reduced to disorderly conduct after you disemboweled a man on Lenox Avenue. And now you are free, too."

"Fresh cold feels different, like I said."

"I am sorry for your partner's loss, as well," she said, looking over to him. "It is very difficult to lose your chosen family. More difficult than losing your blood family."

"Chosen family is blood family. Ain't no difference," he said, too fast, and then, "Thank you."

Mayme Johnson said in her memoir that Bumpy's friend had just died, and Madame Queen acknowledged it at their first meeting almost immediately. "Yellow Charleston, the pimp who shot him. Killed him over a game of cards. A game of chance. In America, when people have a little success, they forget you need the luck more than the skill. High stakes games are high stakes in more than one way."

"He pulled the trigger in my man's face. It didn't go off, but still. They wasn't even playing against each other is the thing. Finley just wanted to move onto the table. Charleston lost eight hundred dollars and wanted Finley to loan it to him, but he wouldn't. Can't blame a man for not wanting to bet against his own money. The Bible says even, don't gamble with money that ain't yours. You know he shot Barron Wilkins, too?"

"Three times in the chest, one time in the belly."

"It's a shame. Barron was good people."

St. Clair nodded. "Yellow Charleston was a bad man."

"He was."

"Was," she repeated, and then looked at him again from the corner of her eye.

He said nothing in reply at first, and then, "Madame Queen, I know you know everything that goes on in Sugar Hill. No sense trying to hide nothing from you."

"I don't know everything about him. Only that the papers say he has been missing for several days."

"Respectfully, ma'am, he ain't missing. Some folks know where he's at."

They sat a few more moments, *The Black Phalanx* still balanced on her knees, her thumb bookmarking the title page. This meeting had showcased all the qualities in him that she had hoped to find: he was levelheaded but still mean as sin, which meant full of potential to be her enforcer. The sun grayed in the winter sky, and they could hear the electricity of the streetlights coming on behind them. A few birds yet to fly south mingled in the old-growth trees of the park. Children bickered over whose turn it was at whatever sport, down the hill.

"What are your plans this evening, Bumpy?" She passed the book back to him as if snapping into herself.

In response, he held the book aloft.

"I won't be coy. I know what you are capable of. We both do. Accompany me to the bank tonight."

"You not scared of me?"

She laughed the way she laughed, once, and huge. "Do you think I have no sense? Of course I am. Any sensible person should fear you. That's why I want you as an ally."

"You scary, too. Too smart."

"I don't want you just for my physical protection," she said.

"You are too intelligent to simply follow orders. Be the eyes in the back of my head. And I will pay you. Enough that if you want to return to school, you may."

She stood, and when she did, he stood also. They were the same height, but with her heels, he had to look up at her slightly.

"Don't worry about my height, ma'am," he said.

She laughed again, and he spied the gold tooth. She said, "The biggest person does not win the fight. The meanest person wins the fight."

He grinned again. "Let's get you back safe, 'fore we talk about fighting," he said, and offered his arm.

"When is your birthday?"

"October 31, ma'am."

She smirked again. "'Don't worry about my height,' says the scorpion."

"And yours?"

"Christmas Eve."

"Holiday babies."

"Party crashers."

She might not have asked his birthday at that first meeting, but it stands to reason that someone adept at tarot reading would also put stock in an employee's zodiac sign, and these birthdays seem fortuitous, right? And those are their real birthdays. It was in this way, over historical literature, that Bumpy Johnson became not just Madame Stephanie St. Clair's number one heavy, but her eventual protégé.

=====

For six months, he served as her enforcer. His intuition was as apt as she anticipated it would be, and he required almost no guidance at all. Bumpy thought of everything because it takes a gangster to think like a gangster. This first peaceful stint was short-lived, though. Bumpy was busted on a B&E in an apartment on West 113rd Street for stealing six suits and $300 worth of jewelry. He didn't really need to do it. It was probably just a bit of fun for him, just a little mess-around with his friends, like teenagers do. Bumpy served a little bit in Elmira Reformatory. It was a short sentence. He was in there just long enough for shit to go down.

AS YOU SOW, SO SHALL YOU REAP

On December 7 of 1929, before Madame Queen's court date and subsequent brief imprisonment, the New York City mayoral election had just occurred in November. Earlier in the year, Magistrate Albert H. Vitale had campaigned hard in favor of the Democratic Tammany Hall cog incumbent, Jimmy Walker. Walker was the one that St. Clair told her readers to vote for in the *Amsterdam News* in October of that year: "Mayor Walker is working very hard to better the conditions in Harlem. You can now see a big change. In order to continue this good work, Mayor Walker must be re-elected next Tuesday. In the same manner that I begged him to help my race, which he is now doing, I now beg you all to vote for Mayor Walker, regardless of any promises the other candidates may make to you. Mayor Walker has proved to be our friend in every way and we owe him our full support."

She knew he was corrupt—but better the devil you know. Walker beat Fiorello La Guardia in the race, and Magistrate Vitale went on vacation to hot springs in West Virginia. A month and two days later, on December 7, Vitale came back to the Bronx. A former magistrate and member of Vitale's Tepicano Club, Michael Delagi, threw him a welcome home party. And it wasn't just any welcome-home-from-vacation party, if you can believe such a thing existed at all. The club rented out the private dining room of the Roman Gardens restaurant on 187th Street and Southern Boulevard. The restaurant was eight stories tall, designed to imitate Old World statues and fountains and bacchanals. The tables were white tableclothed, arranged in a horseshoe around a dais, and served from inside the ring, like a medieval banquet.

If it sounds decadent, that's because it was.

Different accounts say there were between fifty and sixty guests at the party, all men, seated in their finery, eating antipasti and lobster and veal and tiramisu and espresso and then a round of dessert wine, and then Cuban cigars, and then brandy, and then the fine, imported liquors that were illegal to buy. Around 1:30 a.m., Magistrate Albert H. Vitale made his way up to the dais in the horseshoe's center, with his olive oil smile in his sharp tuxedo, to give a thank-you speech to his friends for throwing him a welcome home party after his extended vacation. Years later, when another company bought the restaurant, they'd take down the brown chandelier to clean it and discover the crystals were actually clear. The nicotine smoke from years of parties like this one had stained them brown.

While Vitale was at the podium, seven men burst into the private dining room. The leader was young, and witnesses said "carefully dressed." Only one of them bothered to obscure his face at all. With all their guns drawn, the soft-spoken leader moved slowly to the dais and told Magistrate Vitale to sit down and keep his hands on the table.

Vitale smiled a little and looked irritated that his speech had been interrupted. He wasn't jumpy, frightened, or concerned at all. He didn't move, even while looking seven pistols in the eye.

"Come on now, Judge. This is no joke," the leader said with a welcoming gesture. "Sit down."

After escorting the magistrate to his seat, the leader then jumped up on a chair at the horseshoe-shaped table and instructed everyone to give up their valuables to his associates—only one of whom wore a handkerchief over his face.

"Obey their orders," Vitale said. "Let them take what we have."

Later, he said he gave that direction because he "felt that any resistance might end in murder." It also later came out that while everyone else was forking over their jewelry and cash in fear for their own lives, Vitale slipped off a 4.5-carat diamond pinkie ring into his waistband, and his host Delagi hid his own 3.5-carat diamond ring in his shoe. One other man, an Italian American contractor, threw a $1,200 roll of cash under the table to save it.

It makes me wonder: Where were the robbers while this was happening? Why didn't they see what Vitale and Delagi were doing? There were seven of them. Were they all inside the horseshoe, like the waiters had been, or were they skirting the perimeter?

When the barefaced robber reached to look at Magistrate Delagi's pocket watch, Delagi said, "Don't take that. That was a gift to me by the Elks." *Holstein's Elks?*

The surprising thing, the witnesses said, was that the robbers let Delagi keep the pocket watch for that frail sentimental reason.

Detective Arthur C. Johnson of the Bronx homicide unit was also in attendance. Though he had his service revolver on his person, he never drew it. Instead, the robbers drew down on him, and they took both the firearm and its holster.

"You're a cop, huh? Better sit down and behave so's you don't end up a dead cop."

All told, the robbers collected $2,000 cash and $3,000 in jewelry from Vitale's party guests. On the way out, they also robbed the cashier's desk of $87.

The handkerchiefed man was the only one left behind while the others made their getaway. He waited at the top of the staircase, a pistol in each hand, until the two getaway cars pulled up on the street below. "Stay right where you are!" the man said. "Stay right where you are for three minutes!" Halfway down the stairs, he yelled back up again, "I'm still here!"

Everyone stayed put. Three minutes later, after the thieves had made their full escape, perhaps through the Bronx Park, the victims called the Bathgate Avenue police station. When Captain Charles Nelson and his detectives arrived to investigate, the witnesses gave excellent descriptions of six of the seven thieves—but not of the one who kept his face covered. If no one else hid their faces, Captain Nelson surmised, maybe it's because some of the witnesses might have recognized the one man behind the bandana.

Vitale said in his official statement of the night, "I am glad that Detective Johnson did not manage to reach his gun because if he had pulled it out, the chances are that the gang would have opened fire without delay. In the comparatively small room, someone might have been killed or wounded. I don't see how we could have escaped wounding, at least, with all those guns."

Police commissioner Whalen disagreed. He demoted Detective Arthur C. Johnson to patrolman, after twenty years of police service.

Even more suspiciously, just two hours after the robbery, around 4:00 a.m., Magistrate Vitale invited soon-to-be disgraced Detective Johnson into an anteroom of the executive office of the club. Vitale pulled out a drawer in his desk. "Is that your gun?"

Detective Johnson identified it from the shield number cut into the butt.

"Where'd you find it?" he asked.

Vitale simply said, "It came back."

Detective Johnson pushed on. "How?" But Vitale wouldn't tell any more.

Madame St. Clair read all of these papers, unsurprised by the corruption, but shocked at the blatancy. When Police commissioner Whalen started to really tighten the screws, more incredible stuff came to light—*this is the kind of blatant shit you only think you can possibly get away with if you've been getting away with shit for so long that you're deluded into laziness.*

In addition to the $2,000 in cash and $3,000 in jewelry stolen, the robbers that night also stole a "contract" for a hit that the gangsters had not paid up on, and which the hit man—who was one of the party attendees—threatened to take to the police.

When Commissioner Whalen commandeered the guest list for the party, he discovered that seven of the guests were known criminals—some of whom had been discharged by judges in that very room.

=====

Vitale later told Chief Magistrate William McAdoo that none of the criminals in attendance were invited to his party. Only thirty-two of the sixty had been actually invited, he said. Vitale recognized three of them, but denied four others were there. Even so, he said those three had not "offended against the law in years. It might prove of greater service to encourage their abandonment of unlawful pursuit than to drive them back to it by persecution."

Are people listening? Madame Queen wondered from her cell. *This is all but an open threat.* She grew more excited.

Whalen had dismissed Detective Johnson, the one who got his gun stolen, when he got the guest list for the party. At a later press conference, Whalen said, "We can't expect much of our detectives if we allow them to associate with such characters." The reporter said that detectives frequently had to associate with known criminals, and Whalen replied, "If they're on business it's different, but when they are plea-sure bent, as was apparently the case in this instance, they shouldn't be in company with such characters. It is well to remember that Johnson, as a detective of twenty years' experi-ence, should have been able to recognize some of the seven."

Magistrate Vitale circulated a petition to have Johnson re-stored to detective. He also told the commissioner that there were three other detectives at the dinner, but they threw their service revolvers under the table.

Vitale wrote in an open letter published in the *New York Times*, "One would think that the magistrates of the city of new York are made up of a lot of schoolboys and that the master has the right to call upon them to give an account of their daily doings. I recognize no such master."

That line made Stephanie laugh aloud. *He's saying outright that he doesn't obey the law . . . it's like he has forgotten he is sup-posed to abide by it, let alone enforce it.*

Then: in the same letter, Vitale said it wasn't a welcome home party for him but a dinner hosted by the Tepicano Club, which he served on the board of, and that Judge Delagi was the one who invited all the nonmembers. When Com-missioner Whalen got the roster of the Tepicano Club, he discovered that twenty-eight of the three hundred current members had criminal records.

Next, Whalen brought the charge that the Tepicano Club

was plying a bail bond racket, and that they might even catch a lead from the club to head off the building and arson racket, which was ever growing in New York City.

Just after Whalen charged Vitale with a full Bar Association investigation, a folder labeled with Vitale's name and title was found at Rothstein's residence. Its contents revealed that Vitale took out a loan of almost $20,000 from the known gambler/gangster. Vitale said his friend got it for him, but he wouldn't name the friend.

Even after all of this evidence, Vitale said in a true display of hubris that he "welcome[d] the investigation, for I have absolutely nothing to conceal or fear."

Detective Johnson was determined to clear his name, so he set out to exact vigilante justice. He accosted Joseph Bravate, a twenty-two-year-old out-of-work chauffeur, with sideburns and spats in a barber shop. Bravate was identified as the leader of the robbers. Even then, Whalen did not give Johnson credit for anything but identifying the suspect after he was arrested.

The truth was—and what Commissioner Whalen had either just fully realized or could no longer ignore—all law enforcement associated with Tammany Hall was completely corrupt, or at the very least untrustworthy.

It took months to prove it, but in reality, three criminals who had been invited to Vitale's welcome-home-from-vacation party went downtown and gathered the stolen valuables themselves. When Magistrate Vitale suddenly had his stolen goods returned and hand-delivered by gangsters, police corruption couldn't be ignored or side-lined any longer. Instead, Governor Franklin D. Roosevelt set up the Hofstadter Committee to roust out all corrupt officials, from judges to beat cops, at Tammany Hall. This sent a shockwave through other organizations—what would they do if their iced officials stopped looking the other way? They had counted on buying their legal immunity for decades. How could they get by without it?

Madame Queen was a few steps ahead all along. The very reason she landed in the workhouse at all was because of them. They hadn't protected her despite taking her money, and she gave them up to the incorrupt police. She had established herself alongside the true police . . . in a way. At the very least they would know she was not consorting with any more dirty cops—who among them would collude with her now?

———

It was that event—the robbery of the corrupt judge who saw all the stolen goods back in his own pocket in a matter of hours—that sealed her decision, but three other important events ramped up to it. One, Bumpy Johnson got arrested for breaking and entering and was serving in Elmira. Stephanie had a heads-of-Hydra security system in place of course, but Bumpy was the best. Not only was he cool-headed, but he saw patterns in people's behavior the way Stephanie saw patterns in numbers—it was no effort to peer into the future for either of them, and with his eye on her safety, she could focus on the money.

Bumpy's temporary replacements were big and strong and mean, but they didn't have his foresight, and her safety loosened in his absence. It was bad timing. Right around the time he got locked up, the crime syndicate caught on that the numbers racket was, actually, a profitable game, despite having been dismissed for a decade. Which leads us to the second important event: on Manhattan, the Combination came together. Another elite boys' club, to Stephanie, five Italian mafia groups, known as the Five Families, started working together with Dutch Schultz's organization, piecing out territories and rackets among themselves. Even though he was part of the club, Schultz was an outlier as the only non-Italian, and the only Jew. He compensated for this perceived lack by being the loudest, which was in itself much more dangerous. Besides, he was the Beer Baron of the Bronx, a hugely profitable operation while Prohibition made the legal sales of beer impossible. The Combination was tenuous, Stephanie knew, if only because it was a boys' club. On a long enough timeline, men second-guessed their own power and attempted to prove it to their peers, and they knocked down their own house of cards in the attempt.

Stephanie's concern was not the Combination itself, but that the Combination hired the Four Horsemen. Somehow, the Combination, this all-white Red Rover line of gangsters, looped arms with the four meanest Black police officers in Sugar Hill. If the police force wasn't an elite boys' club, then one never existed. Malcolm X would later say that the worst of these officers had freckles, and his name was Brisbane. The Four Horsemen—undoubtedly a name prescribed to them by the Combination itself, who loved to make up their own nicknames—terrorized the businesses of Harlem, intimidating the owners into paying for Italian and Jewish protection by smashing in plate glass windows and vandalizing the stores or inciting looting. Sure, the businesses were insured, but that kind of damage triggered cascading failures. When they closed down for repairs and restocking, they lost potential sales and profit in the meantime, and their customers took their business somewhere else and gradually forgot about where they used to go. St. Clair saw it for what it was—bullies taking lunch money—but that didn't make it go away. It made it worse. Because the Four Horsemen were Black, it confused the community that had flourished because it was just that, a community full of people who paid their good luck forward. But the logic held for Black men, too: on a long enough timeline, men begin to doubt their own power, so they try to flex it at whomever will pay attention. Still, it gave her a spark of an idea. If a boys' club was a boys' club, why would the corrupt police force topple any differently from an organization of criminals? They were essentially the same construct.

Her next concern: with everyone's hackles up, the Combination's move was to roust out the hold-out banks, like hers. When Stephanie had opened her policy bank, she broke the other banks with her mind. She strategized, ran her figures, and drove them to shutter for a few days, and then she used her winnings to open her own business. It was the honest way to vault herself into success, to start her business, one that happened to be illegal, even if it was legitimate. But as is the case with business, especially the illegal and unregulated kind, it's easy to go about succeeding in a dishonest way, which is what the Combination did. Rather than figure it out with their own minds, they cheated. The Combination had done what Casper Holstein had accused Stephanie of on the stairwell that day: they had a man on the inside.

Stephanie was a little clairvoyant, of course, but because she had bankrupted bankers before, her sense of logic recognized it almost immediately when somebody started running a game on her. Lack of integrity aside, there were still significant differences between Stephanie St. Clair's method and that of Arnold Rothstein, who insisted everyone call him "Abbadabba"—*The arrogance,* she thought. *What kind of silly little man creates his own nickname?* She never tried to put anyone out of business; Madame Queen just wanted her seat at that table, and she had to make the people already sitting shove down somehow. When Stephanie won for herself, she gave it back to her people, too. Rothstein had no such virtues. Granted, he had the skill of a quick-numbering mind. Schultz's lawyer, Dickie Hines, ratted their method much later: at the seventh and final race of the day, the comptroller would rifle through the slips of the day and tell Abbadabba which digits would produce the most winning tickets.

Abbadabba waited for the call at the racetrack itself, and when he got the number, he ran over the sixth race's winning payoffs and the probable returns on the top three races. Dickie Hines outed the details in a court testimony like this:

> Once Abbadabba had that figured out—we're down to split seconds now, mind you—he would have to throw some fast bets into the window to alter the odds and change the payoffs. Abbadabba, only Abbadabba, could do that, and at Coney Island, moreover, he enjoyed a singular advantage. There he had a way to get his bets down *after* the seventh started and while the field was still battling for the finish line. A sure system. He was exercising the final say on the payoffs and maybe now and then snaring himself a winner in the process—and collecting $10,000 a week for the strain all this put on his mental processes [. . .] But it couldn't have been done without the rare benefit of that outside telephone line and the collaboration of the world's most congenial track officials and mutuel clerks.

Not only Abbadabba could do that. Madame Queen could do that, too. The main difference between Abbadabba and Madame Queen, though, was that Abbadabba didn't work for himself. He wasn't an entrepreneur or a hustler. He was the numbers man for the mob. That's all. He was a lackey for Dutch Schultz, yet without his natural skill, Schultz's share in the racket would have dissolved rather than hold or grow. The lawyer thought that Abbadabba was the only one with this so-called "lightning mind," but he was mistaken. For this reason, St. Clair noticed the moment the law of large numbers ceased working. She still paid out winnings, and she was determined to never fold for any amount of time because she might lose the loyal customers she did still have. They crashed three of her competitors, though, all West Indian Black men in Harlem, Wilfred Brunder, Big Joe Ison, and Bumpy's former employer, Alex Pompez. Each man went to his home island to regroup, but when he returned, the Combination had seized his bank. Then, the new banker offered them a job working for them. In this way, the Combination turned three big-time criminal businessmen into working stiffs. Essentially, they did what Madame Queen did, but they did it in a dishonest way, and it took them eight years longer.

As vindicating as it was to see her predictions pan out about keeping all her money onshore despite the taxes and risk of audit, she did not relish the other banks' closures. Now there was no buffer between her and the Combination. She could have squared off against any one of the families individually, but not while they stood together. She knew this was a smash-and-grab, and if she could hunker down long enough, she'd come out on top. But this boxing out went on for months. It was a slow race to see who could hold out, her cash stores, or the Combinations' egos. One night in July of 1931, Dutch Schultz lit her fuse. We know for sure how it ended. The details of how the night *started* aren't written down, but I think it might have happened when Madame Queen deviated from her plans. Here's one way it might have happened. One of Madame St. Clair's regular bettors, let's call him Mr. Jones, hit big. He was so happy, an elderly Pullman porter who had been betting his anniversary every week for fifteen years, never combinating or anything. The same year his wife passed, he struck gold. He tipped his runner fifteen percent. The runner was so happy that with that tip—plus the ten percent of the money he collected from the bank outright as commission—that by six in the evening, he had called Stephanie himself, and he'd wrangled seven other employees of hers to call Madame St. Clair's home line and invite her out. What finally won her attention was when she heard the old man in the background scolding her employees for bothering her.

"Stop," she said. "Put Mr. Jones on the line."

She heard a shuffle as he entered the booth and said, "Madame Queen, I'm so sorry these boys are out here nagging you to come drinking with us. I'm not much of a drinker myself, and I told them they needed to listen to you when you said no the first time. They got to learn, when you push a lady, she don't give in. She pushes back."

"Congratulations, Mr. Jones. How will you celebrate?"

"Only place I go is the American Legion Hall," he said. "Everywhere else is too much for me."

"You've been paid?" she asked.

"Aw, Miss Madame, you know I have."

"Good."

"So, if you change your mind, that's where I'll be, but wherever I am next time I see you, I hope I'll be able to thank you with a drink."

"I couldn't allow that."

"You couldn't? I couldn't let a lady pay her own way! You take care now."

"I'll see you tonight, Mr. Jones," she said, and put down the receiver.

———

Since she'd been out, Stephanie had even less interest in nightlife, but she did prize the daytime fresh air and clean linen and skin moisturizer. Her girdle was loose from her time in prison, but she slid it up over her hips and fastened herself into her most flattering brassiere before stepping into her favorite black beaded gown. Her maid, Jane, buttoned it up the back and clasped a long strand of pearls behind her neck. St. Clair drew on her lips with a burgundy shade and rimmed her eyes with kohl. The maid called her chauffeur, and he waited to open the door at the building's entrance. Madame St. Clair was flanked by two bodyguards, Six-n-Eight and Obadiah, when she entered the crowded Legion Hall 398, and the Mr. Jones approached her with a big, crinkling smile. "Madame Queen—" he pressed her hand "—I sure am happy to see you." He recounted to her the story her controllers had relayed to her many times that day, concluding with, "If only my wife was here today, I know she'd be so thankful for you, too. She was always studying the dream books before she set on her number. I never changed mine. I figured, maybe it's hard for the numbers to hit a moving target. Neither one of us hit anything significant till now. She always told me to remember that you was a real and true lady, and I never did forget it."

Stephanie was charmed. "Your wife's birthday," she said. "It was this week?"

The porter looked stunned. "I didn't tell anybody that."

"You didn't need to tell me. I could tell myself."

"You touched?"

Stephanie just smiled.

The porter pressed her hand again, and it looked like he might cry when he asked her to let him buy her a drink with his winnings. When he asked what she was drinking, she told him Old Granddad. He bought the bottle and passed it around. The crowd was more alive than usual. This was the first shift drinkers of Harlem, the ones who had just clocked out. Mr. Jones said, "I got into the habit of stopping in here for a drink, so as to stay out of Mrs. Jones's way while she got supper on the table. Once in a while, a beer, but most times just coffee so I could stay awake to spend a little more time with her." Because Madame St. Clair was there, though, he lingered longer, until the second wave arrived, the night owls, the younger men stopping in for a cheap round before they headed up to the Cotton Club or High Hat Hut. A few of the young guns talked to Six-n-Eight and Obadiah, asking, wouldn't she come see Cab Calloway at the Savoy Ballroom with them?

Six-n-Eight replied, "Madame St. Clair don't really go for white folks' joints."

"Come on, man. It ain't like Roseland."

She set a hand on her guard's shoulder. "Is Mechanics' Night Thursdays, no?"

Obadiah shrugged. "This is true."

"Let me see how the jitterbug has changed since I've been to prison, eh?"

"Aw, let 'er come!"

Bumpy would have predicted that they would invite her, and he would have asked her beforehand and prepared a gracious decline so as not to insult her customers, but now with Bumpy locked up, his replacement heavy, Obadiah, turned to her, his back obscuring the zeal on the young men's faces. "If this's what you want, we can go," he said. "It is full of white folks slumming. And the Lindy ain't really changed much since Lindbergh made it to Paris."

"Is this the place with the jungle decor?"

He grimaced. The Savoy was one of the three biggest clubs on Jungle Alley.

She laughed and said, "Bien, so long as it's not Connie's."

"What's a matter, Madame St. Clair? You don't like the drag shows? They a trip—them ladies is funny as shit," someone in the crowd said.

"Nah, dummy," someone else yelled. "You know the Dutchman is a silent partner at Connie's."

Stephanie shrugged, more animated than she usually was,
and followed the crowd on foot to the Savoy, almost carried
by her admirers. They rambled toward the blinking lights,
SAVOY written vertically in neon, the strings of bulbs drap-
ing out from the marquee. She paid the eighty-five-cent cover
charge for all who were with her, and the bouncer nodded
his respect to her and then shook hands with her guards. She
passed her summer fur to the pretty coat check girl under the
cut glass chandelier in the lobby and then proceeded with her
entourage onto The Track.

An errand boy set up a small table for her at the edge of the
dance floor, between the two bands that alternated sets so there
was never a lull. The mirrored walls made the pink-painted
space seem even more full than it was—and it was full. Single
men bought a dance card and the Savoy girls taught them
the footwork in one mellow corner, but the other side was
a full-on competition, girls flying into the air, skirts spinning
and knees akimbo on trumpet blatts, the white-haired Lindy
scout overseeing them all with a rapt expression. Stephanie's
face was more alight than it had been in months, and not just
from the bottles of champagne her admirers sent over before
stopping by themselves. She refused all the begs to dance, but
she enjoyed herself nonetheless. The performance and dancing itself was blurred into her memory, with so much glitz
and glam, Cab onstage banging his head so hard his pomade
couldn't keep his hair slicked back, and St. Clair watched it all
from a table brought in special for her, with delight.

Mayme Johnson wrote about Dickie Wells, everyone's favorite dancer. He could move as well as anyone, but he had
the machismo of a cowboy. He had started playing for white
audiences because that's where the money was. He seduced a

white lady in an ermine stole with just his eyes—he was good at that, finding the richest lady in the audience, always in the first or second row, and making her feel like she was seen for the first time. Stephanie had not been there the time he swept that ermine lady off her feet, dripping in jewels, but she heard the same as everyone else, that he gave her about two pumps and a grind before moving on, as choreographed, to another white woman. By the time he regrouped with the ensemble, the ermine woman had slung her cocktail in that second woman's face. It was amazing to watch him pit them against each other, strangers who had never clapped eyes on him or each other before, and then go right on grinning and dancing. He had them all fooled. "He's not *really* Negro," the women stage-whispered to each other. "He must be Cuban. Or his daddy is white." He went with the white ladies, but he'd never really go for them. Tell them to meet them at his brownstone on Striver's Row and then had his dark-skinned disapproving mama meet them at the door. He'd watch from behind the lace curtain in the upstairs window as the white ladies scurried back off the stoop. Rumor had it Dickie had even done Ava Gardner like that, always milking her dry on-stage and vanishing into the wings as soon as she wanted anything more than a performance.

He didn't take a dime off any Black women, though, and Madame Queen knew that. He used his money to buy his mama that house, retire her from her work in a laundry, and he opened Wells' Uptown Club. Now people called him Mr. New York. He usually spent his time at Wells', but when he'd got wind that Madame St. Clair was out tonight, he probably slipped into the Savoy and pulled up a chair to Stephanie's table. She wasn't often off her guard, but Dickie had that way about him. He could turn his high beams on you and make you feel like you were the only one in the room. Again, only the outcome of the night is confirmed in writing, so I have to surmise the dialogue. Without even greeting her, he would have said, "Madame Stephanie, let's see this dress. Stand up and give us a twirl, won't you?" She obliged him, and he whooped politely at every movement of the fringe on her gown.

One of the men in their group said, "We ain't been able to get her on her feet all night."

"And you won't," she said, laughing. "This the Dickie Special." He kissed her hand, they sat, and she said, "You are too charming for your own good."

"No, ma'am, this charm's done me a lot of good."

"I'm sure it has."

"What you doing out tonight of all nights?"

She explained Mr. Jones's big win.

"I been seeing a lot of bullshit in your line of work—not from you, madame, of course. You doing all right?"

She tsked, dropped her voice below the club's boom so that he had to lean in to hear her. "It's taking the shape of a war," she murmured. "I might need help."

"Help from someone like me," he said.

"Not someone like you," she teased. "Only you. No one else will do."

He whooped again. "Might got to try that line out sometime myself, Queenie."

"So, it works?"

"I can contribute a little bit to the war fund. Just because you my girl."

"I'm a lady," she corrected.

"I can stop through . . . tomorrow night?"

"Dear," she chided, "I don't accept visitors after supper."

Dickie grinned. "I'll just have to make an appointment with your secretary, huh?"

"I'll squeeze you in."

"You beat all, Queenie."

"Not without your help, Dickie."

"Well . . ." He made a show of mopping his forehead with his handkerchief. "I'm gone have to dance a little bit to work off all this . . . nervous energy. You still not dancing?"

She demurred politely, and he worked up a lather with one of the young Lindy hop girls in Keds before asking a white lady dripping in jewels.

Six-n-Eight was staring when Dickie left. Stephanie lit a cigarette and bounced her eyebrows at him. "Don't worry, Six-et-Huit. It's only business."

———

Back to the night as I picture it happening: It was much later than Stephanie imagined when she finally got around to squinting at the tiny numbers on her Bulova watch, and she nearly had to close one eye to make out the time even then. "My, my," she said, stamping out her second cigar and standing in a haze of her own smoke. Her men stood with her and they exited the Savoy the way they came, picking up her coat with the ticket and tipping the lovely girl at the front.

Though her guards offered to flag down a taxi, Stephanie insisted on the walk—it was short, and the night was not as hot as the past week had been. There was more movement, and she always savored the fresh air on her face nowadays, even if it was mostly smog, and not all that fresh. She kept her hand in the crook of one guard's arm, her evening bag clutched in her other, until they had her settled on the other side of her apartment door. Stephanie stepped out of her T-straps—what a silly choice of shoe. And now they were nearly ruined. Beautiful as that ballroom was, not a drink went unspilled with all the Lindy hopping going on. She lay down an old newspaper and set them out on the ottoman in the parlor for Jane to work a miracle on in the morning.

Her maid was gone for the night, of course, so she had a time unbuttoning her gown. After she unclasped the top three, she couldn't reach any lower, and she pulled the dress overhead, popping several threads despite her weight loss. She dropped the dress with a tinkling of the beads, and just as she was about to slip into her nightclothes, she heard an urgent rapping at her door.

This next part is hard fact.

Stephanie hadn't let anyone up, and her bouncers wouldn't knock at all if it was urgent. They'd use their key, or just kick the door in. She would never answer the door—barely her telephone—when she was home alone, but at this hour . . . who would knock at this hour? It must be a neighbor.

Stephanie threw her kimono around her shoulders and put her eye to the peephole. It was as she intuited: outside stood a woman she had seen in the building before, holding a hand over her eye, and blood dripped from her nostril. "Who is it?"

I recreated this dialogue, but the gist of each line was documented by Stephanie herself. "It's Catherine, ma'am, from down the hall. Please, can I come in? Please. I'm afraid he'll kill me."

Stephanie hesitated, and then she grew angry at herself. What kind of person was she not to help a woman in need? In her sleepy drunkenness, she unlocked the deadbolt and twisted the knob, only to find that the chain was still looped. She made to close the door again to unlatch it, but before she could, a force blew it out of her hand and snapped the chain off the doorjamb. A big white man stood in the doorway, blocking her exit, Catherine now nowhere to be seen.

He must have seen her face harden, because he said, "My name's Max Renney, ma'am. There's no need to be afraid."

She tried to close the door and he moved his hand up to catch it.

"I need to come in to talk to you, Miss St. Clair, and this will be much easier if you invite me in."

"What is all this about?" she asked. "Why did you hurt my neighbor?"

"Nah," he scoffed. "I wouldn't hurt a fly."

"What do you want?"

"I got a message for yous."

"From whom?"

"From the Dutchman."

At this, Madame St. Clair pursed her lips in a way she hadn't done since her teenage years and nearly rolled her eyes. "The Dutchman? The goddamned Dutch Schultz is sending his boy to talk to me in the middle of the night? He can' come himself? In the light of day, like a man?"

"Now, see here, lady—"

She let out one loud laugh and released the door. She turned her back long enough for him to come into the hall and follow after her before she whipped around and hurled her full body weight at him. He lost his balance and stumbled into her hall closet, where she slammed the door and locked him in the same closet where the police had planted the policy slips. All these things really happened. I only recreated how they happened.

St. Clair fled down the building corridor in her kimono and took the stairs barefoot as fast as her feet could move. When the third shift doorman looked up, he gestured for her to go into the manager's office, where her guards still sat, playing a round of cards. Six-n-Eight and Obadiah jumped to their feet, cards falling like confetti, and took the stairs two and three at a time to take care of the intruder.

The third shift doorman guided Stephanie into a folding chair at the card table, and he poured her a snifter of brandy to settle her nerves. She could barely keep the liquid in the glass her hands were shaking so. He apologized on end: "I would never let anybody up to your place without calling you first—let alone at this hour! I wouldn't even call up unless it seemed urgent."

"I know this. I know this," she said, trying to soothe him in return.

"Oh, are you all right, Madame Queen? I'm so sorry. What can I do to make it right?"

She drew a shuddering breath and said, "First, know that your job is safe. You did nothing to put me in danger. I think he broke in through another apartment, the fire escape. He used Catherine Odlum as bait—she's the only reason I came to the door. It's not her fault, either. But do send someone to look after her."

"Yes ma'am."

"Can you take me to the furnace? The basement?"

"The basement, ma'am?"

"Oui, where is the furnace."

He escorted her down the servant staircase. She gripped the wooden banister the whole way, both feet firm on each step before she took the next, knowing her legs could give out at any moment. She glanced around at the hardware, tools, cleaning supplies, and walked over to the coal reserves. She sat behind them.

"Oh, madame," he said in protest.

"No," she insisted. "I feel safest right here, please. When Obadiah comes down, tell him this is where I am."

———

Her guards took her in a limousine to a hotel nearby. Being Madame Queen, she would have likely gone to the Hotel Olga, and she could not enjoy its luxury for her shaking. They sat in the suite's dining area wondering what they'd done wrong until their daytime relief came, and Jane arrived as well with suitcases packed and an armful of groceries. She convinced Six-n-Eight and Obadiah, who'd been up all night, to lie down while she fixed them some coffee, at least, and she stayed with Stephanie until she regained her nerves. Stephanie slept for most of the day, and when she awoke late in the afternoon, she dressed in a burgundy suit and hat, and she had her limousine carry her to the magistrate court's office, where she filed for a warrant on Max Renney. After she spoke to the police to file a report, and the victim's advocate walked her through the process of setting up a time with a judge, she might have told the girl at the front desk, "Please, be sure this makes it to Samuel Seabury's desk—I know he is a busy man, and I know that these domestic issues are not normally his office, but I think hearing of this assault might help with his investigation. The man said he worked for Dutch Schultz, who is part of the Combination. The men who are corrupting Tammany Hall." At this final name drop, the girl seemed to register the relevance and pledged to let the judge know.

———

Her open letters say that as her driver edged slowly down Lenox Avenue back toward the Hotel Olga, Stephanie spotted Marvel Cooke, the promising young woman journalist at the *Amsterdam News*. She was likely headed home, briefcase in hand. Stephanie knocked on the partition. "Pull over," she told her driver. Marvel stutter-stepped away from the vehicle slowing by the curb. Then she saw the back seat window of the black limousine roll down and reveal the narrowing eyes of Stephanie St. Clair, and she almost gasped. "Good evening, Marvel. I have a story for you."

Marvel was eager to prove herself, both to the queen of Harlem and to her new employers at the newspaper.

"Get in," Stephanie said. "Let me tell you what this goddamn Dutch Schultz did. And what I'm going to do about it."

Marvel tried to walk around the vehicle to the other side, to enter on the door closest to traffic, but Stephanie shouted for her to stop, opened her own door, and slid down to make room for Marvel. It was time for dinner, so rather than have her driver circle the block, Stephanie took Marvel back to the Hotel Olga. The women passed every familiar face of the Harlem Renaissance on the way to the top, everyone from Alain Locke to Bessie Smith. In the suite, Jane took their room service orders and called down to the kitchen.

Marvel didn't go home after the interview. She finished her coffee in the back seat of Stephanie's town car and had the driver drop her at the offices of the *Amsterdam News* in San Juan Hill. She took her time cleaning the machine and brewing a fresh pot at the office. She scrubbed out one of the stained jadeite mugs, filled it, and pulled open the drapes on the New York City night. Marvel was alone in the office, so she sat at a desk that wasn't hers, overlooking Harlem. Behind the typewriter, she started to organize. From the fistful of her shorthand interview notes on Hotel Olga stationery, she drafted the interview. She edited it with the green ink pen Madame St. Clair insisted that she keep, and she retyped it before the following morning. When her editor William H. Davis came to his desk just as the sky moved from pink to blue, Marvel was waiting for him. He sat down, and she dropped this into his lap.

NEW YORK AMSTERDAM NEWS
WEDNESDAY, SEPTEMBER 21, 1932
Page Two
PROMISES TO CRIMP DUTCH SCHULTZ
Threats Disclosed By Mme. St. Clair
"Policy" Queen Asserts That She Will Put End
to White Racketeer's Activities in Harlem—May
Picket His Drops

Mme. Stephanie St. Clair [. . .] promised [that Schultz] is "going out of Harlem" if she has to put a picket at every one of his "numbers" stores from 125th to 155th streets.

"Who does he think he is? [. . .] He's nobody."

[. . .] Armed with the affidavit, Harlem's "policy queen" reveals that she sought in vain to obtain a bench warrant for the arrest of Renney. [. . .]

"I can't find him," said Mme. St. Clair, "so now I'm going after this here Dutch Schultz."

———

The attention Stephanie had gotten from her regular advertisements paled next to this, a professional write-up of events. Stephanie was not finished making assurances, though. Memoirs and exposés of the events say she went to the Black entrepreneurs whom she knew—and whom she knew the Combination was making hell for. She went to see her favorite, first. Dickie Wells, the dancer and performer. At the same time, she instructed Bumpy's boys to pick him up from Sing Sing. It makes sense that they would have arrived in Madame St. Clair's car. Her own chauffeur sat behind the wheel, and one of the very suits Bumpy had been arrested for stealing hung behind the partition. Bumpy laughed when he saw it and changed clothes in the back seat while his friends

popped the bottle of champagne Stephanie had supplied and
cut his cigar for him. She arranged him a hero's return, he
realized when the car slowed in front of Smalls' Paradise on
135th Street and 7th Avenue. Madame St. Clair remembered
that Bumpy loved the club for its Southern motif, with cardboard riverboats motoring around the wall and a cotton field
backdrop, enough to remind him of home without actually
making him homesick—those cotton fields a Sword of Da-
mocles. When he exited the car, he straightened out his tie,
and then smoothed his pockets, and he felt a letter folded at
the breast. He slipped off to the bathroom to read it. Till he
saw that town car, Bumpy thought Madame St. Clair might
begrudge him for his prison time leaving her unprotected,
but he should have known better. This party wasn't only a
party: it was his first job after getting discharged. Eddie Smalls
didn't exactly like white people, but he'd take their money
same as anyone's, and everyone knew that Paradise was neutral ground, a club where rival mobsters spotted each other,
finished their drink, and pulled a U-turn without engaging.

In the bathroom stall, Bumpy read her note, short and
simple. "Welcome back. Schultz has threatened to kill DA
Dewey. Let the Combination know." Thomas Dewey was
thirty-three, and he'd just left government service to work
as an attorney in the private sector. St. Clair knew Dewey.
He was a white hat through and through. Madame St. Clair
respected him for that, even while knowing the paradox that
not everyone could afford to be that white of a hat. One
had to have a certain level of privilege to make that kind of
higher-order decision. Basically, if the choice is to eat or not
eat, everyone steals that loaf of bread. And if it was a matter
of feed your family or watch them starve, everyone would
knock over a bakery. Sacrifice their body, or their time. Send

them alone to a foreign country forever. But not everyone was called to make those types of decisions. Some people got to choose, instead, whether to make their own lives easier by forcing those first-order decisions on others. Dewey was the rare sort of government official who did have opportunities for more power, more money, and more glory at the small expense of his morality—but chose not to exercise those options.

Bumpy grinned, dropped the note in the toilet, pissed on it, and pulled the chain to flush. Bumpy tipped the attendant and as soon as he was out of the restroom, he saw Eddie on the other side of the club, handing over a birthday card and a round of drinks to a white police captain. The Charleston dancers came up behind him to regale the table, and Eddie made his exit. He spotted Bumpy and cut him off as he walked back toward the table. He clapped him on the back and grinned while he spoke, to make his conversation seem innocuous to anybody watching: "Welcome back, homeboy. Listen, I hear Madame St. Clair got a plan to get this Dutch Schultz out of Harlem. Look at his nasty ass over there by the bandstand in his cheap clothes, would you? Set up a meeting with me and Queenie so I can help finance it when you see her, all right? My man!" he said, delivering Bumpy to his own table of friends. "Whiskeys all around?" The table hollered at each other over the brass music and drums while Bumpy thought fast: How best to leak Schultz's death threat of the new district attorney? Dewey was already anti–Tammany Hall and the Combination knew it. He'd walk right up to the Five Families and announce the threat himself, if he thought they'd believe him, but if a straight man like Smalls knew he was affiliated with Madame St. Clair's outfit, that fact was surely common knowledge among the gangsters. His best tack would be the security at Paradise. Eddie had given him one of his first gigs in Harlem as a front door bouncer. As a result, he knew almost every guard in the place.

"Hey, Eddie," Bumpy said. "Steve and Nat working tonight?"

"Working here? Steve? Shit no. He works for the Italians now."

"He in here?"

"Oh. Yeah, he's here. Over there with the Combination. Damn." He shook his head and took his leave.

When Steve went to the bar, Bumpy went to the bar. They stood shoulder to shoulder at the biggest of the three circles, each with full shelves of liquor, and the girls on the stools watched them as if hypnotized. "Thought you ought to know," Bumpy said, "the Dutchman said he was gone kill the district attorney."

Steve lifted his chin. "Thanks for the tip, but the guineas already know."

"Yeah, I'm sure they do." Bumpy peeled off a few bills to tip the bartender. "But do they know that I know? Me, who been sprung all of fifteen minutes?" He shrugged. "Thought that might be too much attention for 'em. But you do what you think."

"Why you telling me this?"

"Maybe one day we'a win you back." He raised his cocktail. "Cin cin."

———

Beyond Bumpy's wife relating his hero's return in vague terms in her memoir, none of the criminals reveal their intentions the way they do in movies, explaining their chess strategies to viewers so we understand how badass the hero is when they finally win. In real life, we have outcomes only, and we have to work backward from them, deducing plots and their execution based on the characters involved. So when I tell you that Bumpy reported for duty at Stephanie's apartment the next morning, hat in hand, I'm saying it's only probable that he said straightaway, "You the wisest woman I've ever known. And I've known some."

I had to surmise the rest of the interaction, too.

"Thank you," she said, rising to shake his hand. "And welcome back. You're here much earlier than I anticipated."

"It's one o'clock," he said.

She settled back on her wingback chair, and him opposite her across the coffee table. "Did you not enjoy your party?"

He laughed. "Yes ma'am, thank you for that. We had breakfast there."

"You haven't slept?"

"First things first."

"Well, I owe you an apology."

Bumpy looked surprised but tried to contain it—maybe this was her farewell.

"The robbery, the theft they arrested you for."

Bumpy stayed quiet. Maybe this was the other shoe dropping.

"I do not want you to resort to any other means of earning your living. I should have paid you more from the start—"

"'Scuse me, Madame Queen," Bumpy said, lifting a hand. "I got jailed, and you giving me a raise?"

She raised one eyebrow. "You wouldn't have to steal if you earned enough money, no?"

Rather than say it was just for fun, just out of habit, rather than talk himself out of a pay raise, he said, "Thank you, ma'am."

She nodded. "If you start to feel like you need to moon-light for more money, tell me first, yes?" Then she changed the subject: "You saw Schultz at the club?"

"I did. They say he looks like Bing Crosby with his nose bashed in, but don't nobody talk about his bad suits." Bumpy chuckled. "It was the first thing Eddie Smalls said when he pointed him out. Eddie wants to help you get rid of him, by the way. You'd hate the Dutchman on sight."

"Dutchman, my ass. Do you know his real name?" She paused and sucked her cigarette. "Arthur Flegenheimer."

Bumpy gave her a bewildered expression. "No wonder he changed it."

"These Jews all give themselves their own nicknames." She threw her shoulders up. "Why? They don't know each other?"

"He says it's so his name fits on the headlines."

"*Merde.*"

"Mine's from bumping people off. Only seems like I gave it to myself because everybody who's said it is dead."

She cut her eyes at him before cackling. "No, but that's what it means now."

He grinned. "That's right."

Bumpy chuckled, leaned forward with his palms together and cut the shit. "So, what we gone do next?"

"Order Chinese." Over lunch, she explained how she an-ticipated all-out gang war. He'd need to prepare. Recruit more soldiers. She was glad to hear that Eddie Smalls rallied with them—she thought that he would, but Eddie didn't like to be pressed, so she had to wait for him to come to her. Which he had last night. Madame St. Clair mentioned her other backers, hesitating at Dickie Wells. According to later memoirs, Dickie had promised a thousand dollars at the Sa-voy, but since then, things got dicey. He'd showed up at her apartment later than he said he would, like any playboy, and then said he hadn't realized that Bumpy would be her general against Schultz. He'd rethought his offer, and he had to withdraw.

The memoirs say that Stephanie had jumped to her feet and with fire in her eyes told him exactly what she thought of him. They don't say exactly what she thought of him, but knowing her how I know her, I think it went this way: "You're a showman and nothing more. Your flash and charm might make you money, but behind that, nothing. A man does not go back on his word. He does not show up late for appointments. He does not abandon a lady after pledging his loyalty—"

"Loyalty?" Dickie had been incredulous.

"Loyalty to this cause, imbecile. I don't even think about who you cavort with in your silly little romances, Tallulah Bankhead, Joan Crawford, mon dieu, you could seduce the Madonna and I wouldn't notice till the Pope announced it. You are a defector. A draft dodger. This is worse than dodging the draft. You're turning your back on your own people. And after you gave your word. You should be ashamed. Your mother—"

"My mother?"

"Your mother would have something to say about this—"

"You gone call my mama on me?"

All this time Stephanie had been walking toward him in the way she'd stalk toward anyone who had cost her money, but now he walked toward her, too, and he was smiling. She put her hands out to stop him, but he took them in his own and pulled her close as if to dance, one palm flat on the small of her back.

"I'm not finished talking," she said, and he kissed her before waltzing her around her coffee table and back toward her bedroom.

All said and done, he changed his contribution from a thousand dollars to a blank check. She didn't need to tell Bumpy why. And he wouldn't ask.

=====

Ever since Mustache Jones extorted her five years ago, she had hated icing the police. They never helped her. They were just more bullies to pay off, but because they were legally backed, she had to pay them—there was no skating around it as if they were petty criminals. After all, it was the violence from police that she was fighting against when the corrupt cops planted those policy slips on her, which had landed her on Welfare Island in the first place. And she had even paid their stupid tax! Madame St. Clair's impulse had been to lie low, which was easy to do for the six months she was in prison. But the other gangs' modus operandi was always to copy every damn thing she did, so now she had to do something different. Now she turned on a high heel and shocked everyone. Madame St. Clair saw this crackdown as a business opportunity. She had to. No more playing in the dirt with these criminals. Her big decision? She was going straight. At least, she was going to the straight officials.

On December 9, 1930, records show that Madame St. Clair, newly released from prison and escorted by her new muscle, Ellsworth "Bumpy" Johnson, walked into the office of former judge of the Court of Appeals Samuel Seabury. He led the Hofstadter Committee—led it so well that everyone now knows it instead as the Seabury Investigation—and all evidence suggests she came clean. She didn't write out the full scene, but I believe it happened like this: She dressed in a demure skirt suit and fashionable turban, and when he invited her to, she perched on the seat of a wingback chair at the foot of his enormous desk in a cloud of French perfume. With Bumpy standing behind her, she said, "I am very grateful that an honorable judge such as yourself has made time to talk to me, a lady who has been to prison. I've read the papers about your committee, and I want to help. Specifically, my colleague has our log of business expenditures—" at this moment, Bumpy passed a red leather folio to Seabury's assistant, who passed it to the judge, who spread it on his desk blotter. "As you can see, the total amount that my business had to pay was seven thousand and one hundred dollars. You'll see thirteen plainclothes officers and one lieutenant named in the second column—"

Judge Seabury held up his hand to stop her midstream. "Just one moment, ma'am."

Stephanie watched his bowed head, the part of his hair crisp, and felt that he nearly vibrated with excitement. "These third and fourth columns . . ."

"The percentage of our income for first state tax and then federal tax."

Seabury smirked. "And the fifth?"

"The police officers' badge numbers, your honor."

He stared at the log for a long time before he finally asked, "Miss St. Clair, I'll need to confiscate these for evidence."

"Of course, do not worry. This is not the only copy of my official records."

He looked up finally, revealing his rounded collar under a dimpled chin. Judge Seabury removed his glasses and stood, so Stephanie stood with him.

"I'm grateful to you for your help, miss."

Stephanie St. Clair reached out and clasped his hand. "Your honor, please, if there is anything more I can do to help, do not hesitate to let me know. I came to this country to escape corruption, and I am glad to assist."

Bumpy held the door for her to exit. As soon as they were

down the steps of the courthouse and in the back of her limousine, he grinned at her. "You so smooth. What you think
they're saying now?"

"His assistant says the judge should not trust me. I'm a
convicted criminal. The judge says the conviction is true
enough, but he says that I'm a lady. Her back never touches
the chair, he says. The aide says, 'But she is foreign!' The
judge says, 'She comes to America for the same reason everyone comes to America.' The aide says, 'She's no better than
any gangster in a zoot suit.' The judge says, 'How many gangsters do you know pay their income tax?'"

Bumpy grinned and glanced out the window. "That's how
they pop all the gangsters. Tax evasion."

"Je suis."

"I know you know. I'm just laughing out loud is all."

Seabury wasn't after St. Clair or her bank. Strictly speaking,
her business was organized crime, but her level of corruption
paled when compared to the mafia. Seabury concentrated on
smoking out the mob. The mafia got greedy, and in addition to their myriad other rackets, they wanted the numbers
game, too. Schultz's crew tried to poach St. Clair's employees
at every turn—they even bullied the businesses in her neighborhood, smashing their windows and posting up outside to
intimidate shoppers. This went on for months, and still she
did not cave.

=====

"Let's talk about the end of Prohibition," Stephanie said in
mid-1933.

Bumpy nodded. "A lot a gangsters fixing to be out of work."

"Exactly. It's not that they love the alcohol. They love the
crime. They won't stay working in distribution when they
have to pay taxes on their products."

"So they coming after us then."

"They already are. And businesses like us. Profitable ones that work outside the law. Even legal ones, if our customers frequent them."

Bumpy winced. "I don't want to get my cart before the horse, but it sounds like we might have a war coming."

She gave a long blink instead of a nod. "I mean to avoid it. Or try to. But we still need infantry."

"I'm with you," he said. "They ready for war, so we got to be ready for war. Hire the soldiers. Traffic the weapons. I follow you." She emphasized that she would be the strategist, and he'd be in charge of the organization of the infantry, with full funds for hiring soldiers and trafficking weapons. He was her enforcer. She gave him full control.

"Mon Machiavelli," she said regretfully.

He shrugged. "Best I can do is make sure the ends justify the means."

"Like President Roosevelt said, America needs a drink."

"New York, at least."

=====

Step one to circumvent the war for which they prepared: Bumpy escorted her to first the Mayor's office, and then the district attorney's. The line was the same for each of them: "I will not be coy, sir. You know that I am among the policy workers, of course, and I am not ashamed for you to know how I make my living, even if it is outside the law. I am a businesswoman, and one day I hope law enforcement will recognize me as that, rather than a criminal. But until that day, I think you should know as well that I have been paying several policemen in the 6th District about $7,100 to protect my legitimate businesses and the businesses of my neighbors from Dutch Schultz and his gangsters, and they offer no such thing in return. The police force—it is becoming a mafia of its own. One must pay a tribute not for 'protection,' but for the bullies not to break your windows themselves. And it troubles me to see the law enforcement of our fine, free, United States of America and the greatest city in the world, so corrupt, as in the Old World. And I need that protection. Now it is Schultz's life or mine. Dutch's men know I am the only one in Harlem who can take back from their boss the racket he stole from my Colored friends, and they know I'm going into action. That's why he wants me knifed."

Before either man could recover from their surprise at such directness, she continued, "I have it on good authority—not the police. Not even Dutch Schultz trusts the street police he ices. But on the authority of someone whose word is trustworthy, Schultz has threatened the life of District Attorney Dewey."

This reveal hit especially hard when she relayed it to DA Thomas E. Dewey himself, with Bumpy standing in one corner of the office and Dewey's own security detail in the other.

"I don't suppose I could convince you to reveal your source?"

"I would, Your Honor, if it did not violate her own trust in me."

"Her?"

"Ah, I've said too much," she said, even though she had planned that seeming slip of the tongue. "This information was passed to me," she said, "so that I would pass this information to you. I only know my own contact's name, and that they overheard this threat at Joe Ward's Uptown Club last night. I do not wish to implicate them, especially when they were trying to do the right thing, and save the life of an important man. Only I know that my people, we love the officials we elected and who have been appointed to their seats of power. We need you, and we do not want an assassination. We are happy to help protect you from the mob, sir."

The men reacted the same: no, no, no. Politely, they said they naturally wouldn't need any help from the likes of another criminal, and she expected as much. The purpose was not to actually provide them help, though she would have, if called upon to do so; the purpose was to tip the first domino over, sending the line toppling down toward Schultz. Already, the lieutenant and thirteen plainclothesmen were suspended over that breach of police etiquette that St. Clair originally brought to the Seabury Investigation. It didn't surprise her at all. And she was even less surprised when officials pulled Dutch Schultz in for tax evasion. *Wonder where Seabury got that idea.*

———

Madame St. Clair was far from the only one who was pressed by the infiltration of the mob into Harlem. Sufi Abdul Hamid arrived from Chicago in early 1935 to encourage the labor force to picket in front of businesses who wouldn't hire Colored people. He organized these peaceful protests as he had done in Illinois when he saw an opening: Harlem was predominately Colored, and the employment rate was down to fifty percent because of the Depression. He installed placards that directed in bold, self-assured letters in front of these businesses "DON'T BUY WHERE YOU CAN'T WORK," an idea that caught on quick. It became such a visual that no one even could pass through Harlem now without seeing and acknowledging the issue. When his name became recognizable, he sold a book titled *The Black Response to White Supremacy* without a license to do it, which ended up being the cause for his first arrest in New York City. Sufi Abdul Hamid, like

everyone else—almost everyone else—wanted jobs for Colored people, and no one was hiring with the mafia posted at
the entrance, preventing customers from spending money. So
like everyone else, Sufi wanted the mob out of Harlem. But
unlike everyone else, he did not say he wanted the mob out
of Harlem: he said that he wanted the Jews out of Harlem.
The mob that was in Harlem was both Italian and Jewish,
and rather than call the Combination out by name—a death
sentence, for sure—he called them Jews.

That cry rallied the ubiquitous anti-Semitism of the time,
but it also meant he called out only one sixth of the Combination, which let the others slide out of focus. He made the
proclamation—to "get the Jews out of Harlem"—in front of
a crowd of four hundred people in an open-air rally where
he spoke from the top of a folding ladder on the corner of
125th Street and 7th Avenue. That one choice of diction pulled
him into the limelight by his very cape and let the public scru-
tinize the bearded face under the white turban. All sorts of
rumors about his origins and affiliations flew while he awaited
sentencing, and they only soared higher when the judge threw
out his case. He earned the epithet of "Black Hitler" as a result. Adolf Hitler had been president of Germany since August of 1934, the previous year. He had already established not
only anti-Semitic rhetoric among his now-Nazi nation, but
established the Dachau camp, boycotts against Jewish-owned
businesses, and limits on Jewish children in public schools.
The Nazi party was banning non-Aryans from working new
jobs on a regular basis, including civil service and journalism, and because these changes were happening so quickly
and with such ardor—and now they were affecting many more
populations in addition to the Jews—the name "Hitler" was
very recognizable. Conflating a civil rights activist championing the employment of people of color with Hitler was at best

a cognitive leap. To be clear, Hamid did not try to repress Jewish people but empower Black people in Harlem who were being oppressed by mobsters who happened to be led by a Jewish boss. But that headline would have gotten a reader's attention, if only through its incongruous absurdity. At its most misinterpreted, conflating these two men would have allowed an already racist reader to become further entrenched in that prejudice without any more research. Either way, the identity of "Black Hitler" made it out of Harlem's local papers and into the *New York Times* itself, which reached a huge audience. Harlem would have recognized it as disenfranchising another Black leader. Madame Queen certainly would have seen it from that perspective, and whether she supported his efforts at the time or not, that moniker would have pissed her off. Sufi would have likely bristled at the insult, too, but been glad for the face time. "All press is good press," and all that. Though that mindset might have attributed to his arrest for disorderly conduct and inciting a riot in 1935.

On March 19, 1935, another small spark started a bigger conflict that no one in the neighborhood could ignore. It was all over every paper and all in the streets. At the E.H. Kress five and dime store on 125th Street, the one right across from the Apollo Theater, Jackson Smith, the manager of the store, and Charles Hurely, a floorwalker, stood on the balcony overlooking the merchandise. They chatted over the people wandering between round racks, watched the small children's delight at hiding in the center of the clothes as if their mothers didn't know exactly where they were every minute of every day. Both pairs of eyes landed at the same time on the sixteen-year-old Puerto Rican Lino Rivera as he walked behind a counter in the back of the store and swiped a ten-cent pocket knife. Lino tried acting nonchalant as he speed-walked toward the exit, even as children darted out in front of him and he gently pushed past elderly women in his path, but Jackson and Charles caught up with him before he could get to the exit. They wouldn't do anything to hurt the kid. Their shtick was the same as store security's always was, just to scare him into not stealing anymore. Still, Lino panicked. At first, he tried to cling to a pillar, but Charles pried him away, chuckling at the resistance, and restrained Lino while Jackson fished the knife from his pocket. The manager frowned and said, "Youse gonna be in trouble for this, son."

Out of fear, Lino bit Charles hard on the hand. When Charles reacted by letting go, Jackson caught Lino before he could scurry off, and Lino bit Jackson, too. Jackson was ready, though, and he kept hold of the boy even while Lino's jaws locked onto his hand like a pit bull's. Shoppers heard the struggle, and they gathered to watch while Jackson called mounted patrolman Donahue.

Officer Donahue saw the curious crowd gathering, and rather than encourage the scene, he walked Lino to the back of the store with Jackson in his wake. Donahue asked, "Do you want to press charges, Mr. Smith?"

Jackson scoffed. "Nah, I think we shook him up enough to keep him from pilfering anymore, right, kid?"

"I still got to take a statement, since I came out to a call . . . but I'll walk him down to the station the back way, since there's a crowd out front."

"Back door'll put you out on 124th Street," Jackson said, and he turned around toward the front of the store when he saw the red lights of an ambulance out front. "Well, this is just overkill, officer," he told Donahue, as Donahue escorted Lino out of E.H. Kress, downstairs through the basement to the back door to take his statement at the police station. That backdoor extradition had the opposite of the intended effect: instead of pacifying the shoppers, rumors started flying. One upset woman who saw Lino disappear down the back stairwell shouted out to the crowd on the sidewalk, "The cops took that boy to the basement to beat him up!" and when the ambulance showed up to treat Jackson and Charles's bite wounds, the crowd took that as confirmation of the story. A few minutes later, the ambulance left, empty, which made the crowd more agitated.

Not much later, an undertaker on the way back to his house parked on 125th Street for a few minutes to see his brother-in-law, and in the few minutes when the hearse was visible rather than parked in his usual garage below the funeral parlor, the crowd noticed the suspicious circumstances: just after a boy disappeared down a back staircase with a policeman after shoplifting, an ambulance came and left empty-handed. And then, there was a hearse parked on 125th. People in the crowd linked those facts together in causality: the police had killed Lino Rivera. One woman cried, "Just like down South where they lynch us."

The police on the scene tried to explain that Lino was fine, but of course they would say that, whether it was true or not. The rage of the shoppers out front escalated, and passersby glommed on to the excitement as well—knowing only what they were told from the gathering mob and their personal experiences with law enforcement. The police let women search the basement for Lino, thinking they'd report back that there was no captive or corpse there, and that would end the excitement. Instead, the women emerged even more insistent on learning what had happened to him. Then, the police shut it down with that old, tired line: it was none of their business, and it was time for them to leave. They shoved the women toward the door. Naturally, that made the tension worse. At 5:30, E.H. Kress closed their store early. That escalated the tension even more.

In response, a group of men who had heard about the incidents gathered on a nearby corner. They just waited, as if holding watch over the area, but it made the store owners nervous.

When police ordered them to move, they followed orders. They walked casually away until they stopped right in front of the Kress store. While the police recalibrated, a chairman of the gathered group introduced a white speaker. Before he could even clear his throat, someone in the crowd threw a rock through the plate glass window of the E.H. Kress storefront. The glass shattered spectacularly, despite the tape the owners had put in place to protect against such an explosion.

The police dragged the speaker off his soapbox stand, and they redispersed the crowd.

The people moved apart, and then they reassembled on the opposite corner of the street, where another speaker climbed a lamppost and tried to rally the crowd there. Police pulled him down and arrested and charged both speakers with unlawful assembly, which only antagonized the crowd further. They had done nothing illegal. Neither of them had thrown that rock through the store window, and neither of them had encouraged the looting that was happening with passersby.

The Young Liberators showed up that evening. They weren't a Communist group like people said they were—they had Communist members, but their mission was to protect the rights of Negroes. The organization's president, Joseph Taylor, heard the story that a little Negro boy was beaten to death in the basement of the five and dime, and he went to the store itself to verify. He was turned away. So he went to the police station, instead. The station turned him away, too. He took this omission as a cover-up.

The Young Liberators started their demonstration soon after, issuing handbills that said "CHILD BRUTALLY BEATEN" and "the brutal beating of the 12-year-old boy . . . for taking a piece of candy" and "11-year-old's body taken out of the store as freight." The Young Communist League did not attempt to verify details either, but started distributing leaflets of the same varieties. To try to counteract this propaganda, the anti-corruption mayor La Guardia sent two patrol wagons with loads of circulars "appealing to the law-abiding element to keep their heads and to assist public officials in getting at the source of the trouble." Patrolmen left thousands of these circulars (large pamphlets printed on white paper) in the Harlem stores for distribution by shopkeepers.

Even as they tried to appeal to calmer heads, an amorphous mob gathered and spanned blocks from 7th Avenue to Lenox Avenue. They smashed store windows with everything available, from glass bottles to stones to flower pots, and they looted as they went, sometimes taking things that could have no immediate use, and sometimes just destroying in frustration.

Five hundred police officers were summoned to put down the disturbance.

All counted, two days later, over two hundred stores were sacked. Stores owned by Black proprietors displayed signs in their windows as a precaution, saying "This shop is run by COLORED people," and obliging white store owners announced that "This store employs Negro workers." These businesses were not always spared. Property damage was estimated at two million dollars. Eight police officers were injured with bricks and rocks thrown by the mob. Four civilians (three Black people) died from injuries of that night's riot. The first confirmed death was that of nineteen-year-old James Thompson, who was looting the A&P on 138th Street and Lenox when shot in the chest by Detective Nicholas Campo. Sixteen-year-old Lloyd Hobbs was on the way home from a movie with his brother and they happened upon the riot. When police pulled up in their patrol car and took aim out of the window with their service revolvers, everyone ran. Lloyd ran the wrong way, though. Patrolman John McInerny said nothing at all before he fired one fatal shot that passed through Lloyd's body and into his hand. Both teenagers died within days of being shot by the police.

The Harlem residents might have been incorrect in the specific facts, but they were not wrong. They had incorrectly assumed that the police beat Lino Rivera to death in the basement of the five and dime store on the afternoon of March 19. But within twenty-four hours, their assessment of law enforcement's brutality was supported twice over.

The next day, police tried to placate Harlem by photographing Lino Rivera with an unarmed Black police lieutenant, Samuel Battle—but Harlem wasn't having it. They had yet to learn the truth of his safety. They saw it merely as confirmation of what they already knew: that Lino was already on probation for putting a slug in a subway turnstile, and that this photograph was from that offense, not the one at the five and dime.

Over the forty-eight hours of the Harlem Riot of 1935, one hundred civilians were arrested on grounds of inciting to riot, burglary, disorderly conduct, and carrying concealed weapons. Most of the suspects were held for further hearing at the magistrate's court, but several were immediately sentenced to serve between five days and six months. The two speakers arrested at the inciting assembly were held in custody for twenty-four hours without food, water, or the ability to notify anyone (including their lawyers) of their whereabouts.

Officials responded with varying degrees of appropriate address. DA William C. Dodge launched a grand jury investigation into Communist influence behind the rioting. Reverend

Adam Clayton Powell wrote in the *New York Post* that the unrest wasn't because of radical agitation but "empty stomachs, overcrowded tenements, filthy sanitation, rotten foodstuffs, chiseling landlords and merchants, discrimination in relief, disenfranchisement, and [. . .] [a] disinterested administration." Mayor Fiorello La Guardia said in an early morning statement at city hall that, "The unfortunate occurrence of last night and early this morning was instigated and artificially stimulated by a few irresponsible individuals," but because he knew that wasn't all there was to the story, he also appointed a "Committee on Unity," to sleuth out what the hell had happened. That committee evolved over decades into the City Commission on Human Rights, fighting against discrimination.

Lino Rivera, the child shoplifter whose disappearance incited the vigilante mob, intentionally gave the wrong home address at the police station, but he was ultimately escorted home to his widowed mother, who harangued him in Spanish as reporters looked on.

Madame Queen did not write in to the *Amsterdam News* about the riots as she might have done another time. Perhaps she saw fit to forego it because Harlem was already aware of their rights, and that they were already fighting for them the way she would have encouraged them to fight. Nonetheless, she knew what was happening in her neighborhood: there was no way around it. Maybe now, people outside Harlem would see that the police didn't just target criminals like her, but anyone at all, even innocent children.

=====

It certainly got the attention of people like Adam Clayton Powell and Mayor Fiorello La Guardia; they worked hard to identify the injustices that agitated the mob and provide solutions for them—and not just the obvious cause, that a little boy went missing after shoplifting. The problem went far deeper than this one instance. It was a big project, one that's still not rectified, and they were just getting started.

Others, like Sufi Abdul Hamid, were complete opportunists. He utilized the Harlem Riot of 1935 to his own advantage, to sweep back onto the scene as a heroic civil avenger, gold braid–trimmed cape swirling behind him . . . never mind that there's no written proof of any action by him during the Harlem Riot. They needed a hero, and he had a cape.

Still others used the riot as a distraction. Like the worst Jewish mafia member, Dutch Schultz, who beat two tax evasion charges while the city was distracted.

———

1935 was a tense year, not just for Madame Queen, but for most of the world. Europe was trying not to panic about the rise of the Nazis, while Adolf Hitler had just abolished the title of president and become Germany's full dictator, which made headlines across the world, even if his other extremist, exclusion laws were less known. The US was trying to climb out of its Depression and hoping that the situation in Europe wouldn't go where it was inevitably going. The New Deal was under way but not fully enacted. The Wagner Act forced companies to acknowledge unions. Civil unrest ran all through Harlem. Madame Queen, like America herself, was getting ready for a war she hoped wouldn't happen—or at the very least she wouldn't be called to fight. St. Clair was still operating, but like the director of an illegal outfit should, she didn't say much about it.

She had long ago accepted icing the cops as a part of business. She didn't like it, but it was a necessary expense. Her rival, the one who had threatened her life and business, and the livelihood of much of Harlem, Dutch Schultz, didn't like it, either. And that was common knowledge, written in multiple newspapers, memoirs, and interviews of the time. In fact, a later tell-all account of the night said it was this part of the bookkeeping that Schultz and his guys spread out on a stained tablecloth at the Palace Chop House in Newark on October 25, 1935. Schultz ranted about how there was too much coming off the top of their profits, drawing attention to himself as always. He had just threatened to murder the new district attorney, Thomas Dewey. Stephanie St. Clair had relayed that threat to Dewey himself, and Bumpy had tipped off the Italian families that word·was out. Even with the Combination breathing down his neck to chomp it off, Schultz couldn't keep his fool mouth shut. That night, two guys from his own outfit walked into the Chop House, and sat at the bar. One of them, Charles "the Bug" Workman tipped his hat back on his head, and ordered a drink. When Schultz went to the john, so did the Bug.

While Schultz stood at the urinal, the Bug fired his .45 twice through the stall. One bullet lodged into the peeling wall above the second urinal, and the other hit Schultz in his stocky torso, blowing through his large intestine, gall bladder, and liver before exiting and embedding into the floor next to the urinal he'd been using.

Schultz reeled out of the men's room and bled onto the white tablecloth, telling his guys to call a doctor before his head bounced on the table. He didn't know that the other guy, Emanuel "Mendy" Weiss, had already shot his lawyer, Otto Berman, in the chest, shot his lieutenant, Abe Landau, in the neck, and got several shots into his bodyguard Lulu Rosencrantz all before Schultz made it out of the stall.

Abe and Lulu were full of bullets, but they followed the Bug and Mendy into the street, emptying their clips the whole way. Mendy was ahead. He got to the getaway car first and screamed to leave the Bug behind.

By this time, Abe was unconscious. Somehow Lulu staggered back into the bar and yelled for the bartender to "Get the fuck up and make me some change!" The hidden barkeep made change for a dollar, and Lulu called his own ambulance. You know it's bad if a gangster agrees to go to a hospital, let alone calls his own ride. Lulu and Abe went in the first meat wagon. The ER was so shocked that Lulu was still alive— let alone conscious—after that much blood loss and trauma that they didn't even know where to begin treating him.

Otto and Dutch Schultz got into the second ambulance. Apparently, Schultz thought God had granted him one of the tax evasion acquittals and had converted to Catholicism just before this hit, which was why he asked a priest to give his last rites before he went into surgery. The surgeons operated on his internal hemorrhage, quick and efficient. He reacted well to the extraction and closure, but then he got blood poisoning, and his paranoia skyrocketed. Police thought among all the jibber jabber he might reveal some secret, confess some connection they hadn't put together, so they installed a stenographer in his recovery room. He said all sorts of crazy stuff while he was on the record: "John, please, oh, did you buy the hotel?" and "Oh, oh, dog biscuit, and when he is happy he doesn't get snappy—please, please do this" he said. He called his morphine "bonbons," and was out of his mind for days. The whole time, the stenographer transcribed every fever dream.

And what a job. Stephanie St. Clair was almost jealous of that guy taking deranged dictation: how wonderful would it have been to hear Dutch Schultz's paranoid delusions at his very dismal end. She was delighted to read about the dramatic irony, even secondhand. Schultz had tried to kill her, to take away the business she'd worked her whole adult life—and, in fact, five years of her childhood—to build. Worse yet, he had delegated the hit. He had not even shown up himself. Now his mouth had gotten him clipped by his own guys . . . with only a little assistance from her. It took a while for the domino she had tipped over to make it down the line toward his come-uppance, but Madame Queen was patient and levelheaded.

People sent her newspapers that updated the curious public of his demise, and memoirs recall the substance of their vic-tory conversation even if I recreated the details here. "Ain't it just the cherry on top, Queenie?" Six-n-Eight said when he saw the papers. "His own mouth turning against him!"

"Listen at the wild things this sick fuck was screaming. Some tough guy," Obadiah muttered.

"Dear," she told her thrilled employees when they brought her news, "any man with a tough guy persona and a loud mouth is just a scared, childish coward."

"Yes ma'am, you know that. And we know that. But now, everybody knows that."

"Listen at this, Queen—" and here, Bumpy shifted into a cartoonish Bronx accent. "Oh, sir, get a doll a roofing. You can play jacks and girls do that with a softball and do tricks with it . . ."

"I didn't know you had that voice in you, man!"

The whole room howled in vengeful laughter.

"Look, listen," he said, returning to his lampoon. "A boy has never wept nor dashed a thousand kin for nothing."

Madame Queen smiled her big smile, the one that showed her gold tooth, and she asked her secretary, "Can you get me the telegraph office, please?"

———

Anyone with good sense knew the hit on Schultz was an inside job. No one but his own had the tip on Schultz, and hardly anyone knew yet that he had threatened the life of the district attorney. Besides Madame St. Clair, that is, and the people she chose to leak it to, namely Dewey himself and the mafia soldiers. They had informed the bosses about Schultz's hotheaded threats, and they knew that kind of big mark would bring all kinds of attention down on their mob. Whether he actually said it or not, that couldn't stand. While Schultz lay on his deathbed, a wire telegram came for him:

Don't be yellow. As ye sow, so shall ye reap.

Madame Queen of Policy

How's that for a nickname.

STORMY WEATHER

"Bring down organized crime." That's what Fiorello La Guardia said as soon as he got elected mayor on his anti-corruption platform on January 1, 1934. He developed a task force for that purpose. Of course, the first few times the task force was assigned, the corrupt New York state governor made sure it fell into the hands of other men in bed with Tammany Hall. It was 1934 when Thomas Dewey had been considered for the position of district attorney. The salary Dewey was offered for this post was only about a tenth of what he might have made working in private practice. To Stephanie, he was a class above any other officials she'd come across. When she had told him she came to America for opportunity, she had meant it. If Stephanie had had an option to do what she did legally, she'd have been so much wealthier, safer, happier. But that option didn't exist for her, and she didn't like to dwell on improbable outcomes. Suffice it to say, in another world, Stephanie thought she'd be like Dewey. Hell, in another world, Dewey might have been like Madame Queen.

Dewey had big conditions before accepting the job. He required total independence from the existing city government. He would work on a separate budget entirely, he needed a separate office nowhere near the corruption, and he wanted to handpick every single member of his staff. He wouldn't hire anyone who had worked in Tammany Hall, he said. He wrote them all off as corrupt. All his conditions were met. He set up shop on the fourteenth floor of the Woolworth Building on lower Broadway, and he renovated the suite for security. Every door was made of solid wood, every pane of glass was frosted opaque, and every window blocked with venetian blinds. He hired detectives familiar with the mafia to serve round the clock as lobby security guards, just in case a mobster tried to sneak in—or break in and steal their records. Telephone lines were direct, no switchboard interaction. Each of his assistants would have their own office in a special corridor, complete with a private waiting room.

Special prosecutor Thomas Dewey had fixated on Dutch Schultz from the beginning. That fixation is what made the Dutchman threaten his life, and that death threat is what made the other organized criminals take Schultz out . . . expedited just a little by the ingenuity of Madame Queen. Since then, the Combination lay low, which let Stephanie reestablish her own numbers racket. Everybody on the island knew she'd blown the whistle that set the Combination against itself. The Five Families then understood what kind of power they actually held, if they could stick together, and they grasped, too, how easily they could come apart at the slightest division. It took only one person to get sloppy to put everyone at risk. After Schultz's murder, they had to catch their balance. Most people thought Salvatore "Lucky" Luciano was the one who made the call for the hit on Schultz because Luciano was in line to succeed as the capo. He was the head of the Genovese crime family, and after he'd got the tip that another don was going to kill him, Luciano killed him first. The first thing he did as head of the Combination was restructure the whole thing. No one person should be in charge. That's what led to wars of paranoia. Instead, the Five Families became the Commission, sharing the power. But no one outside the Commission knew that yet . . . though even the G-men had plenty reason to believe it. They just didn't yet have the hard evidence required to prove it in court. That was the problem with the law: even if someone broke it, you had to make a charge stick without breaking the law yourself. There was no level playing field.

═══

When they called for applications to work on the task force, three thousand lawyers threw their hats in the ring. That was one sixth of all the lawyers in New York. Dewey hired twenty of them. They were young and ambitious, fresh out of school and eager to prove themselves. The salaries were low, but this was the Depression, after all. And the prestige in working for Dewey was huge. There could have been any number of reasons why eighteen of the twenty hires were Jewish men: women were seldom lawyers, and maybe Jewish people had a harder time finding work at large Protestant firms due to still-growing anti-Semitic attitudes. Listing this task force as a line on their résumé might fast-track them later. Maybe they'd already been on the business end of the extortion and bullying from Jewish gangs led by men like Dutch Schultz, the Beer Baron, during Prohibition. Maybe Thomas Dewey was exceedingly progressive for the time. Or, most likely, all of these causes affected the outcome. Of the two remaining lawyers, one was a white man. The other was Eunice Hunton Carter, a thirty-four-year-old Black woman living among the elite in Harlem.

Later, Dewey said he just hired the best of the applicants, period. Eunice had earned some clout by serving on the special session that Mayor La Guardia appointed when he investigated the Harlem Riot of March 19, 1935, plus she had campaigned for Mayor La Guardia in Harlem during his election period, too. Even the Associated Negro Press called her hire a consolation prize after she lost the election to the New York State Assembly against a tough incumbent the year before. Despite the fact that Carter was the first Black woman to graduate from Fordham Law School, popular opinion said that she was a token: Dewey hired a woman to satisfy women. Or a Black lawyer on his staff to satisfy Harlem, because the force would be targeting racketeering, and a Black woman would naturally know all about the numbers racket. In reality, against all odds, Carter didn't even play the numbers, and Dewey didn't put her on that side of the investigation anyway.

When the team was up and running in August of 1935, Dewey made a simultaneous broadcast on three radio stations, calling for tips of all kinds: "There is today scarcely a business in New York which does not pay its tribute to the underworld," he announced. "A tribute levied by force and collected by fear . . . the object of this investigation is to rid this city of racketeers. If you come to my offices in the Woolworth Building, you will be seen by a responsible member of my staff. He will welcome your help. He will respect your confidence. He will protect you. You will not read your testimony in the newspapers, nor will the heads of your union learn you have been to the office. Your cooperation is essential. Your confidence will be respected. Your help will be kept secret, and your persons protected." In allowing witnesses to remain anonymous, testimonies flooded in via phone calls, letters, and in-person visits.

Dewey assigned segments to his task force based on which industries were run by organized crime, focusing on markets like dry goods, bakeries, and racketeering, too. Petty crime wasn't his mission, and he didn't want it to involve his staff or exhaust their energies. He also did not expect the majority of the complaint deluge to be about sex work. He didn't want to pursue prostitution because he didn't want this task force to police morality. He held the common belief that prostitution was the world's oldest profession, and as such, wherever there were men, brothels were inevitable. Under that mindset, sex work was just an organic manifestation. There were too many whorehouses and too many women for that kind of crime to be "organized." He wanted to swing big. Still, he had to cover as much ground as possible, and with so many people complaining about prostitution, he had to cover it somewhere. So, he had Eunice Hunton Carter man the sex worker tip line, a line he didn't want to establish in the first place. She was tucked away in a corner of the office, where she read letters, took notes, and waited for the black telephone handset to ring. Even when people showed up at the Woolworth Building without appointments, walked into the glorious antechamber with its wide staircase, and took the elevator up to fourteen, their journey ended on the other side of Eunice's desk.

She took every interview seriously, taking detailed, complete notes. The women who worked in prostitution came to Eunice Hunton Carter because they couldn't go straight to the police: the police would book them and miss the whole point. The women's courts were where testimonies went to die; they were disgusting and dismissive and more corrupt than any court division, and the women's words would doubtlessly fall on the deaf ears of bored clerks anyway. Plus, it was easier for women to talk to a woman. Prostitutes in too much perfume and too little clothing complained to Eunice about the points all the sex workers had taken out of their earnings before they ever saw any money. Their pay got skimmed by the madam, their pimp, and then a bonding fee. That last payoff got their bail paid and kept them out of jail. Carter noticed that all the prostitutes had the same bondsman.

Plus, not all the tipsters were criminals. Other women came to Eunice, too. Women who didn't interact in the criminal world but lived nearby it. They noticed that even when brothels were raided by police, they seemed to open back up right away, with all the madams, pimps, and whores out of jail in mere hours. They saw the beat cops collecting next-door payoffs twice a week in exchange for squashing any new, competing whorehouses that might try to open.

Giving Dewey credit for knowing he'd tap into a new community by hiring Carter would be too generous, but that's what happened: a whole vault of unpredictable criminality opened through these tips, and her tip line specifically. Carter composed her evidence in such a compelling way that he couldn't ignore her argument. After weeks of work, she now had the most thorough map of sex work in New York City that had ever been compiled, and she was convinced that whoever had taken over when Schultz died was in charge of the prostitution racket now. She presented her findings three separate times before she finally got Dewey's attention. Even though he didn't want to pursue such a low lead, it was the strongest one they had, so he had to follow it.

And then, someone leaked that lead. It showed up in the *New York Evening Journal*, which was how Madame St. Clair and the rest of the city knew that Dewey's team was about to make an arrest on the head of the mafia.

As soon as that intel appeared on newsstands, Lucky Luciano fled New York City for a gambling den in Arkansas called Hot Springs. Dewey couldn't use that as evidence in court, but it was a huge tell. And very embarrassing for the other gangsters.

Funny thing was, the leak was wrong. Dewey wasn't anywhere close to making an arrest yet, but now they knew where to focus. Eunice Hunton Carter's mission became the entire task force's mission, and they started organizing the raid.

On January 31, 1936, all the bookers and bondsmen were quietly detained. Dewey's team stationed one hundred and sixty policemen (no vice policemen, as he considered all of them fully corrupt) on street corners around the city. The police at those stations had almost no information until they received hand-delivered envelopes at 8:55 p.m. on February 2, which instructed them to raid every brothel in New York at nine o'clock. The simultaneous raid of forty-one places from grand townhouses to tiny tenement apartments jailed over one hundred sex workers. With just an average of two policemen per establishment, some sex workers and some patrons gave the slip, but they only wanted the johns' testimonies to confirm that there was prostitution happening, not to police vice. The police booked everyone they caught at their station houses, taxied to the Woolworth Building on lower Broadway, and lifted to the thirteenth floor of the Woolworth Building by freight elevator. With no bondsmen to bail them out, no one was going anywhere. Not for days. On a long enough timeline, people started to talk. Especially the people whom Luciano thought unimportant. Eunice Hunton Carter tagged each person as they arrived at the commandeered space. The more they talked to Dewey's staff, at hotels and offices commandeered for this specific purpose, the more they realized that with Luciano behind bars, they stood a much better chance at living a normal, happy life. February moved into March, and many withdrawal symptoms of madams and prostitutes subsided. Like coming out of a bad hangover, it was as if they could see clearer than ever before. By the end of the month, Dewey had enough evidence. He declared Charles "Lucky" Luciano public enemy number one on April 1, 1936, and gave orders to law enforcement every-where that he was to be arrested on sight.

Madame St. Clair watched it all unfold from a safe distance. Meanwhile, no one was watching her. As a result of being left to her own devices with both law enforcement and mobsters distracted, she could focus on expanding her business.

=====

Dewey knew that Luciano would flee—he fled before he'd even been named. What no one anticipated was how much ground Luciano would cover in forty-eight hours. He was a gangster, and like Queenie, he had eyes all over. When he got the tip from the manager's office that detectives were on their way up, he left his room at the Waldorf Towers through the freight elevators. He drove from Manhattan to Philadel-phia, where he bought a new wardrobe at Jacob Reed & Sons with an IOU and four thousand dollars of his walking-around money. He switched his car for a Cadillac with Tennessee plates and drove to Cleveland, where he ditched the Caddy and took the train down to Little Rock, Arkansas.

It was serendipitous, really, that Bronx detective Jacob Brennan just arrived in Little Rock the day before to inves-tigate a completely unrelated murder. He saw Luciano walk-ing with his buddy and stopped him on the way to the hot springs. "Why don't you come back up to New York with me on the train?" he suggested.

"You're a nice guy, but that's the craziest suggestion I ever heard in my life. I'm havin' a good time here. Why don't you just stay out of it?"

"If it comes out later that I seen you, I could lose my badge. I hafta let 'em know in New York."

And he did. Little Rock authorities extradited Luciano out of the bed of crime that was Hot Springs, and eventu-

ally they removed him fully back to New York. At the pre-
liminary hearing, he learned that if he was convicted on all
ninety counts of the indictment, he'd could face 1,950 years
in prison. His bail was set at $350,000.

———

Luciano was in court by mid-May of 1936. Three women the
task force interviewed had dated men in Luciano's inner circle, and even though Dewey would ultimately have fifty-eight
women testify against Luciano in court, these three drove the
nail in the coffin.

Mildred Harris, Nancy Presser, and Cokey Flo Brown
were not the type of witness that jurors typically trusted.
All of them were gangsters' molls. They all had at one time
been prostitutes, and they were all drug users. They were all
also white women in their midtwenties who looked decades
older. They had each been enticed into sex work at a young
age, and all of them had escalated in drug usage because their
boyfriends turned pimps and strung them out intentionally.

Cokey Flo Brown was a waif in a dirty blue dress when
she showed up to testify against Luciano, fingering her di-
sheveled marcel curls out of the way as she was sworn in and
looking—one newspaper said—like innocence destroyed.
Florence had been one of the soldiers' girls, and he'd enticed
her into prostitution when she was in her teens. That's how
she knew Luciano, although he didn't remember her.

In the audience, Luciano's lawyer turned and hit him in
the arm and said, "Who's she?"

Luciano paused to squint at her and replied, "How the
fuck should I know? I ain't never seen her before."

The lawyer shook his head as he watched tiny Florence
float up to the witness stand and brush aside her hair. "Char-
lie," he said, "I've got a feeling she's real bad news."

Florence testified that she had been a madam of the syndicate's brothels until the February bust. But she had been clean of both drugs and prostitution since then, thanks to the Women's House of Detention. Luciano might not have remembered her, but she remembered every meeting with him, and she'd been to all the meetings of the vice ring.

====

Back in early winter, when Florence had been one of his madams, she sat right next to Luciano at the table during the discussion of expansion.

His underboss, Little Davie Betillo said, "There's been a lot of pinches, and that took money out of the Combination. But when we get them all in line, it'll be okay."

Even then, Florence had tapped her fingers and sniffed and said, "Dewey's investigating. We may get in trouble. It may get tough. I think we better fold up for a while."

Lucky said, "I'd like to quit awhile. Maybe then we could reopen and we could even syndicate like they did in Chicago. We could have one Combination instead of three or four.

"I don't think it'll be so tough. The Dewey investigation won't get us. They'll just pick up a few bondsmen and let it go at that.

"We could syndicate the places on a large scale same as a chain store system. We could even put the madams on salary or commission. It would take a little time, but we could do it." He brought it up at every meeting, how to beat, torture, threaten, and hook the girls on drugs so they would work hard without complaining. "Step on them. Talking won't do no good. You got to put the screws on." Without realizing his irony, Luciano had looked right at Flo, who would later be the key witness against him, and said, "I'm gonna organize the cathouses like the goddamn A&P." Florence was much more present of mind than Luciano thought, even after having endured the same beating, torture, threats, and drug abuse that he encouraged his cronies to inflict on the next generation. He'd dismissed her so outright that he did not even recognize her when she came to the stand.

———

Nancy Presser was the next to testify, and she confirmed the conditions. She was a faded twenty-six now, but she was thirteen years old when first enticed to sex work. She'd been the high-priced call girl of every gangster from Dutch Schultz to Joe the Boss Masseria, which was how she met Lucky. She gave him her phone number, as well, but he didn't call. It wasn't until she started dating, and then prostituting for, Ralph Liguori that she got booked into one of Luciano's brothels. He substituted her opium pipe for a needle and morphine. "Low prices but big volume," he instructed her.

It was like working on an assembly line, she told the courtroom. "Every ten minutes, he beat on the door. Told me to finish up because somebody was waiting his turn."

Since February 1, the day of the raid, she had also been clean. In fact, all of the sex workers who were busted in the raid had gotten clean since. Their newfound sobriety further supported that the women were under duress when they became the "junkies" that undercut their testimony.

———

The bust and Luciano's arrest sent the Commission scrambling, but because Luciano had eliminated the system where there was a single head of all mafia families, there was instead a counsel of multiple bosses who shared the power. Dewey hadn't brought down organized crime, not completely. But he shook them up enough to distract both the Five Families and the law from St. Clair's racket, and she knew this even as she followed the news of the trial over the next few weeks. After hearing Luciano's rap sheet, and that there were fifty-eight women willing to testify against the biggest mob boss since Schultz, St. Clair no longer hoped that they ruled to lock him up under the jail only for her own sake. She would have hired the women herself if she hadn't seen how happy they were to be living straight—even her spite against the Combination couldn't let her wrestle the Dream away from someone who'd earned it at such a high price. A few years later, she'd come to learn that the two key witnesses bought a gas station on the west coast together with the payment from an interview about the case. *Imagine*, she thought. They were thriving now, now that there was no one to jab a needle into their veins and convince them they were worth nothing. What might they have done with all the time lost to being drugged out of their minds. At least they turned that bastard into a windfall.

———

Not long after Dewey's radio announcement calling for tips, December 23, 1935, to be exact, Casper Holstein's Turf Club was raided, too. Police had confiscated what they called "numbers paraphernalia" from the basement, and then they'd arrested Casper and his runner, Carmen Lopez. They spent that night, Monday night, and most of Tuesday in jail till bail of $5,000 was arranged for Casper's release. On the record, Holstein said he'd rented out the basement to someone else, but officials did not believe he'd extricated himself completely. They thought he'd had ties to Dutch Schultz, and then assumed a connection with the Combination, so just for good measure, it seemed, they'd pull him in to see what he could tell them about Luciano.

The answer was nothing. Holstein didn't work for any of

them, and he never had. To the hardnosed new committee, though, there was no honor among any thieves at all—and many of them considered gambling stealing.

The Friday following his arrest, Holstein was in good enough spirits when he told G. James Fleming at the *Amsterdam News*, "They just like to pick on me." Holstein had just helped remove Governor Paul M. Pearson from the Virgin Islands, and he thought his political enemies were out to get him, even in New York City. "On the other hand," he thought, "every time the policy racket is mentioned in New York they just like to connect me with it."

To everyone's shock, Holstein was convicted, along with Carmen Lopez. Lopez was sentenced to thirty days in prison for possessing policy slips. Holstein was sentenced to three years, and they led him to Cell 136 in the Tombs. The *Amsterdam News* made sure to print his cell number so his supporters could write to him, and when they reported on the trial, the journalist did not focus on the conviction. They did not attempt to expose his innocence—everyone knew he was guilty. "On a long enough timeline," and all that. Rather, the newspaper took a different tack: on February 15 of 1936, they wrote, "Despite his record of philanthropy and the pleas of his attorney, Casper Holstein, Sportsman, was sentenced last Friday," and praised his work in a detailed, two-part story, as if rallying a crowd instead of divulging facts. It wasn't enough that he kept up the Chrysties, who gave him his start in the world of business. He aided the building of a Baptist church in Liberia, right alongside Casper Holstein Hall, a dormitory for girls. In Gary, Indiana, he funded a home for orphaned and deserted children. When he learned that the family who had long ago employed his own lost everything in the stock market crash, and that their son whom he never met might have to drop out of Columbia University, Holstein sent him a check. Holstein donated to Fisk University and Howard University to further the education of boys like him who would have excelled in school if given the opportunity. He loaned $20,000 to Vincent Sanitarium hospital because he thought it would give opportunities to Negro doctors. He financed the construction of several houses for Negro families in Neppherhan, upstate. He even contributed to Jewish and Catholic funds. He made Christmas happen for five hundred poor Harlemites. And speaking of all he did at home, the Elks Monarch Lodge No. 45 wouldn't exist without him, and neither would that Turf Club everyone loved so much. More importantly, he invested in first mortgages through Louis Jacobson's firm, which gave homes to Harlemites. When people in Harlem died without insurance, their families still called Casper to help them. When people were threatened with eviction from their homes in Harlem, they went to Casper for help. He funded every business venture from hot dog stands to steamship lines. *This guy?* the papers seemed to ask. *This guy is the one you want to put in prison?* As if they were waiting for someone, anyone, to speak up and say to take Barrabas instead.

═══

The Five Families still ran a lot of the rackets in Harlem, but with the heat and spectacle from the Luciano trial, and since Holstein's bust, they weren't fixated on numbers anymore. What was a little penny game when your mob boss was facing charges of sixty-two counts of compulsory prostitution? And they'd probably promise to reduce the boss's sentence if he gave out just a little more information. Like Schultz's lawyer, Dixie Davis, did. Sang like a canary when the Philistine temple started to crumble.

Stephanie enjoyed reading the serialization of his confession in *Harper's* as it released. She and Bumpy had more fun reading Schultz's deathbed ramblings, of course, but this exposé was almost that vindicating. Stephanie loved having been right all along. She loved being right all along almost as much as she loved making money. With all this attention on men's organized crime, Stephanie intuited that she could thrive without rallying any unwanted attention. But losing her business wasn't an option. She had to do something more to demonstrate that she, like Holstein, was serious about going straight. Yes, she had already talked with Dewey directly, but she needed to remind New York that she, too, was a philanthropist, a Harlemite, and sincere about improving the city. The next time Stephanie set foot in a courthouse, it wasn't regarding anything criminal at all—at least, not directly. The next time she went to the courthouse, it was to make the Declaration of Intention. With these first papers, as they were so called, she pledged under oath that she intended to renounce all allegiance to any foreign governments and become a loyal American citizen. She also filed these papers under her legal, married name, Stephanie Gachette, because she had never bothered to get properly divorced.

———

Summer of the same year, 1936, Stephanie was back on top. If being out of the boys' club had worked to her detriment before, it was paying off now. All her competitors had burnt out, from Schultz and the Combination to even the ones she didn't mind, like Casper Holstein and the West Indians. Her numbers bank was so stable that she was now able to focus more attention on her other business ventures. She employed more runners and comptrollers; those she couldn't employ, she helped by spotting their rent or networking to find a job that suited their skills; and because her business was now flourishing again, she could fund Black entrepreneurs in Harlem. St. Clair met Sufi Abdul Hamid—the papers still called him "Black Hitler"—in person for the first time at one such pitch meeting. She was not impressed. She remembered him from the boycotts in '34 on 7th Avenue. She supported that cause, but she couldn't abide his clothes. He wore a rhinestone-studded turban and cape, which was certainly a brave choice, but it wasn't the flamboyance that put her off. As a former professional seamstress, she could see their craftsmanship was lacking. Besides, it was June in New York, and he had sweated through nearly every layer. That's how this generation was, she knew: lots of flash to distract from their shortcomings. Never mind that she'd been lying about her age for so long that she never really considered he was just six years younger than she was. Sufi met with St. Clair to ask for money. He and his friend McKenzie came to her with a business proposition for a moving venture. She listened to their theatrical pitch in her office at the bank before politely declining. They thanked her for her time, and she believed that to be the end of their interactions.

But the next day, Hamid came to 409 Edgecombe, where she lived, intent on speaking with her about business. Jim, her doorman, called up, saying, "A man named Snoofi is here to see you, madame." She was busy, and he had not made an appointment, so she told Jim as much. Before she hung up the receiver, she probably heard Sufi in the background demand, "Busy with what?" and even though Jim covered the mouthpiece she overheard his shut-down: "It don't matter what, Snoofi, busy is busy, and she said no."

Hamid next wrote to her for an appointment, and she refused—she was used to people wanting a second shake at her startup capital. She'd already determined that the plan for Hamid's moving business was too loose for her, especially when he already had a palm oil company on which he needed to focus, and only three days had passed since the first meeting, which was not nearly enough time for the full revision the business plan needed.

Hamid wrote to St. Clair a second time. It was his fourth time trying to meet with her. She could appreciate tenacity in a business person as much as anyone, but she did not appreciate that he ignored her answer. She said so later, in an interview about him. All the points of what follows are from her interviews, but this part, the part where Sufi gets Stephanie's attention, was the hardest part of this whole book to write. Harder even than the portions of her life that were barely documented. It was not in keeping with her character to give him anything but a courtesy nod, so this is the only way I can believe it went down: with Madame Queen being courteous, and Sufi being charming through his self-deprecation. It only makes sense if he knew he wasn't good enough to talk to her, and if he let her know that he knew he wasn't good enough to talk to her. The dialogue below is how, after long rumination, I think their meet-cute might have happened.

Stephanie threw the letter away without reading it. It wasn't until she left the bank that evening that she saw him sitting on the bench across the street from her, watching a shirtless man walking a wolf on a leash. He muttered at the wolf, "Don't you know you wild? Take a bite out a that man titty." Madame Queen laughed at his absurdity aloud, the man in the cape and turban talking to feral animals in the city. He jumped to his feet. "Madame Queen!" he shouted, and broke into a sprint across the street at her, nearly getting hit by a city bus in the process. He whirled around, spinning his cape in front of his face like Dracula and continued his beeline. He was breathless when he reached her. "I been—" He huffed. "I been thinking about what I would say to you for three days. Ever since I first started stalking you."

She was so surprised by his candor that she laughed again. "Get on with it, then."

"You didn't read my last letter, did you?"

She sighed.

"It was blank anyway."

"It was blank?" she asked.

"Yeah, I just . . . I thought it might get your attention."

"That's absurd."

"I know," he said defeatedly. "Getting your attention was all I could think about. I can only do one thing at the time, see. So, I didn't think about the next part yet. Just give me a second—" He snapped his fingers, interrupting himself. "Look, I know you don't want to do my gravel business idea—"

"You brought me a business plan about moving trucks."

"That one, either. I know, they're half-baked ideas, but I'm an ideas man, see. I got a million a minute and I know there's one good one in there if I could just sift it out of the bad ones."

"I don't have time to listen to all your ideas." She shook her head and started to move around him, but he stepped in her path again.

"Of course you don't! You a busy woman, and I know that. I can't expect you to listen to all my ideas—hell, I don't even want to hear half of 'em. The one good one I had was not buying at a business where you can't work—but I don't have the long game, see. I don't have the long-term vision. I change my mind too much. I can get their attention." He boomed his voice and spread out his arms so that passersby glanced over in expectation. "But I don't know what to do with it once I got it."

"What do you want from me?" she said, exasperated.

"I want to hear how *you* did it, Madame Queen. You a bad motherfucker—excuse me. You the best in the game. Let me take you to coffee and listen to you."

"Coffee?"

He fast-talked her. "I can't afford much else. And to be honest we'a be lucky if ain't just chicory and dirt and they pour it into your hands because I don't have but one cup and it cracked this morning—wait! I'm serious. I just talk this much when I'm nervous. This is your one shot. Just let me hear you out."

"Let *you* hear *me* out?"

He smiled. "You like how I spun it around, huh?"

She moved to walk on again.

"Walk with me," he said, as if she would be pitching him the ideas.

"You are ridiculous," she said.

"Yeah. Yeah," he admitted. "But I'm here to learn, Madame Queen."

By now they were in the lobby of 409 and he trailed her until they passed by Jim's counter, which was when Jim's eyes caught Sufi. "Madame St. Clair—" he warned, pointing at Sufi.

"Aw, shit!" Sufi said dramatically. "I thought I'd Trojan horse my way in, try and hide behind Madame Queen so you wouldn't see me."

Stephanie chuckled again, nodding hello to Jim.

"You all right, Madame? You need me to get him off you?" Jim asked, completely confused.

Stephanie slowed down as she approached the elevator. As a rule, she did not bring men to her apartment, especially without appointment or chaperone, but her butler was there, so at least there would be a man nearby. She hesitated and said, "I'll be back down in twenty minutes. If he is not out by then—"

"If I ain't out of her hair by then, you come kick the door in, Jim-bo."

"Bombastic," she muttered as he carried on in the elevator about how there was no dust anywhere, the floors looked like they'd been waxed and he'd just need some slick-soled church shoes to pick up a hockey game in the hallway.

As soon as he stepped into the apartment, he marveled again. (Madame Queen related all these plot points to her friend, the journalist Marvel Cooke much later, but the dialogue I have invented. I feel confident that the mood is correct even if the actual lines are lost to time, simply because there is no other way he could have convinced her to let down her guard other than his complete fascination with Stephanie and total awareness that she was out of his league.) "Purple in the entryway, look at this wallpaper . . . your whole kitchen is white. Red in the parlor and blue in the bathroom . . . how'd you decide which room for which color?"

She answered him shortly, sure he was just making small talk, "I read the energy of each room."

He glanced at her, and then back to the carpets, touching the furniture gingerly with his fingertips, "How did you read the energy?"

Stephanie hung her coat on the rack and called quietly for her butler, Bridget, to bring in a pitcher of tea and any leftovers she had on hand before she answered him, again, "I clear my inner eye, and then I look for it. Sometimes I consult my cards."

He had more questions, but not in the childlike way of having a list prepared, or asking "why" ad nauseam. Sufi listened to every answer carefully, drawing her out so that she stopped replying with clipped, minimal answers by habit, but rather fully explained, even venturing into a story once when he commented on the art deco design gilded on the rims of the dessert plates, how it matched the style of her furniture:

"I saw these plates at a tea house downtown, when I was living at the White Rose Home. The place wasn't whites only, but they sat my church group and me at the very back of the house, near the kitchen door, even though the dining room was almost empty. It must have been five years later, I heard they were going out of business—because of the Depression. I had my driver take me all the way down from Sugar Hill and bought every dish they had for a penny on the dollar. Dropped a saucer on the way out and watched the shards scatter into the corners. Just out of spite. I regret that, now. It's not good to dance on a grave."

"Bet it felt good at the time, though," he said. He was cooling off in the breeze from the fan by the open window, and he finished all but one of the cookies that Bridget put on the matching platter. "The dead know not anything."

"Neither have they any more a reward," she said, finishing the quote.

"When did you live at the White Rose Home?" he asked. His ankle was crossed over his opposite knee, and if his sock hadn't been threadbare, he would have looked the part of a gentleman. Not exactly mannered, but the type who didn't need to have perfect manners because of their own self-assuredness.

"Only a short while. Years ago. When I first arrived in America. They helped me learn trade skills, money management, English," she answered.

He drew her out again. "Seems like they were good teachers. How'd you learn such good English?"

"I was only thirteen. I don't know that I could learn another language so easily now."

"I knew it. You're younger than everybody thinks." And then he spotted the clock on the mantle. "Look at the time," he said. "I've kept you longer than I promised. I'll be on my way now, and thank you for your hospitality." He got to his feet.

Stephanie rose, as well. The time had passed quickly, though it had only been about twenty-five minutes. The impulse she had next surprised her: don't go just yet. She of course did not say this—she knew better than to invite a man to stay when he had one foot out the door.

"Can I take this tray to the kitchen?" he asked.

She brushed off his suggestion. "I'll pick at it for a while."

Stephanie followed a few paces behind as he walked down the hall. At the door, he turned to her and said, "I sure did enjoy talking to you, Madame Queen. Maybe I could come back and visit another time."

She blinked and gave him her hand, but she remained non-committal.

Sufi was smooth. He wouldn't have lingered or dragged out his departure the way his fellow Midwesterners usually did. He thanked her again and whirled out the door. When she stood alone in the foyer, her ribs felt light. He had not flattered her or tried to charm her, didn't hold her at a distance like most men who revered her and respected her out of their own unacknowledged fear. Sufi seemed to know she was ahead of him. He was in awe, but not in a fearful way. He was curious.

═══

When she found him waiting outside her building again the following evening, she allowed him half an hour. The day after that, a full hour. Each time he visited, he asked her more about her life, and the period of his visits lengthened every time. In turn, he told her about his travels to Greece and India during his military service, silly missteps in business and personal affairs, his dream of leading a church that combined some Christianity with some Islam and some Buddhist practices. Stephanie thought he was teasing her, so she said, "If you waver in your beliefs, your followers won't take you seriously. Make sure you have all your tenets clear before you start your little cult." St. Clair found herself looking forward to his visits. They carried on for weeks, every day extending longer. She settled on her settee and he leaned back cross-legged in the wingback chair. He never stayed longer than she invited him. The afternoons stretched into the evenings, until she called in supper for them both.

———

He still waited outside on that same park bench because Jim did not trust him, and Sufi knew it. Monday, July 6, he did not wear his cape. It had become so much a part of his persona that Stephanie noticed immediately, and she asked about it before he stood to full height, turned around, and showed that his shirt itself had been ripped almost off his body. The ribbed, sweat-stained undershirt showed through the slashes, as did stretches of his smooth skin. He said, "When I tried to wash the cape, it just about fell apart, see."

Madame St. Clair clocked that he washed his own clothes, and she noticed that he washed them in preparation to visit her. She did not wonder why he had not worn a different shirt—there was simply no way that this was his only one. "So, you wanted to show me that you had been in an Independence Day fight?"

His sheepish grin spread across his full face. "It was getting to be too hot for the cape."

"I should think so."

"It wasn't a real fight, anyway. Just drank too much whiskey on too hot a day."

"Who did? You did?"

"Everybody did, I won't lie."

"You won't, eh? What set off this brawl?"

Sufi saw that she was not impressed by the fight. Of course she wouldn't be, he should have known. This was a woman who got death threats. A bar fight would be stupid to her. "Oh, it wasn't . . . nothing important."

"No, I insist. What started it?" She stood in the middle of the sidewalk, and she had not invited him up to her apartment.

She watched the fight drain from his face. "This dummy . . . a girl I know sells dream books. She helped this man interpret his dreams to bet on his numbers, and when he didn't win on Saturday, see, he came at her. This happened when I was getting her into a taxi." Sufi shrugged.

"A girl you know," she said. "Predicts the numbers down to a digit."

"She's just some girl—"

"I know," she said, surprised at her own jealousy. "Why are you coming to see me? What do you want from me? What do you have up your sleeve?"

Sufi looked hurt. He said, "Nothing."

Stephanie looked him over for a beat before she said, "I can't entertain today. I have had an appointment come up."

"Okay," he said in a rush. "I'll come back tomorrow, and maybe you'll have some time then."

She was already walking away, into her apartment, when she said, "Maybe."

"Good afternoon," Jim said at the desk, and when he saw no one trailing behind her, he added with relief, "you're looking mighty stylish today, Madame Queen."

But Sufi was back on Tuesday. For the first time, he brought a bundle of flowers and he waited in the lobby when Jim reminded him that he was under specific instructions not to let anyone upstairs, especially not any men, even if they did have on a full, clean shirt. Sufi looked completely hangdog when Madame Queen entered the lobby, flustered in spite of herself at not seeing him waiting on the bench across the street. Jim did not hide that he was watching. When Stephanie spotted Sufi, his clean shirt, and the roses, she stopped midstride and clenched her eyes closed. She would not speak to him first, but she didn't have to: "Good evening, Madame Queen," he said.

She opened her eyes but stayed silent.

"I wanted to apologize for yesterday," he said, and then stopped.

"Let's hear it, then."

"Ma'am?"

"Let's hear your apology, then."

"That was . . . I did."

She scoffed and made to walk around him. Sufi side-stepped into her path, and Jim stood from his post.

"I'm sorry," Sufi stuttered. "I shouldn't have showed up here with my clothes that way."

She and Jim both stood, silent.

"And I shouldn't have said or done all that nonsense over Independence Day." He was catching his stride now. "You're a lady, and you're too dignified for that silly stuff. And I want to make it up to you by spending the afternoon with you."

"How?"

Obviously, he had not thought this far in advance, but thinking ahead was his biggest shortcoming by his own acknowledgement. When Stephanie had thought he was there for business purposes, she could let him into her parlor to conduct business meetings. Now here he was with flowers. She was a lady, and ladies did not court in their own homes.

"Let's go to the movies," he said in a rush. "We can catch *The Great Ziegfeld* at the Star on Lexington." He wouldn't let her decline. "And we can get dinner afterward, at, uh—"

"One thing at the time," Stephanie said.

He smiled and held out the flowers to her.

She accepted the flowers and said, soft, "I'll be back down in a minute."

Stephanie had her chauffeur take them downtown, rather than wait on delayed trains and buses that never came, and they arrived at the Star Theatre just before 5:00, when the prices changed. Sufi bought their tickets and escorted her into the air-conditioned viewing room. By the time the cast was dancing on the dining room tables, Stephanie had nestled into the warm crook of his arm, so unaccustomed to the drafts as she was.

She had dismissed her driver after their arrival, not knowing how long the film would run, so they meandered through public transit on the way back north to 409. They stopped to eat at Bumpy's favorite diner as the sun set, both of them thrilled more by the intricacy of the costumes than the dancing or singing.

"You think I should grow a mustache like Flo?"

"I thought you'd already done that once. I've never seen pumps like that in Harlem. If I saw them in a store, I would buy a pair in every color."

"Wouldn't matter. They'd be gray as they were on screen by the time you got from the bus stop to the apartment."

"The *bus stop*?" she joked back. "My feathered crown will not fit on the bus."

"Where you think they get those ostrich feathers?" Sufi asked. "They got a farm upstate somewhere? Or they run wild in California?"

The second shift operator was on duty when they came

into the lobby. Stephanie walked to the elevator with Sufi as she had been doing for weeks, without a second thought. Her maid and butler had gone, so she poured gin for them herself in the kitchen and brought it into the parlor where they clipped the ends of their cigars into a freshly emptied ashtray. They talked about the movie until he saw her yawn behind her hand at eleven o'clock. Sufi took his glass to the kitchen sink, and she smiled at him when he left, seeming to hesitate before slipping out of the door. Madame St. Clair locked the door behind him and turned out the lights all around the apartment. In the bathroom, she combed and wrapped her hair in a silk scarf. She washed her face with the newest line of Madame CJ Walker—even though A'Lelia had died, she was still a loyalist to the Walker brand, being neighbors— and rubbed in the moisturizer. She brushed her teeth and changed into her green satin nightgown, lay down to sleep and pulled the woven emerald coverlet over her when her doorbell rang.

A jolt of fear shot through her chest and her eyes flashed open in the dark. The last time someone rang her bell at this hour, it was her neighbor, Catherine, held at gunpoint so Stephanie would open the door and Dutch Schultz's henchman could come in and murder her. Her heart raced as if the bell had been a gunshot. She stayed hunched on her side, hoping whoever it was would realize they had the wrong door and move on to wherever they were supposed to be, or they'd lose hope that she would wake up and leave a note with the doorman out of courtesy, and tomorrow she could call back and give them a piece of her mind. *Why wait till then?* She thought as her heart hammered on and the doorbell rang again several times in succession, frantic.

Stephanie flipped on the light and pulled on her matching robe. She grabbed the .38 from her nightstand drawer and stomped down the hallway to the front door. She didn't bother looking through the peephole as they'd surely have their thumb over the lens like any coward. "Who's there?" she demanded.

There was a pause and just as she was about to yell again, she heard a soft "It's me" in the hallway. She then slid aside the peephole cover and saw Sufi in its fish eye, wringing his hands like a child in trouble.

Stephanie drew the chain lock and opened the door. With her jaw fixed, she said, "What you want? I'm tired."

Sufi held his hands up to his face and rubbed his eyes before he said, "Oh, madame. I fell so much in love with you that I can't go home. I went as far as 145th Street and couldn't go further. And so I had to come back, see. Oh, madame, won't you marry me?"

Stephanie blinked a few times before a smile broke through her confusion.

Sufi grinned and grabbed her up and kissed her against the wall. She kicked the door shut behind him and as he made to carry her into the apartment, she said, "Lock it!" and he did, with difficulty, still carrying her and both of them laughing at how clumsy it made them. He said as he stumbled back through the parlor, "I will marry you and love you and stay with you until death," over and over. He carried her toward the office, and when she tried to correct him saying, "The bedroom is that way," he said, "No—it's not the right energy. This is not green. It's yellow. It's gold." She left out the details when she recounted the story, though, saying only that they spent the night in the yellow room.

———

When the sun rose behind the drawn curtains, he was still murmuring, "I will marry you and love you and stay with you until death" while they rested on the scallop-backed sofa and its mustard velvet. In her interview with Marvel Cooke, she said he asked again, "Won't you marry me?" and she put him off, since it was a serious decision. How she put him off she didn't say. I imagine it was like this: Stephanie sat upright, her minty robe pooling in her lap. The roses he'd brought her the day before were on the side table. She pulled one stem toward her, circled the bud between her forefinger and thumb, and pushed down with a cracking sound. His hair curled on the arm of the couch, one of his own arms thrown up to prop up his beautiful head. His chest alone was too wide for this sofa. How had they managed to stay on it without tumbling off? She blew open the bloom and twirled it toward him.

"Let me think on it," she said.

"What is there to think about? You love me, don't you?"

"This can't be rushed, my dear."

He smiled when she called him that and reached for her cigarette. "When will you know?"

Stephanie stretched over and lay on top of him, placing the rose's stem between his lips. "Shut up," she murmured. He laughed and bit down on the stem in a jack-o'-lantern grin. "Give me a few days to think." She turned her head to the side and saw the detritus scattered on and around her desk, papers feathered where they may and an ink bottle overturned on the blotter with handprints all across it. *Looks worse in here than when the police broke in*, she thought. Jane and Bridget would arrive soon. She sat back up and pulled her robe around her.

"Aw now, don't do that," Sufi said, removing the rose from his mouth and pricking his finger on a thorn in the process.

She motioned for him to follow her. "Bring your clothes," she said. They had sex again in the shower—in the blue bathroom—before she told him to get dressed. She said on

the record that she took him shopping after the proposal.
Knowing her expertise as a seamstress, she must have taken
him to the fashion clothiers of bespoke menswear, or at least
the Wanamaker's mens' department in the Lincoln-Liberty
Building, and she told Marvel that she bought him everything
he desired. I don't think she would have bought anything,
though, before he modeled it for her. If I had to guess, based
on the fashion of the time and photos of them together, she
bought the fishtail back pinstriped maroon trousers only after
he squatted in them, posed, bent at the waist, walked down the
store and back to make sure they didn't ride between the
thighs. The soft collar brass pins only after seeing them by his
throat. How did they look when he smiled? And what about
when he winked? The double-breasted wool overcoat with
the wide lapel, only after he raised his arms and checked his
watch. Did he prefer it in the charcoal or the camel? At the
haberdashers, the fedora had to not only fit when he shook
his head as if in a strong wind or disagreement, but it had to
look good between his hands, as well, since he would seldom
wear it in her presence, anyway. "And wouldn't it look nice
with a gold band on this finger here?" he might have chided.
"Let's get a feather for it. Stick it in my cap there. What you
think, girl? Is it macaroni?" She was confused. He forgot that
she wouldn't have learned all the same Revolutionary War
history and rhymes about Yankee-Doodle as he had in Chicago because she grew up in the Indies, so he sang it for her,
making up the lyrics he forgot as he galloped about the store
modeling spats to protect his new patent leather shoes, weav-
ing through the mannequins and racks to make his way back
to her, breathless, at the end of the measure. She still didn't
get the joke.

"What history did you learn, instead of Yankee-Doodle?"
he wheezed.

St. Clair shrugged while she examined the pants. "I only went to school till I was thirteen, but before that? Ah, my favorite was the French Revolution. The slaves on Guadeloupe were freed during the Reign of Terror. And then when Napoleon became emperor, he re-enslaved everyone. Or he tried to. Solitude was my favorite. She was pregnant when she helped Louis Delgrès lead the slave rebellion."

"Oh, shit. Did they win?"

"No. He blew himself up in the fortress at Pointe à Pitre while he played the violin. He said, 'Long live death.'"

"What about her?"

"After she had the baby, they executed her by guillotine."

"That was your favorite story?"

"The one I remember best. Her last words were 'live free or die.'"

"You learned that in school? About a slave rebellion?"

"No, of course not," she said. "The pants need a cuff. They don't break properly. No more bad clothes," she told him. "Only suiting fit for a Ziegfeld from now on, understand? Macaroni, sure, if you like, but no more rayon."

—————

Three days passed and he barely left her side all that time, standing outside her office door like a puppy while she took meetings, thinking she might forget him if he let her go long enough. She told Marvel Cooke that at the end of the third day, she accepted his proposal with the condition they would have a contract, "like we do on the Continent," she might have said to soften the blow to his ego. They would have a one-year trial period, and afterward, they would be man and wife for ninety-nine years. Sufi didn't know anything about love contracts, but he wasn't bent on tradition, and he happily signed. He moved in with Stephanie at 409 right away. He loved being able to say he lived there. People who mattered lived at 409: activists, businesspeople, socialites, professors. Truth told, Sufi arrived at her apartment before his new tailored clothing. He hadn't had all that many clothes to begin with, and compared to these new fabrics, he could see now that they were cheap. Each time a new garment arrived, he put it on right away, and when the effect wore off on Stephanie, he called his friends to come over so he could show off.

He and his friends drank till all hours. She came out of their bedroom at two or three in the morning, and she would only have to look at him before he cleared his friends out the door. She told him that she needed time alone—or with only him, sometimes—to clear her inner eye. "What you need to see out of that thing for?" he might have asked, a little drunk. "All the rooms decorated already."

"It's not for that, clearly," she said. "I have to conduct business tomorrow. It's the business that supplies you with these new clothes to preen in like a new rooster. I can't focus if I have too many energies around all the time." She clenched her eyes again, frustrated. "I'm tired. I should not have to explain that I need rest in my own home."

"All right, all right," he said. After that, he didn't keep parties going after ten o'clock anymore. Rather, when his friends left, he left with them. Once, just before they left for a second location, Stephanie sought him to say goodbye, and she overheard him say from the parlor, "She's like a Jew. Stingy, see. Give me a little time to wear her down. We'll get this chicken business off the ground yet!"

Stephanie did not engage with it that evening, she said in her interview—she was, as she said, tired. Instead, she asked him about it after lunch the following day, sideways, the necessary way when dealing with ego. I think she would have approached him sensibly, after the fact maybe as they ate at the apartment. Again, she told the plot points, not the details, so I've approximated the dialogue and setting for the conversation: Jane had made chicken and dumplings, the roast broccoli that was becoming fashionable, with a baked apple for dessert, and while this was plenty for Stephanie, Sufi still enjoyed the new fads, so he had a plate of Lay's potato chips next to him, too. The trend reminded Stephanie of the fried fish fins of her childhood. They were good, but they weren't anything new, so she remained apathetic while he crunched audibly, leaning back in his chair to stretch. He must have just recently woken.

"What has been on your mind?" Stephanie asked. "What are my husband's dazzling new ideas."

He leaned forward and swigged the Kool-Aid out of the delicate, footed Mayfair tumbler. Its pink tint made it look even more red. "McKenzie and me, we thinking of starting a chicken business."

"What kind?" she asked with the undertone that she was going to say yes, whatever he said.

He frowned and shrugged. "Just chicken."

"A chicken farm?" she led.

"Yeah, a farm."

"Can I help?"

"What you mean?"

"I mean I want to support my husband's dreams." She tried to keep the edge out of her voice.

"Do you, now?"

He had his forearms on the table, threatening to upturn the whole thing with his bulk.

Seeing her failure, that his pride still fueled this growing resentment toward her, she sucked her teeth, pushed her chair back, and stood. "If you don't want special treatment, so be it. I have no problem not wasting money on half-hearted schemes."

When she saw the business plan, it was full of holes. She offered a small startup amount anyway, as a gesture of good faith, though even that was waning.

The creep started gradually, like moving off to another location when Stephanie needed to wind down for the night. Showing up late to Bumpy's birthday celebration with a crew in tow as if they'd taken an intermission from their own, more important party. Sufi always kissed her goodbye, said he wouldn't wake her up when he came back home, but it felt like a hot-bedding situation, like when she woke up, he'd only just lain down. Then, on Thanksgiving of the same year, when they had been married for six months, Sufi went to the watering hole after their afternoon feast, and he didn't come home till the next morning. St. Clair told in her interview that she wassick with worry; and even though he apologized and kissed her and smelled only of alcohol, the holiday just continued the pattern. The pattern's nuance is what I've intuited.

Sufi slipped out without telling her where he went, or with whom. She told herself that she trusted him, that he wouldn't dare set up with another woman. Any man with a brain knew that would be suicide. She hadn't backed down from actual mobsters. Why would some average man get a free pass?

The door closing behind him on the third night in a row woke her from a dead sleep. The green bedsheets tangled around her, and she realized that her sleeplessness was anxiety. Her intuition had served her well her whole life, and the likelihood that it had stopped working now was less probable than that Sufi's secrecy veiled something awful. She dressed herself, wrapped herself in a plain gray coat, pulled her hat down low, and exited through the servants' staircase to follow him at a distance.

Where he led her was awful, but it was not another woman's

place. In all the finery she had bedecked him with—all of it at once—he traipsed into Harris's on the corner of 132nd Street and 7th Avenue, a gambling den run by the Combination. She did not follow him inside. She'd rather die than step foot on their territory—and stepping foot on their territory might have well resulted in that, since despite the truce after Luciano's arrest, Bumpy had outfitted her whole crew for war. Rather, she called her captain when she got home, left a message with his girlfriend, Mayme, one that a wife can only confess to another woman whose lover was nefarious: tell Bumpy to find out what the hell he's doing there.

By morning—before Sufi's return—Stephanie had her answer. He wasn't with anyone else that she knew. He was just a bad poker player. As embarrassing as it was to be married to a man who couldn't count cards, her worry released, though not as fully as it should have. She lounged in her pink robe in the pink parlor with a cup of coffee so black it looked like motor oil on the surface. But when the sun started to peek in through the window, she leveled up. She dragged her favorite wingback chair directly into the footpath from the hallway to the rest of the apartment. There was no way around her. If she'd been knitting, she would look like a worried mother upset that her teenager broke curfew—and she very well felt like his disciplinarian even as she sat there and resentment brewed at the bottom of her upset stomach.

He came in clumsy, knocking over the hat rack as he tried to hang his coat. He jumped and swore when he saw her silhouetted at the end of the hall. "Shit, Stephanie, you scared the hell out of me, girl."

She wasted no time, knowing that he'd redirect the conversation if she allowed him the chance. "I know you've been at Harris's."

"So?"

"You know that place is run by the Combination. Don't play stupid with me."

Sufi's eyes glinted despite his drunkenness.

"Have you forgotten they are my competitors? That their man tried to have me killed more than once?"

He said nothing, just swayed on his feet.

"You should be ashamed at this disloyalty," she said, trying to drive her point home. "I don't mind spending money on you, and you don't mind living off the profits of my business. But you have to be loyal to it for that to continue. If you want to lose at cards, do it in a Colored-owned place. Live by your own principles."

"You got a nerve telling me what to do."

"Oui, I have a lot of nerve. You think a coward could do what I've done? I'll clear your debts, but I don't like paying white men, so you're not to gamble at Harris's anymore."

Sufi slapped her so hard that it broke the charm off her earring. She relayed this fact to Marvel, for her to print in the interview.

Stephanie stood up and turned to stone. "Don't bite the hand that feeds you. It's odd that the thing you liked best about me now emasculates you so. Get out."

He slammed the door behind him and she shook with rage as she reeled down the hallway, sending paintings awry when her shoulder ran the length of the wall. There was no point in locking the door when he had a key, she thought. The strike itself was a thing apart, but what cut deeper was the knowledge that her intuition had failed her. She'd been treated worse, no doubt, but never by someone she trusted. Her hands trembled while she cranked open the fire escape's window and lit her cigarette in the brisk air. She had to restart dialing the front desk twice on the rotary phone, she was so shaken. When Jim answered, "Good morning," he heard the edge in Stephanie's voice immediately. She told Marvel about the following ask. "Hello, Jim. I have an urgent request. I need the apartment locks changed as soon as possible, and of course, I'll pay for the rush."

"You all right, Madame St. Clair?" Jim asked. He watched Sufi stumble through the lobby without his trademark cape. He pushed out through the antechamber and into the December morning without any coat at all, nothing on his head or hands. He must be headed somewhere quick, somewhere warm in an instant. "I'm glad to help with a locksmith, ma'am. Anything else you need?"

She paused for a moment. "Jim, I know you never said, but you were right. You were right about . . . about my . . ." She sighed.

"You won't hear me I-told-you-so-ing, ma'am. I don't like to be right about this, but I'm glad we're taking care of it. I'll call Mr. Johnson for security till we get the locksmith up."

"Thank you." She hung up the receiver. Jim knew that behind Bumpy's soldiers was the safest foxhole in the world.

Stephanie poured herself another cup of coffee and drew on her cigarette. She couldn't quite grasp why her wealth and success had suddenly turned into a point of contention. Men didn't like when she bested them at their own game, and that was no secret. But her success was never a surprise to anyone with a working knowledge of Harlem—and after all, they'd met because Hamid wanted an investor for his ridiculous business idea. She had even funded one of them just to keep him happy, with play money. It wasn't even the same idea he'd brought to her a few months ago, that was how featherbrained he was, zipping from one idea to another. And now that she required him not to patronize certain businesses because of it, he resented her. The irrationality of this paradox led St. Clair to believe it was erroneous; that it must have been something else to cause his violence. But it didn't matter. It was out of her control. She was a great success through her own hard work and luck, and that was not going to change because it made her man feel threatened. It was just time to get rid of the man, regretful as she might be about it. Violence was something she wouldn't tolerate from anyone, not her enemies, and certainly not her beloved. At least she'd had the foresight to create her own contract rather than sign a true marriage license. This thing would never hold up in a court. Imagine, God, if all her wealth was tied up in the law over a careless personal mistake! She poured a jigger of whiskey into her coffee to steel her nerves, while the cold air whipped in and made her eyes water.

Bridget arrived within the hour, already briefed by Jim in the lobby. They saw to it that the locksmith finished that morning, replaced the key on her ring, and only mentioned it in passing at lunch, that the job was complete. Stephanie had already called and had a ham delivered to the homes of both men, and I think after this fight, she called their wives to explain their service and declare how much she appreciated them. It's a courtesy she would not have realized to extend until she had been in a loving marriage herself, not just one of convenience. It made a big difference to know that other women were fighting your corner, or at least appreciated you. How many wives and girlfriends had she unknowingly irritated just from her lack of manners? Not anymore. These women would know where she stood from now on.

=====

She walked through the park that afternoon, a long walk in the brisk air in ugly flat shoes, just to get her bearings again. She thought of inviting Shirley DuBois or Marvel Cooke or Bumpy's then-girlfriend Mayme for company but decided against it—coming on too strong all at once would be more alarming than absolute silence, and carrying a conversation, even with these brilliant women, sounded exhausting, so she went alone. People greeted her with a nod, but kept their distance at her countenance. It was good to clear her inner eye. She'd been trying to for weeks.

When she came back that evening, she told her interviewers that Sufi was back. He sat weeping in her bedroom with a tattered bouquet of flowers and a box of chocolates for her. She thought of the gun in her nightstand, and Bridget still tidying up in the apartment kitchen behind her.

"What the hell are you doing here?" she said, low.

"Don't worry, they wouldn't let me up. I had to break in after Jim sicced the hounds on me, and Bridget wouldn't even take my calls."

"I told you—"

"I climbed up the fire escape," he said, his head in his hands. "I thought the lady downstairs was gone shoot me I looked so much like a crook."

"I don't want you here," she said.

"I don't blame you," he said, weeping. "I wouldn't want me here, either. I just wanted to apologize—I'm so sorry. I'm not gone drink no more. It brings out the bad in me, and people always told me so, but I didn't see it till last night. I'd kill anybody else who laid a hand on you and here I've gone and done it myself. I understand you don't want me, and I don't blame you. You deserve everything in the world, and you worked hard to get what you already got. I just needed to tell you face-to-face."

So he had learned to apologize. And she forgave him.

BLACK COFFEE

It was a mistake to take Sufi back, but Stephanie said that she did it. She knew it was a mistake, I imagine, even as she took him into her arms that night, even as she stood naked at the foot of the bed and picked the chocolates with nuts out of the box for herself while she watched him sleep, flung like a starfish across the mattress, sheets twisted around his limbs in such fascinating knots that she knew she would never make a space for herself without waking him. She felt the sinking feeling, she watched him snore, and she ate the chocolates. *He will be gone as soon as he wakes*, she thought. *He will wave to Jim on the way out the door, and Jim will stare baffled until he drops his chin to his chest in disappointment. And when it ends predictably in a ball of flames, the doorman won't even condescend to say I told you so.*

Stephanie didn't give Sufi a key. And she never said that she changed the locks again. It seems like she just stopped locking the door all together. If she couldn't count on herself for her own preservation, why waste anyone else's time on security? Sufi came and went as he liked. He brought friends over again, first one or two at the time, then an elevator full, and soon enough to fill the whole place. He wormed his way into

409 the way that water forms a pothole, freezing and melting and freezing and melting until even the concrete breaks down and gives way. So gradually overstepping the boundary that it went unnoticed until it was irrefutable. One night when he missed dinner, I imagine she walked down to his favorite watering hole, where he sat at a two-top with some unimpressive woman. "You must be the wife I've heard so much about," she said. Stephanie was speechless that she was even in this situation, so she left.

Back at 409, she wouldn't have even known what to say. Where to begin. So she asked, "What the hell?"

"I talked to her *about you*," he said.

"If you are a married man, you don't need to be in a club talking with any woman about anything at this time of night."

"So I'm not s'posed to talk to anyone at all if I'm married to you?" he misdirected.

"That's not—"

"You knew when you met me that I don't sell shoes for a living. I'm an *ideas man*."

Stephanie was baffled beyond speech for the second time in a single night.

"Can we just skip this fight?" he suggested, as if it was reasonable.

Stephanie scoffed. "No."

"I just can't go fifteen rounds with you tonight. I can't."

"Why? You have somewhere you need to be in the morning?"

"You know, you think you're somebody special, and you are. Other men, they might notice these little things about you, and they might can get past them. They might can tolerate you being all in their business or nagging them about dinner—" She didn't get the chance to ask *What business?* Or say, *You are the one who asked for steak on a Tuesday night.*

"—but nobody will love you for your crazy mind. Nobody's gone think those little things about you are the good things, the way I do. Nobody can love you better than me. And you don't appreciate me at all."

To be honest, as a researcher, I never understood what was so great about Sufi. It only makes sense that he was charismatic and manipulative in the way of a public speaker with a following, a prosperity-gospel–type orator, and he would have had to be a great debater to win out over Stephanie St. Clair, a woman of iron will. For that reason, and others that will reveal themselves, I can only conclude that Sufi's arguments ran irrelevant circles around the original thing that made her so upset, which varied between loyalty of one kind or another and his drinking to black-out. By the time this fight happened repeatedly, at two or three in the morning, she was too exhausted to realize that he redirected the entire argument, twisting around his misdeeds until she felt like, maybe she did have something to apologize for . . . even though at the start of this conversation she was the one who was angry, and she could point to the exact reason why. The word games, which were all in her second language, were so disorienting that more often than not she just gave up. She did have somewhere to be in the morning, and she couldn't fight every little battle with him and still show up fresh-faced and sharp-minded.

Everyone around them also knew of the gambling dens he frequented, in addition to the dens of other women. He was so unabashed that no one even had to mention it. They weren't withholding information from her. It was simply no secret. No one mentioned his trespass, not her security detail, not her doorman, not her butler, not her business associates. Everyone knew; everyone knew that she knew; and no one would dare embarrass her with a confrontation. But she was a woman who did not bring the same problem to the same people twice, and she certainly did not try the same solution and expect different results. Rather than turn Sufi out again, Stephanie instead removed herself. She rented a second apartment at 580 St. Nicholas Avenue, closer to the bank, in an attempt to refocus her energy and attention. Still, she seldom ate unless it was to binge from stress, whole bundles of grapes, whole boxes of chocolates after days of nothing but whole pots of black coffee and cartons of cigarettes. No one spoke to her of her personal life. Only business. Stephanie thought she might give Sufi some time to realize his success and either attribute it to her generosity or boost his self-esteem so that he was no longer intimidated by her. But he hardly seemed to notice her absence anymore, let alone her presence. It was inconceivable that he could dismiss her out of hand, not when so many young men who worked for her revered her and respected her. So, she waited. In the meantime, she gave her butler and the doorman strict instructions not to allow any men access to her new apartment.

She found out about his cult, but she didn't say how. I imagine that Bridget, her butler and as loyal as any of her employees, came the closest of anyone to broaching the subject when he brought her the paper one morning on her coffee tray. He laid it with toast and butter and jam, just in case an appetite should strike her, and he folded open the *Amsterdam News* to an article about her husband.

A few moments passed before she saw it. Stephanie stirred from her half sleep when the door clicked shut behind Bridget. She wrapped a blue kimono around her shoulders and plucked a cigarette from a decorative dispenser on the side table. A blue-painted porcelain music box. Lift the top of the carousel, and the cigarettes splayed for the taking. If she wound the key at the base, it played *Swan Lake* till it stalled midmeasure. She couldn't quite remember which of her long-ago admirers had given it to her. Likely a veteran of the Great War, since surely this thing was French, or at least Italian. She studied the pastoral scenes on its tiny panels as she took her seat by the window. She lifted the box into the light to inspect its fields of gathered hay, a thatched-roof cottage. She couldn't tell what country. Still gazing on, she gulped down a full cup of black coffee before reaching over the tray for the carafe to refill when she spotted the newspaper's headline. It was far from front-page news that Sufi was named bishop at the Universal Holy Temple of Tranquillity in Harlem. This accomplishment was his own racket. He'd opened his silly little cult that she had warned him against. Not only was the concept ludicrous, but after she realized the idea wasn't a joke, she balked on the grounds of integrity. A cult was not an honest business. It was predatory. And, Harlem already had one profitable cult leader in Father Divine. Why would his followers change loyalties to a charlatan whose name they couldn't even pronounce? One who did not preach equality like Father Divine (on the surface), but held a platform near anti-Semitism? Seeing his promotion in writing turned her stomach. *All he wants is money*, she thought with watering eyes as she felt her diaphragm spasm. And then she felt even sicker when she realized, *No. He doesn't even want money. Not even power, like most men. He only wants attention. Like a little boy who is not particularly intelligent or athletic or charming . . . he puts the thumbtack on the teacher's chair because any attention will do.* She was disgusted, and she retched until she threw up her morning coffee and whatever acid she had created to digest it.

She rang for Bridget and asked for milk to drip into her next mug. He was happy to see the toast half-eaten on the plate when he arrived, and she said, "It seems the acidity no longer agrees with me."

———

One day when she arrived at her apartment on St. Nicholas, Stephanie said in later interviews, a small woman sat in her parlor. She was wrapped in a white dress that made her look even smaller than she was, and she carried one of her self-published dream books with the typical misspellings and misprinted margins clutched to her chest. Stephanie could tell from the exposed back cover alone that Edison McVey was the woman's publisher. He would publish just about anything. Nice enough man, but no discernment. They were on friendly terms. Stephanie would have to remember to call him for a reference on this character.

"Who are you?" Stephanie asked as her maid helped her with her fur coat.

She relinquished her empty-looking handbag to Jane and answered, "Are you feeling well enough, Madame St. Clair?"

Stephanie sucked her teeth and went about her business, unpinning her hat. She asked, exhausted and irritated, "What are you doing here? Who sent you here?" She was tired of people she didn't want to see showing up unbidden in her own apartments.

"I'm Madame Fu Futtam," she said, "The Negro-Chinese seer." This was, in fact, how Madame Fu Futtam described herself.

"Okay," she scoffed. Stephanie squeezed the bridge of her nose between finger and thumb. This woman was a walking migraine. "What do you want?"

Fu Futtam popped her tongue. "I always like to be nice to the sick," she replied and presented the dream book to St. Clair, along with several colored tallow candles—Madame St. Clair didn't specify which colors, but after a little research, I think she brought pink to invoke celestial happiness, orange for lucky dreams, and a black one to ward off evil. Fu Futtam said that she knew as well as everyone in Harlem who Madame Queen was, but when she had persistent recurring dreams about Stephanie falling ill, she took the initiative to visit her. Stephanie did not trust anyone's clairvoyance over her own, but she allowed Fu Futtam to stay and visit because she had, in fact, been losing weight. She'd thrown up just a few days ago, though she attributed that to nerves and poor judgment, and she was not feeling well generally. She might have been more alarmed at the sudden interest in friendship had she not just recently resolved to make more of an effort with the women associated with her employees as a gesture of courtesy. Stephanie kept a polite, formal conversation with her for a quarter hour or so, never fully relaxing into her seat, until Bridget came to interrupt them as he had been coached to do at meetings with anyone who had not made an appointment. Stephanie politely excused herself, and when Bridget returned after escorting Fu Futtam out, she thanked him by letting him go home early.

She did not know that Fu Futtam would take her good manners as an invitation to return. St. Clair said she did return, many times.

Fu Futtam brought over delicacies every day after that—wine, candies, and finally, chicken. St. Clair threw it all up, but she also learned more about the "seer" with each visit: she was born in Panama, she lived in Jamaica, and her real name was Dorothy—which St. Clair only clocked after noticing a piece of mail in Futtam's handbag. It was harmless enough for Futtam to change her name; but to prey on the desperate with this faux fortune-telling, lying about their hopes and fears, it all left Stephanie uneasy. Stephanie had no illusions that she, too, provided a hopeful gamble, but hers wasn't a gaff. She didn't mislead anyone, and she always paid out when they won. Most importantly, the game was winnable. Fu Futtam gave very specific predictions about which numbers would hit for whom and on what day. What baffled Stephanie was when people lost but still came back to her for more advice.

When the continuous vomiting finally compelled St. Clair to seek a doctor, he said that she was likely allergic to something in the air of her new apartment building, and he advised her to move. Because she was sick, though, Stephanie did not have the energy to search for a new residence, and she moved into the Braddock Hotel at the corner of 126th Street and 8th Avenue.

Fu Futtam seemed to understand her temporary weakness. St. Clair's record says that Fu Futtam brought matzo ball soup to her next visit. All the plot points of Madame Fu Futtam's rent swindle are mentioned there as well, though some of the dialogue has been re-created to string documented quotes together. "I know of a nice apartment," she said, walking the soup into the parlor with steps so small she looked like she was gliding. "It's further downtown, at the south end of Harlem, 45 West 110th Street. I'm going that way tomorrow, and I'll be glad to check on it for you."

"Yes," Stephanie said almost immediately. Before even tasting the soup, she retrieved her purse from her nightstand, gripping the furniture in her vertigo on the way, and slid two five-dollar bills from her clip. She returned and gave them to Fu Futtam. "I have not seen mold in this building, but I must be allergic. My doctor said I need to move, that I will continue this sickness until I do."

"Oh, yes, you should see about moving as soon as you can, then." Fu Futtam tipped her head a little to the side, her wide hat's brim dwarfing her already diminutive face on a neck so narrow Stephanie sometimes wondered how she swallowed.

"I wonder if I might . . . well, there's no use beating around the bush. I have a business idea, Madame St. Clair—wait, wait, I know now is not the time or place, and I wouldn't want you to make any decisions until you're completely well. I'm just excited about the idea, and I didn't want to surprise you by trying to make a business appointment, not after we've become such fast friends."

Stephanie's vision swam for a moment before she nodded. She didn't have the presence of mind to frown at being fast friends when she had only learned of Fu Futtam's existence mere weeks earlier. *Why do strangers assume that I am fond of them? Am I so approachable now? When did that change?*

"I think there's a real profit to be made in humus, even among industrialization. Upstate, there's still a lot of farmland," she prattled on. Stephanie had to excuse herself to lie down before the door fully shut behind her unwelcome visitor.

Fu Futtam returned the following evening. She settled on the wingback guest chair in the office, and before long she said the landlord needed the first month's rent in total, seventy more dollars. Stephanie gave it to her. When she asked about it the following week, Fu Futtam claimed that she had lost the receipt of payment. Stephanie was sure this was why she'd come to visit at all, to run a short grift on a Harlem patron who was running a fever so high she couldn't think straight, but then the landlord sent over a lease with the full eighty dollars totaled in receipt. The notice did not offset the anxious feeling in her belly.

It had been a few days since she saw Fu Futtam, and Stephanie was feeling a little better. She made it down to Braddock's bar just for some air and, and because they both lived nearby, I think she met Ella Fitzgerald at least once. At least, I like to think she did. Maybe she didn't, but it feels real, so I'm leaving it in. Ella had just become famous outside of Harlem for her sweet rendition of "A Tisket, A Tasket," but she'd been in the neighborhood for years trying to make it as a dancer. She wasn't a great dancer, but she could sing.

"I like 'Holiday in Harlem,' myself," Stephanie said as they chatted.

"I'm sure you do! They told me to think about you when I sang about sophisticated ladies with danger in their eyes."

This gave Stephanie the first true laugh in weeks. Her eyes watered up as she pressed a palm flat to her chest. "Oh, dear," she said. "If only you knew how much I needed to hear that."

"Good. Almost makes me feel absolved for running for a different bank when I first got to New York. I didn't know the lay of the land yet, understand—"

"I understand. They knew a good thing when they saw you, and everybody has to make a living."

Ella smiled. "What are you drinking tonight, Madame Queen?"

"Just tonic water. My stomach has been upset."

"Let me put a little ginger in that, to settle you. My official apology."

"Apology accepted. Long as you keep thinking about me when you sing 'Holiday.'"

"I'll tell Chick we got to perform it tonight. Madame St. Clair's special request."

———

That lightened feeling diminished soon after. The following events are told in newspaper interviews, though I've recreated the details. Her belly went into full, blooming heat when her phone rang the next afternoon, and Sufi was on the other end of the line. "Stephanie," he said, and even through the static she knew it was him. "What are you up to?"

She would not mention that she didn't feel well. "I'm on the way to the bank," she said, though she sat at the gossip table in her slip and robe.

"It's almost three."

"A late lunch appointment."

A pause extended. Stephanie propped her head on her hand before saying as gently as she could muster, "Did you need something?"

"I wonder if you might have dinner with me tonight. At the apartment."

Her heart hammered. She wasn't sure what caused its acceleration, this conversation or her rising fever. She let another silence drag, as he had, just to fuel his anxiety.

"I'll stop by after work."

"All right."

The line crackled.

"It's been too long," he said. "I'm looking forward to it."

Stephanie pressed between her eyebrows, "All right."

Stephanie didn't mention Sufi's call when Fu showed up unexpected not a full hour after she hung up the receiver. It was no oddity. Fu Futtam never gave notice, only ever dropped in. The little woman tottered in on tiny heels and waved to Stephanie as if she happened to run into her on the sidewalk, not at all like she was a visitor in Stephanie's apartment.

Stephanie was curt for a reason she couldn't pinpoint: "What a surprise."

"Oh, I won't keep you. I'm sure you have plans. I just stopped in to collect the eighty dollars."

Stephanie glared at her. She'd been feeling a little better, despite the worry. Her vision was straightening out at least, and she didn't like the cut of Fu Futtam's cloth. "I don't owe you any money."

"No, no. It's for the apartment I found you. I put up the money while you were sick. You remember."

"I already have the receipt from the landlord. I don't owe you anything. Now is not a good time, besides."

Fu Futtam's face fell from the demure little smirk as she huffed, "I was trying to help you. I'll come back when you're feeling better."

It was true that Stephanie didn't feel well. Better, but not well. She never felt fully well nowadays, and she was reminded that she never felt this anxious before, *not even when I was a target for the fucking mafia.* She was more scared then, sure, but she knew what she was afraid of. She could put a name, even a busted face to the fear. But now, she didn't know when the other shoe would drop—and why was it even bothering her. No one could touch her nowadays. She had the whole world at her feet. Still, she felt her senses heightened like a deer who doesn't realize that peculiar smell is a hunter, a human, as she dressed for dinner that night. Evening wear, but nothing all that romantic. Black, with darts that helped the shift fit better to her waist, pantyhose with Cuban heels and a pump with three buckles across her arch, silver fox fur, and a velvet turban. *I'll show him how to style a turban.*

———

She expected to feel relieved when she walked into 409. It was nice to see Jim grinning at the front desk, and to talk with him about his family on the elevator, but the symptoms of her allergy didn't lift immediately like she was hoping they would. The apartment itself had been cleaned by someone who didn't know how. She saw scuffs on the walls and grease smeared on the kitchen counter. Someone had wiped up a spot without cleaning the whole area. The height of laziness. Sufi bought Chinese takeout. It was still in the little paper boxes in the dining room. No tablecloth under it. No table settings. He brought her a plate from the drain board—he must have only just done dishes when he realized the time because they were mountained up and ready to crash at the slightest touch. Rather than feel lighter to be in his presence, like they were on the mend, or that he'd gone out of his way to do something special, she rather had the impression that all his other social plans had fallen through, or that he was running out of money and thought he needed to butter her up to get an allowance, but he'd forgotten the first time he won her attention was through his genuine admiration and conversation about her life of success, not with a half-assed dinner befitting his second choice to a high school dance.

He tried to be charming, but she saw through it for the vim of insecurity that it was, even as she willed herself to be wrong. The pressure in her ribs wouldn't release, even as he yammered on about which of his friends had shacked up with which lounge singer, and did she know that Billie Holliday only wore those gardenias because she'd burned her scalp so bad with the curling iron that her hair wouldn't grow back?

It all seemed inconsequential.

Sufi talked only of himself and his friends and doings until he got hungry, and then he asked her about business before shoving a huge bite of orange chicken in his mouth.

"It's flourishing," she said, and though she was proud of her accomplishments, that, too, seemed diminished in the current setting. Why try to impress? To what end? She was back behind her own smokescreen. When her head was clear she would wonder what if anything he could do to restore his stature.

"You had any weird investments come across your desk lately?"

Her smile was sad. "Nothing weird. I haven't been taking as many chances lately. My cards have warned against it for now."

"You and these cards." He chuckled. "Most people are up on dream books nowadays."

"You have to trust the author of those, and most of them are anonymous. How accurate can they be, if they won't sign their name to it?"

He shrugged. "That works if you trust yourself more, I guess."

"Mon dieu, of course I trust myself more."

He continued chewing.

Their conversation was dying.

"I do have one different meeting. About a humus business."

At this, Sufi shrugged, seeming to reoccupy his animated body and said as nonchalant as if directed to act cool: "I don't know much about farming, but you don't have any schemes like that. Maybe it'd be good to change it up?"

She hadn't even taken the meeting with Fu Futtam yet, and she knew no details, but in a rare act of desperation, Stephanie decided on the spot that she would fund the start-up, just so she could show him that she had listened.

Sufi carried on with his chitchat and bravado, and though she listened, she listened like he was a radio on in the other room. Why was she here? Why was she acting like this? How had he twisted her around so that she was playing to his whims, trying to get his affection? She was Stephanie St. Clair! She was Madame Queen!

He fixed her some whiskey drink with ginger in it when she said her stomach hadn't been right lately, and she took a few sips of it before she stood to leave.

"You ain't got to go," he said.

She looked into his eyes for a long time. "Do you want me to stay? Or are you being polite?"

"If you want to stay, then I want you to stay."

It wasn't enough, and she knew it. "I'm sure you have plans tonight." She heard Fu Futtam's passive aggression echoed in her own voice.

"No, I don't."

She waited for him to continue. He didn't. *How is this the time when he learns to negotiate?*

"I haven't been doing right—"

"No?"

"Now, don't make it sound like I admitted to something I didn't. All I meant was I know you're mad at me, and I would understand if you wanted to leave."

Even this half-hearted confession made her bristle. It was another misdirection, as if her anger started the problem. Would it go any differently if she did stand her ground? No, she'd leave two hours later even more upset. It didn't matter that she dreamed about him every night, nor that she second-guessed her own memories of them together. Were they just thoughts she had, daydreams about their life together and how it could be? Did she ever have the experiences of him that she remembered? Did he just say things, and she conceptualize them? Was their relationship—the goodness of it that she remembered—in her imagination? What if none of her other perceptions were grounded in reality, either? And what other whore would be here within moments of her leaving.

He watched this monologue play on her face and said, "Of course I want you to stay. You my wife."

She looked down on him, stretched at the head of her dining room table. She deserved to be here, and that's where she landed, on entitlement.

She stayed, and in the morning, she felt a little better and a little worse. Of course he was looking for attention and money. What if he had finally, only just now realized that their marriage was not a legal contract? What if only yesterday he had consulted a lawyer from outside Harlem, one of the only lawyers who would hazard his career to represent him against her, and what if that lawyer informed him that not only was a divorce impossible without a marriage contract, but in the nonevent of a separation, he was entitled to exactly nothing?

No, she thought as he snored beside her. No, he was too hotheaded for that. If he knew that she had outsmarted him in his own confidence scheme, he would have reacted with rage first, not Chinese takeout.

———

When she granted the loan to Fu Futtam, the tiny woman showed little gratitude. She signed the contract and slid the check into her beat-up pocketbook that loudly clicked closed. Fu Futtam then slid her palms out on the upholstered chair arms, and with her chin lifted, said, "There is something I can do for you in return." She closed her eyes. "For two hundred and fifty dollars more, I can go into the cemetery and call the spirits of our ancestors. I can command them to make your husband do right."

When Fu Futtam opened her eyes, St. Clair was leaning over her chair, fingernails digging into the backs of her hands like a cat, staring at her violently. "Go home and make your own husband do right," she said, according to her own written accounts. She snatched up the tiny woman by her wrists and shoved her toward the door till Fu Futtam fled on her own.

Fu Futtam returned again the next day, prim and stoic,

with more gifts and apologies. "I shouldn't have implied I knew something that I don't," she said.

=====

Stephanie was at the bank when she got a phone call from Bridget, who had just returned from 45 West 110th Street to schedule her move in. "Do you have a moment, Madame?" he asked with a voice full of worry. "I hate to bother you with such things, and I want to tell you I did try to work it out—"

"What is it, mon ami?"

He sighed at the end of the line, leaning against the island in her kitchen with a sweating brow. "I talked to landlord, and he said he had no record of your deposit. He said he never talked to anyone at all about an apartment vacancy, madame."

"A dishonest man."

Bridget huffed again. "Actually . . . respectfully, I don't think so. He was worried to death that he would offend you. He knows who you are, of course. Seemed flattered you would want to live in that building, which, now that I seen it . . ."

"Show him the receipt of pay that he mailed."

"I did, ma'am," he said haltingly. "I brought it with me in case he wanted proof that I was who I said. The man, he wanted to help. When I showed him the carbon copy, he showed me his ticket book. They didn't even match up. They were different pages, different tickets themselves, if you catch my meaning."

"What the hell," she said.

"I don't know, madame. I don't know what might have happened. I wanted to talk to you—to get your permission to call Fu Futtam if you think it's right. I don't want to accuse her of nothing . . . but. . . ."

"Thank you. Yes, I'll handle Fu Futtam. Be sure she won't go unaware that she embarrassed us both."

Bridget inhaled heavily on his end, turned around to face Jane, the maid, before he asked, "We making good progress packing up house, madame . . ."

She took his meaning. They had to go somewhere.

"Bien." She made sure that Bridget heard the smile in her voice when she said, "It is a good thing that I own an apartment in the most prestigious building in Sugar Hill, oui?"

She felt Bridget's tension ease as she ended the call, and she asked to be connected to 409. Jim answered, and he was delighted to hear from her. He told her all about the New Years' ham that his wife's Scottish employer sent home with her. Here it was almost King's Day and they were still eating high on the hog. "What can I do for you this fine afternoon, Madame Queen?" he asked.

Stephanie asked him to connect her to her apartment.

She heard the joy leave his voice and the business manner return when he said, "Just one moment, madame."

Stephanie didn't let it deter her. When Sufi picked up—answering his own phone, she noticed—she cut out all pleasantries. "I'll be moving back into 409 at the end of the week," she told him. "I expect for you to accommodate the change with no obstacles. But of course, if you find this disagreeable, I'll understand if you need to make other living arrangements." He barely had time to acknowledge he heard her before she disconnected.

═══

Even after the move, Fu Futtam found Stephanie. She came to visit within a day of her getting settled, and she saw the tiny woman talking to her husband in the doorway when she emerged from the bedroom. Fu Futtam said, "I was just making your husband's acquaintance, madame."

"What do you want?"

"Stephanie," Sufi chided with a be-nice expression.

Stephanie raised her eyebrows at Fu Futtam.

Fu Futtam pushed in. "I was hoping madame would grant me a short-term loan. Because I've been so hard at work on the humus business venture, I've fallen behind on my rent a few months—"

"A few months."

"Yes, four months I'm not ashamed to say."

"You're not ashamed to say you're four months behind on your rent?"

"Stephanie!"

"Well, I'm not ashamed at the reason why at least. I was hoping I could impose on your generosity again."

"I don't have four months' rent in cash on my person. That would be irresponsible."

Sufi interjected, "Surely in the safe?"

Stephanie was so baffled at their heavy-handedness that she answered with a flat, "What safe," and walked back into the bedroom to finish dressing, shouting a firm "No" over her shoulder before she shut the door behind her. The nerve of them both. Her having stolen money already; him assuming she had a safe in her apartment like a fool. Maybe that was the reason he stayed around. Fool's gold.

Fu called several more times over the next few days and left messages when Stephanie would not take her calls. She had one hand on the shoe horn the first time Bridget knocked. He poked his head in and said, "It's Miss Fu Futtam on the telephone for you," with a face so placid it looked like a farce. He continued, saying Fu Futtam wanted to make a good impression at some appointment with some motion picture people, and could Stephanie lend her some jewelry?

Stephanie scoffed.

Bridget smiled and closed the door.

Stephanie left her messages unanswered.

———

Fu Futtam did not take the hint, not even when Bridget relished relaying the message that her calls were no longer welcome and dropped the receiver with a big flourish. Instead, the little mosquito started calling on Sufi. Bridget knew better than to connect them. Instead, he politely excused himself and left the receiver off the hook on a cloth napkin in the kitchen to muffle the sound. He tapped at the office door of 409 with his Masonic seal ring.

"Oui," Stephanie answered.

Bridget stepped in and discreetly closed the door behind him.

She recognized the cue and looked up from the fistful of paperwork.

"Madame—" the lines that bracketed his mouth deepened "—I've just received a call for Mr. Hamid." He paused and wrung his hands that were already clasped behind his back. "From Fu Futtam."

Stephanie looked down for a moment. She squared her shoulders and relaxed her face and asked, "What did she want?"

Bridget tried his best to keep his face calm and said, "She didn't want anything. Only to talk to him."

Stephanie rose from her desk chair and strode in stocking feet to the gossip table in the parlor. She removed her sapphire earring and took the call, "Hello."

Fu Futtam giggled on the other end.

Stephanie's nostrils flared. "Were you not aware that your calls are no longer welcome here?"

"Oh, madame, I knew *you* didn't want to talk to me. I just thought Bishop Sufi might."

"You are a foolish little girl to ask to speak to my husband. And what is it that you want from him? Because everything he has belongs to me."

At this, Sufi strode half-dressed out of the bedroom. Stephanie met his eyeline and kept it, and she did not stand. Into the receiver, and into his face, she said, "You are not to make any more contact. Do you understand?"

In her interviews, Stephanie says that Sufi swiped his hand back across her face. He picked up the telephone receiver and threw it down on the marble tiles, smashing it to bits. "You been keeping my calls from me, bitch?"

Stephanie stared at him, even while the side of her face colored from his strike.

"I be damned before I let some hincty bitch tell me what to do and who I can see." He towered over her, even as all her employees moved to stand in the parlor as her witness. "I could do to you what I did to this telephone. And if that didn't break you, I'd kick you within an inch of your life, stomp you out, and throw what's left out that window."

As soon as he slammed the door, Jane rushed over to Stephanie, and Bridget collected the pieces of the telephone. "Are you all right?" Jane asked, examining her face while gesturing for the other maid to bring over the steak from the icebox. She placed it on her eye, and Bridget held in his palm the sapphire and its setting, now separated from Sufi's violence. "I'll have George & Sons reset this, madame."

Stephanie shook with rage as if she was in shock. Jane brought her a cup of black coffee and set the ashtray and cigarette holder down on the gossip table beside her. Stephanie fumbled the cigarette to her lips, and Bridget struck the match. "Have one," she said to all three. "Please, if you wish." She drew another breath. "This kind of scene is not what you were hired to care for," she said. To her surprise, tears leaked from her eyes and straight down both cheeks. Bridget held out his handkerchief.

"Madame Queen, we are here to serve you," he said.

"Yes, ma'am," Jane agreed. "We here for whatever you need."

Stephanie dabbed at her face and drew once more on the cigarette before stubbing it out. She nodded, and with shaking hands and a deep frown, and a steady, heavy voice that belied none of her turmoil, she said, "Help me wrap his things in newspaper."

He was back in ten minutes, mad and erratic. Bridget greeted him at the door with the parcels in hand, and Sufi shoved him aside, sending the butler and the packages sprawling, before he marched into the apartment.

I have not re-created the following dialogue.

Sufi screamed, "What I say? I'll throw you out that goddamned window—"

"I would not do that if I were you." Stephanie stood in front of the big parlor window, where she overlooked 409 Edgecombe Avenue and exhaled a cloud of smoke. She didn't even look over her shoulder when she said, "This won't end well for you." She nodded at her security detail who was entering the building on the ground floor below.

Sufi was quiet for a long time, huffing like an angry stallion who had worn himself out bucking and was about to finally break. She was not startled to feel his big hands on her shoulders and a kiss at her cheek, the other cheek, she noticed. Not the one he struck before. He went back into her bedroom, and to the best of her knowledge, he went back to sleep.

Stephanie did not go to sleep. She dismissed her employees, and she told her body guards that they could go home, as well. When Sufi came out of the bedroom fully dressed in the middle of the night, Stephanie was sitting in the darkened parlor still smoking like a chimney. He did not notice her, but instead wrapped his cape about her shoulders—the one lined with red satin, one that she had bought for him—and softly closed the door behind him. When he was out of the building, Stephanie stuffed his .38 into the pocket of her jacket and followed him to 209 West 125th Street.

ST. JAMES INFIRMARY

No one saw what happened on the stairs of 209 except for the two parties concerned. The only things that all accounts corroborate are that there was an argument, three shots were fired, and no one was seriously injured.

Mrs. Nettie Roach was visiting the office of Eustace Dench when she happened upon the scene on the stairs from above. "I'll shoot you," she heard Sufi mutter.

Both Mrs. Roach and the second witness heard the shots. Two together, and then one.

Clarence Dade had just ratcheted open the gate of the elevator he operated when he heard Sufi shout, "I'm shot!"

When he rounded the corner, Sufi was on a higher step than Stephanie, and he had control of the .38.

Mrs. Roach also saw that Sufi had the gun in his hand.

Madame St. Clair looked up at Mrs. Roach, and then down at Clarence, and she said to him, frantic, "He's lying. He was shooting at me."

"All right, all right," Clarence said, his hands in front of him. "Don't nobody panic. Important thing here is that no-body's really hurt, and we want to keep it that way."

Stephanie's hand was shaking and bleeding, and he let his glance linger on it before he asserted that it would be all right to leave it for the moment.

"Thank God for you," she said to him, though she seemed not to be seeing anything.

"Sir," Clarence said to Sufi, who was staring and sneering at Stephanie. "What's your name, sir?"

"Bishop Amiru Al-Mu-Minin Sufi Abdul Hamid."

"Mr. Bishop," he said in a low tone. "I know you don't want to hurt nobody. Y'all, I'm just gone reach in my pocket and get a handkerchief for both of y'all, all right?" He withdrew two handkerchiefs. The first, he unfolded and said, "Mr. Bishop, do me a favor and hand me that firearm. I'll just hold on to it till we can get everything settled, if it's all right with you."

Sufi considered for a moment before he broke into a wild smile and looked Clarence in the eye before handing the gun over with both hands, like a politician grasping at a handshake.

"Thank you, Mr. Bishop." He folded the cloth around the hot metal and slid it into this pants pocket.

"Miss ma'am," he said up the stairs to Mrs. Roach who stood frozen to her spot. "Would you please see to this lady here." He redirected his attention to Sufi and said, "Won't you come walk into the manager's office to cool off with a drink of water?"

Sufi followed him into the lobby and behind the counter, where the doorman was putting the phone back on the receiver. He stared as Clarence ushered the strutting Sufi away from Stephanie St. Clair, who collapsed sobbing onto the stairs and into the arms of a perfect stranger. "I only wanted to scare him," she said. "If I had killed him, I would have died."

NEW YORK AMSTERDAM NEWS
SATURDAY, MARCH 19, 1938
MME. SUFI UP FOR SENTENCE
Black Hitler's Frau Punished
By Marvel Cooke

Sufi was the first witness on the stand. In his best Oxfordian English [he said], [. . .]

"I turned my head quickly and reached for her hand trying to grab the gun from her. The first bullet whizzed by, nicking my front teeth. The second passed through the breast pocket of my overcoat my top coat and shirt coming out through my sleeve. By that time I grabbed her hand and the third bullet went up singeing my forehead and landing in the ceiling."

[. . .]

Q. The first shot nicked your teeth and didn't go through your mouth?

A. I wouldn't be here now if it had.

Q. You tell me that all of those holes in your clothes were made by the second bullet?

[. . .]

When the judge asked him if he had ever threatened to throw his wife out of the window, Sufi said:

"Your honor, I weigh 234 pounds and it is highly improbable that if I wanted to do her bodily harm that I couldn't."

[. . .] I am sorry for her [. . .]. But if she ever tries shooting me again, it mightn't be so lucky for either one of us."

Stephanie went back to her jail cell for seven days after the trial. To anyone else, it would have been a stressful, sleepless week, but it was more likely that after this resolution, her anxiety released and she resigned herself to the reality of prison time. Now she knew what would happen, at least in part, which meant she could prepare for it. Philip Levey would have schemed with her, advised on how to keep her business going in her absence. He advised her on the legality of how to liquidate and distribute her assets so the government would not seize them. That was her priority, pending incarceration, that the police not steal any more of her money. Her legal bank accounts had been frozen, but like any criminal, the bulk of her wealth would not be found there anyway. For those who could not meet her, who could not risk incrimination themselves, she wrote coded letters at Levey's expertise. Letters to the wives of each of her business associates, and enough cash for two Easter hams and a coat for each of them. Typed letters of reference for each of her domestic workers to be delivered to her neighbors in 409 for them to sign, along with a token of her appreciation.

She did not expect Marvel Cooke to visit, but she did. When she arrived, Stephanie handed her the letter she had already written, thanking Marvel for her transparent reportage and directing her where to find pieces of her favorite jewelry that she wished Marvel to keep.

"Madame Queen, I'm not here for that," Marvel said. "Thank you, I mean, but I don't expect anything from you. I think you know you have my support in this, just like you had it when you were fighting the Dutchman—"

Stephanie gave a startled laugh. "How the mighty have fallen."

"You? No ma'am. This is just another . . . what are they calling it in baseball? Pop-up slide? You'll take the base. I'm not worried about you."

"What did you come for, then?" she asked gently.

"For one, to tell you that. And two, to get your statement."

"My statement? He did me wrong," she told Marvel, "and he'll get his just desserts! He's a vile, evil man and he has no right to live."

"That is a statement," she laughed. "But I have to break some more news to you, madame. It's bad. It looks like Sufi's going to marry Fu Futtam."

Stephanie grimaced, even as her eyes welled. Her chest felt like it would cave in. "My statement to that is, they are two peas in a fucking pod, and they deserve each other. But . . . I am broken hearted. I married Sufi because I loved him . . . but now I know that he married me for monetary reasons. When he got all he could, he was through with me."

Bumpy arrived in person, too, and although no one knows exactly what they said, everyone knows it was a changing of the guard. If she had to sell out, she would sell out to her protégé, the one person she trusted to shore up with her taxes and accountants, and to roll her business into his own.

The official write-up from the *Amsterdam News* listed the facts. After her conviction for first-degree assault and gun charges, the judge sentenced her for two to ten years in the state prison. It read that Madame St. Clair "kissed her hand to freedom as she was led out of the courtroom. Sufi, one of Harlem's most colorful figures, was not in court when the sentence was pronounced."

EPILOGUE:

NOBODY KNOWS YOU
(WHEN YOU'RE DOWN AND OUT)

What's the truth about the end of the story. The truth about the end of Madame Queen. Truth is, nobody knows the truth. Not for sure. While she served her sentence for shooting Sufi—for shooting at Sufi—the newspapers were her window outside. She went back to making dresses, which was her trade while incarcerated. But after the mind has adjusted to freedom and strategy and imagination, it keeps roaming even if the body is chained to a sewing machine. The monotony of the patterns. *Spool on the peg. Wrap thread around tension knob. Loop down the lever. Loop up the lever. Loop down the lever. Thread the needle. Join the bobbin thread. Pull threads to the back. Feed the fabrics. Drop the foot. Push the fly wheel. Foot pedal. Guide. Turn.* Those rote commands are not very exerting on the mind. Mastering the zipper enclosures resisted her a little, but the body follows instructions, carrying out its tasks while the mind takes flight. It follows its own whims, makes conversation with itself, laughs at its own creativity. *Can you believe we came up with that?*

Such was the case with Madame Queen. She saw Sufi's name in the *Amsterdam News*, in an article written by her own friend, Marvel Cooke. "Bishop Sufi A.A.M.M.S.A.H. Unveils His Universal Buddhist Holy Temple to Public" Marvel wrote, as if looking at Stephanie from the corner of her eye like, *I had to abbreviate his name.* And then the subtitle, "Black Hitler Intones Mystic Phrases for Crowd Attending Cult Opening," like, *y'all won't believe this.*

> Curtains hiding the altar were slowly pulled back by kimono-clad usherettes revealing His Holiness wearing a black and gold biretta at a cocky angle and a chartreuse brocaded robe over which was a "twenty-two carat solid gold vestment." His head was bowed in solemn prayer and he slowly crossed the platform and salaamed before the altar.
>
> "O, arach lo cha, gyah gyah, oon she foorah. Allah she foorah, she susa she susa, shu sheelee," His Holiness intoned.
>
> Later he explained that this was a manifestation of reincarnation, "for how would I know Chinese if I had not been reincarnated?" he asked the audience. There were no Orientals in the offices to doubt the authenticity of his Chinese [. . .].
>
> "God do not associate with dumb folks," he declared. "He manifests Himself in that which objectivizes itself in all things that be."
>
> Later explaining the old "I am that I am" theory, His Holiness said: "If you was I am that I am you wouldn't have to be here."

It was the type of article meant to be read aloud in front of an audience howling at the accuracy of its absurdities. In highlighting his various forms of fraud, it was like Marvel wrote to Stephanie specifically—but, of course, she didn't. Her beloved shyster "Harlem Hitler" marrying that little "Negro Chinese Seer." Records revealed their license, but the temple's secretary claimed to know nothing when Marvel asked about it. The reporter talked about Stephanie more than she talked about his new wife, which Madame Queen appreciated. And Marvel called them by their given names, Eugene Brown and Dorothy Mathews, which stripped them of all their put-on exoticism. She explained Stephanie's contractual agreement with Sufi from two years ago, and how they didn't have a ceremony, so their marriage was not recognized in New York. In the very next thought, she explained that Stephanie was serving time for "allegedly taking a pot shot at Sufi," and objectively listed the new couple's litany of ridiculous contradictions.

Stephanie could easily read between the lines of Marvel's journalism. In one feature in the *Amsterdam News*, she quoted Stephanie saying, "He's a vile, evil man and he has no right to live." She went on: "No one thought much of Stephanie's prediction at the time. It was a natural thing to say under the circumstances. Stephanie was howling mad. When he was told what she had said, Sufi laughed, shrugged his shoulders, and said, 'poor Stephanie.'"

Still, Stephanie's mind must have run wild picturing an absurd ceremony between Sufi and Fu Futtam at the cultish temple. Melding together what she knew of Sufi's' clothing taste before she taught him better and the general tackiness of Fu Futtam, she could all but see rough fabrics swathed around them both, leaving their dye behind as they sweated. The red from his turban concoction might stream into his eyes like blood from a head wound that changed his personality from charming to evil. Purple bruised her neck from being choked so hard for so long that it left her brain dead. These were not visions. They were not wishes. They were interpretations.

=====

When Stephanie invested in Sufi, she had lent him the respectability he needed to dupe other investors. Her reference of character, the others believing in him, those ego boosts probably gave him the confidence to buy that plane. Since

Lindbergh's flight some decade ago, everyone with enough money to buy a vessel thought themselves entitled to the sky. Sufi said he was inspired by Douglass Corrigan, who flew across the Atlantic "by mistake." So he set out to copy Corrigan. Fewer than three weeks later, he found a monoplane, a Cessna, that was nine years old and had belonged to a man who died fighting with the Spanish Loyalists. Sufi bought it for $2,000. He determined that the pilot mattered more than the plane in matters of longevity, and he decided they would take just a couple test flights before they would make the first direct flight from California to Liberia. First, they had to get to California.

But the sky rejected Sufi.

Stephanie saw the first notice of it in the *Syracuse Herald* on Monday, August 1, 1938.

She had watched Sufi die a thousand slow deaths in her mind, but even the slow twisting of limbs from his body as one savors plucking petals from a flower did not prepare her to see in the newspaper, "Harlem Hitler and Pilot Die in Crash." Her brittle, carbon-coated fingers held the paper, and she blinked long and slow, assuming one of her interpretations had invaded her waking thoughts. But no. She realized it was not her own mind exploding his viscera into a ball of blue flames when she learned the reason why: his plane ran out of gas.

THE AFRO-AMERICAN
SATURDAY, AUGUST 6, 1938
WAS IT THE CURSE OF FATHER DIVINE OR DID
MADAM ST. CLAIR KILL SUFI?
Corrigan Flight Made Sufi Buy Ancient Crate
Cult Head Thought He Could Fly It to Japan
By Ralph Matthews

NEW YORK—If Douglass Corrigan, white, had not flown across the Atlanta Ocean by "mistake" nearly three weeks ago, Bishop Sufi Abdul Hamid, who crashed to his death Sunday afternoon, would be alive.

Sufi, always a colorful and daring character, was driven to his death by his desire to prove that this race was no laggard in the field of aeronautics. He bought the 9-year-old plane in the hope that he could duplicate the feat of Corrigan and take some of the edge off of the achievements of the Nordics in aviation. [...]

Because some chiseling pilot of a private plane pilfered several gallons of gas out of the tank of Sufi Abdul Hamid's nine-year-old J-5 Cessna plane, two persons were killed instantly and a third seriously injured, Sunday.

Sufi had the plane only ten days and had been up twice before he made the fatal attempt.

[. . .] Pilot Fred Burkhardt, white, who was killed with Sufi knew that the tank was filled [. . .] and did not bother to examine the gas supply again after two short trial flights in which Hamid's wife accompanied him. Knowing that this flight could have consumed but a few gallons of gas at the best, the plane immediately took off [. . .].

SUFI'S PILOT TOLD TO GET MORE GAS
By Harry B. Webber

NEW YORK CITY—For the first time since her husband was killed almost before her eyes [. . .], the widow of Bishop Sufi Abdul Hamid cried as she sat in a big roadster at West 124th Street and Morningside Avenue, Monday afternoon telling about his death.

"I haven't shed a tear since the tragedy," she said [. . .]. She wore a red figured dress.

If it hadn't been for Stephanie's stuttering grief at the death of the man who had won her heart against all odds and against her better judgment, imagining his precious airplane crashing in front of thousands near Long Island's Southern State Parkway, his body ejected from the plane and bent double the wrong way because he was too irresponsible to fill up the goddamn gas tank . . . it would have been hilarious. The kind of gleeful reverie that would have had her lift her foot from the sewing machine pedal and crack her knuckles in defiance before loading the next sleeve, chuckling at her ingenuity the rest of the day. But because she had not imagined it, because it was the real death of a real love, his fiery demise brought her no joy, no peace at all. She clipped the many write-ups from the many papers and pasted them onto her cell wall. Most of them ridiculed him, saw him for the cult leader he was. Marvel's homage was perhaps the fairest, since it told a fuller story. She acknowledged that he lied about who he was, and that even though he had come from a racketeering background, he had done good for the community in championing the riot of March 19, 1935, and campaigning for jobs for Negroes before his "energies were misdirected" and he "began his campaign on anti-Semitism." Her friend went on to editorialize more than she ever had before, saying Stephanie "might have saved herself the trouble of attempting to rub Sufi out, for he was killed in an airplane accident just four months after she began her prison sentence."

Madame Queen was eligible for parole less than a year later, on June 13, 1939. Then she disappeared. There are no more records of her until she died at Central Islip Psychiatric Center in 1969. That leaves thirty long years unaccounted for . . . almost half her life scrubbed from the record. She was that good.

But just because we don't know what happened doesn't mean we don't tell the story of what happened. Some people say she moved into a group home after the prison discharged her. Some say it wasn't a group home. It was a poorhouse. Triple bunked, sewing from before dawn till after dusk because the government seized everything she ever owned. And that would make sense, knowing the character of the government. It took them decades to realize her business was a good idea, that it was giving a lot of people a lot of hope. After they popped Queenie, they stole her idea and called it the New York State Lottery. Established 1967, they said.

Some say watching the government co-opt the business they'd prosecuted her for all her life was what put her into her grave two years later.

Loyalists say Bumpy did it. He was eating hominy grits at his favorite joint, the Wells Restaurant on 7th Avenue, like always, when he had the heart attack that finally killed him. And Stephanie did die within months of Bumpy. Some say the death of her best friend is what took the life out of her. There are folks who say that's what she'd want us to believe.

Others say she wouldn't want anyone to think she died of loneliness. She didn't go to the poorhouse. She went back to domestic service, same as she'd done when she was thirteen years old. The loyalists say that even if she had done that—which we doubt to begin with—she only went back to being a maid because she had to, not for the money. She was too smart to let the government seize everything. She'd have squirreled some investment away to Bumpy or her brain trust to take care of her when she got out. No, she did it because she had to tell her PO about her gainful employment, same as any parolee. Stephanie was proud, but she wouldn't have let that pride stand between her and her freedom. Just because she told her parole officer something doesn't mean she really did it. Or at least it doesn't mean she did it for the reason he told her to do it.

It's hard to imagine she still had the knack for housework anyway, not since she'd been living like royalty. Imagine her arguing with the lady of the house. She'd tell Madame Queen to polish the silver one way and Queenie would do it the way she knew was correct. It wouldn't matter that she was right, though, since everyone knows the person footing the bill is paying not for the service itself, but to be in power. Besides, can you imagine Madame Queen in a White Swan uniform? In her sixties?

======

Most Harlem folks don't want to believe St. Clair ever fully retired, behind bars though she may have been. They believe that Bumpy Johnson took over her bank and business ventures. Her final investment paid off as Bumpy eventually expanded into the drug trade for which he became infamous. And it was probably overdue to call in a favor from Bumpy, seeing as how she put him on all those years ago, and how good he was doing by then. That would make sense. Maybe he put her up in some mansion like the one he lived in later, somewhere discreet where she could live in peace, dabbling in her side hustle just for fun, and not because she needed money. Even Bumpy's widow, Mayme, said St. Clair died far from penniless.

======

Some say Stephanie started over when she got out, and she bought an apartment complex or two in 1960. With what money?

Same money she started her bank with, they say.

But where'd she get it from?

At the getting place, come on.

They say she bought a four-story brownstone in 1966, too, with a first-timer's loan.

That doesn't mean it was her first time, though—if anyone could game a system it was Madame Queenie. They say that when it came down to the wire, rather than lose the building, she ran in front of a laundry truck for the insurance payout. She was wearing a silk dressing gown and she was barefoot.

Loyalists can't believe that. Queenie was never not in high heels—and have you ever tried to run in mules? She was hit. She didn't run in front of the truck. Even the records say so. Even if she admitted "contributing negligence," you know they made her admit it. You wouldn't sign to that if they were giving you $2,000 to do it?

They say, too, she sold her buildings to her tenants after that, at the end. She wanted them to own a piece of Harlem, tend it like their own, which it was. She lived her last nine months in the Islip asylum.

She wasn't crazy. She was too sane. It was the best way to get the care she needed and still give back to the people she loved, and who loved her.

Another version of the ending goes like this: in 1963, she filed a report with an Immigration and Naturalization Service investigator, and she listed her hometown as Marseilles, France. Everybody who knew her knew she was the Tiger from Marseilles. And wouldn't it be just like her, slick and clever, to trick the government into deporting her to her vacation? That's where she lived off the dividends her people kept for her, sitting in a café chair on some cobblestone walk, laughing at all of them, smoking a cigarette, *I was bred and born in the briar patch! Bred and born!* Maybe the reason we never saw her after she got discharged is because she hightailed it right on out of here, hopped off to France where they know how to treat people.

———

However you want to slice it, the problem is the same. What bothers people most is not that they don't know how the story ends. It's that they don't know the beginning or the middle, either. They don't know Queenie at all. They live in her apartment building, walk right in front of her bank, and never heard her name. Not as a businesswoman who succeeded despite the odds and defended it against police corruption and the Mob. We don't like that despite the huge impact St. Clair had on her community, her story still fell through the cracks in history. People know about Bumpy Johnson. Dutch Schultz——some people even know about Sufi Abdul Hamid. But Madame Stephanie St. Clair's story has been forgotten, reduced to a footnote in the biographies of her male contemporaries. Is it because she was Black? A woman? An immigrant? Because she didn't go out with a bang like Sufi? Or a whimper like Schultz?

No, it's because Stephanie St. Clair, the numbers queen, was a Lady. And she was too good at her job to tell people about it. Glamorous and dangerous and powerful, but ladies don't brag about their own legacies—that's for other people to do.

★ ★ ★ ★ ★

ACKNOWLEDGMENTS

Thank you so much to my incredible agent, Kayla Lightner at Ayesha Pande Literary, who saw potential in this work long before its existence, and without whom this book might not exist. Park Row and HarperCollins, especially my editors Erika Imranyi and Annie Chagnot, first had the faith for the project and then brought the book over the finish line. I couldn't have written this book without the detailed archives of *The New York Amsterdam News* and Marvel Cooke's writing there in particular, the research of Shirley Stewart, LaShawn Harris, and Claude McKay—and the special collections at the Atlanta University Center Robert W. Woodruff Library who let me pore over the out-of-print materials in person. And, of course, the Museum of the American Gangster on St. Marks. Without that docent who first tipped me off to Madame Queen's existence, she might have stayed secret from me forever.

Personally, I'd like to thank Rachel Blankenship and Mimi Denaris, my fun, New York–local friends, for researching with me. We walked Lenox Avenue, explored 409 Edgecombe, and hung out at NYPL's Schomburg Center (by day), and checked out live music at the American Legion Hall and ordered off crumpled handwritten menus with two options (by night). They also helped me mull the unanswerable question, "*What* is so *great* about Sufi?" while drinking out of a trophy at a random bar in Sugar Hill and get in the headspace of a boss who got hoodwinked by a smooth-talking man. Because who (among us) has never been in that headspace? Mike McDonald and Max Bowen, too, were incredibly helpful lawyer friends who explained intricate laws to me without ever losing their patience.

And of course, the most gratitude to my husband, Chase Dickinson, and all of my family who emotionally supported me day-to-day . . . and just humored me in general. Chase endured everything from pausing everything we ever streamed so I could tell him how it related to Stephanie St. Clair to bursting into his office while he was on a video call to announce, "You're not going to *believe* what she just did."

There were many more people along the way who helped me, and whom I have forgotten to acknowledge here. Please forgive me. And please know that I will remember to include you as soon as it is too late to edit this section.

BIBLIOGRAPHY

Afro-American. 1930–40.

Anderson, Jervis. *This Was Harlem: 1900–1950*. Farrar, Straus & Giroux, 1982.

Baldwin, James. *Go Tell It on the Mountain*. Alfred A. Knopf, 1953.

Breznican, Anthony. "Francis Ford Coppola Rights a Wrong by Restoring Black Scenes to *The Cotton Club*." *Vanity Fair*. September 12, 2019.

Campbell, E. Simms, Cartographer, and Publisher Dell Publishing Company. A night-club map of Harlem. [New York, N.Y.: Dell Publishing Company, Inc., ©, 1932] Map. Retrieved from the Library of Congress, https://www.loc.gov/item/2016585261.

Carter, Stephen L. *Invisible: The Forgotten Story of the Black Woman Lawyer Who Took Down America's Most Powerful Mobster*. Henry Holt and Co., 2018.

Chepesiuk, Ron. *Gangsters of Harlem: The Gritty Underworld of New York City's Most Famous Neighborhood*. Fort Lee, NJ: Barricade Books, 2007.

Coloured Domestics from Guadeloupe, 1910–1928 (RG76 B1A, Vol. 475, file 731832, microfilm C-10410) (MIKAN 1434358).

Cook, Fred J. "The Black Mafia Moves into the Numbers Racket." *New York Times*, April 4, 1971.

Cotton Club Encore, The. Director Francis Ford Coppola. Performances by Richard Gere, Diane Lane, Gregory Hines, and James Remar. 1984. Film.

Cruce, Ashley. "A History of Progressive-Era School Savings Banking, 1870 to 1930." Working Paper. Center for Social Development, Washington University in St. Louis, George Warren Brown School of Social Work.

"Cult Leader and Pilot Die in Plane Crash." *Syracuse Herald.* Monday, August 1, 1938.

"Cult of Father Divine." *The Nod*, January 28, 2019. Podcast, https://gimletmedia.com/shows/the-nod/49h39j.Davis, J. Richard "Dixie." "Things I Couldn't Tell till Now." *Collier's.* July–August 1939.

"Dimes Make Millions for Numbers Racket; 600–1 Payoff Lures 500,000 a Day to Make Bets Here." *New York Times.* June 26, 1964.

Dubois, Laurent. "Solitude's Statue: Confronting the Past in the French Caribbean." *Outre-Mers. Revue d'histoire.* 2006. 27–38, 350–51.

Durn, Sarah. "Stephanie St. Clair, Harlem's 'Numbers Queen,' Dominated the Gambling Underground and Made Millions." *Smithsonian Magazine.* Published May 21, 2021. Accessed July 30, 2021. https://www.smithsonianmag.com/history/meet-stephanie-st-clair-immigrant-turned-millionaire-who-dominated-harlems-gambling-underground-180977759.

"Dutch Schultz Courted Death before Killing: Retribution Hinted in Telegram from Mme. St. Clair. SWIPED NUMBERS RACKET BY LOANS Reputedly Took Holstein for a 'Ride.'" *Afro-American* (1893–), Nov 02, 1935, p. 1. ProQuest, https://www.proquest.com/historical-newspapers/dutch-schultz-courted-death-before-killing/docview/531093237/se-2.

Ellison, Ralph. *Invisible Man*. Random House, 1952.

"Episode 1—Madame Queenie." No Man's Land by The Wing. Host Alexis Coe, guests LaShawn Harris and Karen E. Quinones Miller. November 2018. Podcast.

Farley, Helen. *A Cultural History of Tarot: From Entertainment to Esotericism*. Bloomsbury Academic, 2009.

Fleming, G. James. "Millionaire? Bosh, Casper Holstein Declared when Asked about the Stories of His Fortune." *New York Amsterdam News* (1922–38), February 22, 1936, p. 1. ProQuest, https://www.proquest.com/historical-newspapers/millionaire-bosh-casper-holstein-declared-when/docview/226203863/se-2.

Gautier, Arlette. *The Sisters of Solitude*. Rennes University Press. 2010.

Gosch, Martin A., and Richard Hammer. *The Last Testament of Lucky Luciano*. January 1, 1974. Enigma Books, 2013.

"Gunmen Hold Rich Clubman, Want $70,000." *Daily News*, New York, New York. September 23, 1928, p. 2.

Harris, LaShawn. "Madame Queen of Policy: Stephanie St. Clair, Harlem's Numbers Racket, and Community Advocacy" Chap. 2 in *Sex Workers, Psychics, and Numbers Runners: Black Women in New York City's Underground Economy*. University of Illinois Press, 2016.

Harris, LaShawn. "Playing the Numbers: Madame Stephanie St. Clair and African American Policy Culture in Harlem." *Black Women, Gender & Families*. Vol. 2, no. 2, (Fall) 2008, 53–76.

Hay, Mark. "In 1930s New York, the Mayor Took on the Mafia by Banning Artichokes: Gangs and Mafiosos Have a Long History with Food Crime." *Atlas Obscura*. January 2020. https://www.atlasobscura.com/articles/strange-mafia-histories.

Hewlett, B. Gregory. "Dutch Schultz Near Death; Two Bodyguards Killed in Gang War at Newark Tavern." *Daily Home News*. New Brunswick, N.J., Thursday Afternoon, October 24, 1935.

—. *Home to Harlem*. Northeastern UP, 1928.

—. "How Dutch Schultz Became a New York Digit Baron: Shooting of Dutch Schultz Recalls how He Muscled in on Harlem's Numbers Racket Bronx Dutchman Stole Policy Game from Colored Barons with Killings and Kid Nappings; Feud with Mme. St. Clair, "Policy Queen," Led to Federal Charge; Took $20,000 Daily from Harlem Pockets." *Afro-American* (1893–), November 2, 1935, p. 23. ProQuest, https://www.proquest.com/historical-newspapers/how-dutch-schultz-became-new-york-digit-baron/docview/531102803/se-2.

Johnson, Mayme, and Karen E. Quinones Miller. *Harlem Godfather: The Rap on My Husband, Ellsworth "Bumpy" Johnson*. Oshun Publishing Company, Incorporated. May 13, 2008.

Kasinitz, Philip. *Caribbean New York: Black Immigrants and the Politics of Race*. Cornell UP, 1992.

Lacour, Auguste. *Histoire de la Guadeloupe (History of Guadeloupe)*.

—. "Law Regards Holstein as Menace while Throngs Recall Good Deeds: Sentenced as a Policy Banker, He Tells of Early Struggles." *New York Amsterdam News* (1922–38), February 15, 1936, p. 1. ProQuest, https://www.proquest.com/historical-newspapers/law-regards-holstein-as-menace-while-throngs/docview/226196646/se-2.

Malliet, A. M. W. "Dewey Calls Alex Pompez: See Doom of Numbers Racket in Hines Trial Takes Stand." *New York Amsterdam News* (1922–38), August 20, 1938, p. 1. ProQuest, https://www.proquest.com/historical-newspapers/dewey-calls-alex-pompez/docview/226150871/se-2.

Matthews, Ralph. "Looking at the Stars: Harlem Happenings." *Afro-American* (1893–), January 2, 1932, p. 14. ProQuest, https://www.pro

quest.com/historical-newspapers/looking-at-stars/docview/530962464
/se-2.

McGinnis, Laura. "Mother, Daughter, Slave, (Re)sist(e)r? The Female
Body in Antillean Visual Commemoration" in *Essays in French Literature
and Culture*. No. 56. October 2019.

McKay, Claude. *Harlem: Negro Metropolis*. Harcourt Brace Jovanovich, 1968.

Meriwether, Louise. *Daddy was a Number Runner*. New York: The Femi-
nist Press at The City University of New York, 1970.

Moitt, Bernard. "Slave Resistance in Guadeloupe and Martinique, 1791–
1848" in *Caribbean Slavery in the Atlantic World*. 919–50.

Morrison, Toni. *Jazz*. Alfred A. Knopf, 1992.

Negro in Harlem, The: A Report on Social and Economic Conditions
Responsible for the Outbreak of March 19, 1935. The Mayor's Commission on Conditions in Harlem. New York, 1935.

New York Amsterdam News. 1929–39.

New York Times. 1928–40.

"Prison for 'Digit Daddy': Man Who Invented Numbers Game Jailed in Al-
leged Operation Casper Holstein Is Given from Six Months to Three Years
as Onetime Fabulous Wealth Dwindles; Charges He Was Framed." *Afro-
American* (1893–), February 15, 1936, p. 1. ProQuest, https://www.proquest
.com/historical-newspapers/prison-digit-daddy/docview/531160793/se-2.

Sann, Paul. *Kill the Dutchman!* Popular Library, 1971.

Schwartz-Bart, Andre. *A Woman Named Solitude*. Bantam Books, 1973.

Sherman, Augustus F., and Peter Mesenhöller. Augustus F. Sherman: Ellis
Island portraits, 1905–1920. New York: Aperture, 2005. https://scalar
.usc.edu/works/let-me-get-there/guadeloupe-women-1911.

Stewart, Shirley. *The World of Stephanie St. Clair: An Entrepreneur, Race Woman and Outlaw in Early Twentieth Century Harlem*. Peter Lang Inc., International Academic Publishers, 2014.

Vaz, Matthew. *Running the Numbers: Race, Police, and the History of Urban Gambling* (Historical Studies of Urban America). University of Chicago Press, 2020.

Watkins-Owens, Irma. *Blood Relations: Caribbean Immigrants and the Harlem Community, 1900–1930*. Indiana University Press, 1996.

Watts, Jill. *God, Harlem U.S.A.* University of California Press, 1992.

Whitaker, Jan. *Tea at the Blue Lantern Inn: A Social History of the Tea Room Craze in America*. Macmillan. December 1, 2002.

White Rose Mission and Industrial Association collection at the New York Public Library. 1899–1981.

White, Shane. *Playing the Numbers: Gambling in Harlem Between the Wars*. Harvard University Press, 2010. https://login.proxy.kennesaw.edu/login?url=http://search.ebscohost.com/login.aspx?direct=true&db=nlebk&AN=447976&site=eds-live&scope=site&ebv=EB&ppid=pp_Front_Cover.